Hearts ON FIRE

JILL LOWRY

ISBN-10: 0-692-17915-1
ISBN-13: 978-0-692-17915-4

Hearts on Fire

Cover, Scripture Images, and Watermark Designed by
Kerry Prater.
Interior Design by Katharine E. Hamilton

DEDICATION

This book is dedicated to my Lord
who has set my heart on fire for Him.

To my husband and my children who have always
stood by me and supported my dreams and passions
for ministry.

And to my father and my sister who
supported and encouraged me to keep on writing.

ACKNOWLEDGMENTS

I am so grateful to so many people for supporting, encouraging, and praying for me as I wrote my second devotional, "Hearts on Fire." My heart's desire is to encourage all of you, my readers and friends, as you read a treasure of truth from scripture each day.

I would like to thank my wonderful family who faithfully love me and encourage me to keep following my dream of ministry through writing and speaking. I love you so much and am grateful for your love and support!

I would like to give a special thanks to my publishing consultant, Katharine Hamilton, who has gone above and beyond for me again with this book. She is a wealth of knowledge and so fun to work with. Also, many thanks to her sister, Kerry Prater, for her awesome cover designs for both of my books. This team of sisters has impressed me!

I would also like to extend a heartfelt thanks to my friends who stand beside me in prayer and have prayed for my writing. Your prayers have made a difference in my life. Thank you for faithfully praying!

Finally, I would like to give thanks to God for giving me His son, Jesus Christ, who died for me and for His gift of the Holy Spirit who lives inside me. I give Him all the glory and praise for helping me write this book of devotionals for you!

INTRODUCTION

This is my second devotional book written out of my desire to bring to life the word of Jesus to ignite hearts for Him. As I was writing my first book, "Finding Joy in Jesus," a weekly devotional, that was inspired by my mother, I discovered that my heart sparkled with the light of Jesus because I spent time daily in His treasures of truth. I knew that I wanted to continue writing encouraging words, but this time I saw a need to write a daily devotional so that you could seek Him daily and deepen your relationship with Jesus!

In "Hearts on Fire," you can read a passage each day of the year that will give you a promise found within the scriptures from His living word. His word is sharper than a two-edged sword and is a daily manual or guide for living a full and abundant life. Open your Bible as you mediate on each scripture and discover that the Holy Spirit will speak to you through His word. Each scripture is italicized at the beginning of each day so that you can have a reference to look up in your Bible and read.

Do you want to revive and soften your heart? Try planting it in the good soil of faith and see how you will grow much fruit for Jesus. Your life will be a harvest of glory as you discover that the true road to joy is found on the path where Jesus leads you. Jesus Christ is the answer!

I am so glad that you have joined me on this journey as we spend 365 days in the Bible together. My hope and prayer is that you will make time for Jesus every day. The Lord wants your heart 24/7 as it says in Jeremiah 24:7: *"I will give them a heart to know that I am the Lord, and they shall be my people and I will be their God, for they will return to me with their whole heart."* Return to your Lord Jesus with your whole heart and let Him set your heart on fire!

FOR I KNOW
the plans
I HAVE FOR YOU,
declares the Lord,
plans for welfare
AND NOT FOR EVIL,
plans to give you
A FUTURE
and
A HOPE.
JEREMIAH 29:11

JANUARY 1

Jesus is the Light
John 1:4

In Him was life, and the life was the light of men. Jesus has come to give you life. The life that He gives is everlasting and real. He has made a way for you in the darkness and has brought you His light. See the light that He gives and follow Him to sweet freedom. There is power, life, and freedom through *Jesus Christ*!

Only *Jesus* can give you the freedom that you desire. He will never leave you. Because once you believe, His Spirit lives inside you. This Spirit is the same Spirit that raised *Jesus* from the dead! You can live with hope, because His Spirit is alive and active in you. You will experience a freedom like never before with *Jesus*. Give it all to *Jesus*. He takes all your worries, tears, and fears and makes a way for you in the darkness. His light shines brightly to light your way. Do you see His light? Are you giving all to *Jesus*? Are you believing? Start today by simply believing and trusting Him completely to meet all of your needs. He is waiting for you to come to Him just as you are. Surrender all to *Jesus*!

JANUARY 2

Shine with Love
Matthew 5:16

Let your light shine before others, so that they may see your good works and give glory to your Father who is in heaven. Shine on so that others may see this light in you that comes from *Jesus Christ*. People need *Jesus*! You can be that person who shines His light so that others may believe. Yes, you can show *Jesus* by your example of love.

Love one another like *Jesus* loves you, and let His light shine on others as you live in love. Be an example of love through your acts of kindness and grace. Humbly serve today where *Jesus* has called you. You can make a difference for *Christ*. It is possible to bring others to *Jesus* through your good works and faithful witness. All glory to *God* for these opportunities to shine radiantly!

Do not miss your time to shine for His glory! Today is the day you have been given by your *Lord* to shine. You will be blessed when you do as you are called. Go shine brightly so that others will believe that all things are possible with the *Lord*. Let them see Him in you. It is time to shine as the favor of the *Lord* is upon you!

JANUARY 3

Christ in the Center
Psalm 130:5

I wait for the Lord, my soul waits, and in His word I hope. The *Lord* is ready to bless you when you trust in Him. His timing and His will are perfect. Trust that He knows what you need and when you need it, even before you ask Him. He knows the best plans for you: plans for a future and a hope.

Believe in the beauty of your dreams. Put *Christ* in the center of them and see how and when those dreams are answered. Know that He wants the best for you and will give you the desires of your heart. What are your utmost desires? Have you trusted *Jesus* to give you all that you need? Have you surrendered all to Him?

Feel the freedom that exists for you as you wait, trust, and surrender all to *Jesus*. He will give you more than you can ever dream or imagine. Believe that He will give you more as you give Him more. It is possible to have it all with *Jesus*! Yes, you will see His promises of new hope as you keep trusting and waiting faithfully upon the *Lord*!

JANUARY 4

Set Your Sights on Jesus
Psalm 145:18

The Lord is near to all who call upon Him, to all who call upon Him in truth. Call upon the *Lord* and He will rescue you. Make Him the *Lord* of your life. He wants to know you more deeply and wants you to abide in Him. As you abide in Him and His love, you will find complete and everlasting joy!

Yes, your joy is in *Jesus*! This joy from *Jesus* cannot be taken away from you. It grows as you grow closer to *Jesus*: the direct source of your joy. Are you searching for more joy in your life? Do you believe that you can find joy? It is possible to those who keep abiding and staying connected to the love of *Jesus*. Draw nearer to *Jesus* and discover this pure joy!

Jesus wants you to know how much He loves you. He works all things for good to those who love Him and are called according to His purpose. His glory will shine through you as you aim to please Him first. Set your sights on *Jesus*, your Savior, and see how your life will be joy-filled! Find your joy in *Jesus* and you will never be alone!

JANUARY 5

Healing Power of Jesus
Psalm 147:3

He heals the brokenhearted and binds up their wounds. Jesus has come to rescue you. Through His wounds, you are healed. When you let *Jesus* comfort you, your heartache will turn into rejoicing. Let His grace cover you completely. His grace is something that no one can ever take away from you. Your Savior, *Jesus* has given you grace upon grace so that you can move forward to your new life with Him. Leave your past behind and forge ahead victoriously with *Jesus Christ*!

No sin is too big for *Jesus*. Nothing will keep Him from loving you. Do you believe that *Jesus* has a good plan for you even when you cannot see all the details? Are you following *Jesus* to freedom? Your freedom is found with Him and not by yourself.

There is hope for you when you let *Jesus* work in you. Your salvation is promised through His sacrifice. Your heart and soul will come alive with the joy of *Jesus* when you let Him heal you. Do not let your heart be troubled any longer, for *Jesus* has overcome the world for you! Yes, He has overcome all for you through His pain and suffering on the cross. Receive His love and His grace and come alive with the Spirit of the living *God* working inside of you!

JANUARY 6

Experience Life to the Fullest
Psalm 139:17

How precious to me are your thoughts, O God! How vast is the sum of them! Your thoughts are higher than our thoughts Lord. Your ways are greater than our ways. We know that you want the very best for us as you made us in your image. You formed us perfectly to be your children who would be able to follow you to freedom. You also gave us free will to decide on our own how we would live. The choice is ours to make. We can choose you, *Lord* and experience life to the fullest. You want us to live abundantly, and you have given us every opportunity to know and love you. You are calling us out of the darkness of sin and into your great light that leads to freedom. The path to life is narrow and those whom follow it are few. The ones who choose *Jesus* will live with joy. Believe it is possible for you to have joy with *Jesus*!

Yes, all things are possible with *Jesus Christ*. He is waiting for you to come to Him. He needs you to follow Him to the life He has made for you. There is more for you. Do you want all that you were created by your *Lord* to have? Do you want to live a joy-filled life? Are you searching for hope? You will find it all when you meet Him at His throne of life. He is waiting there for you!

JANUARY 7

Salvation for All Who Believe
Ephesians 2:8

For by grace you have been saved through faith. And this is not your own doing; it is the gift of God. Salvation is available to all who believe. As we confess with our mouth that *Jesus* is *Lord* and believe in our heart that He was raised from the dead, our sins will be forgiven. Every sin, trespass, and temptation will be wiped away. What hope we have in our *Lord Jesus*. He is our living hope!

Jesus is alive and actively working in you as you believe. Let Him show you His glory. See His majesty and beauty all around you. He is searching for you and wants to bring you out of hopelessness and into His great light as He shines His rays of hope upon you. The light is upon you, do you not feel it?

Bask in the glory of His promises for you. Feel the warmth of His love. Find shelter and comfort in His arms of peace. Every day you spend with *Jesus* will bring you closer to His great love! Thank *God* that salvation is real through *Jesus Christ*. Spread the good news of hope so that others may believe! Salvation through *Jesus* is *God's* greatest gift to you!

JANUARY 8

Perfect Timing of the Lord
2 Corinthians 1:20

For all the promises of God find their Yes in him. That is why it is through him that we utter our Amen to God for his glory. The timing of the *Lord* is perfect, and He will answer your requests prayed faithfully. Do not give up. Pray steadfastly and fervently. The *Lord* hears you and is waiting for His perfect time to answer. He sees your heart and into your soul. He is the King of your humble heart and the Overseer of your sweet soul.

Take time to listen to His voice and feel His Spirit calling you deeper. He wants a relationship with you. Abide in His love and keep talking to Him in prayer. Listen for His guidance as you read His words of hope. Trust Him through every situation and circumstance, even when you do not understand. Faithfully follow Him by loving Him first. Be patient. *Jesus* knows what you need even before you ask. He wants the very best for you. His yes will become your best yes. The *Lord Jesus* has made you different so that you will stand out for Him. Stand firm and believe even when no one else is believing. Look up and see a whole new world with the *Lord* guiding your every step in a real way. A real relationship with the *Lord Jesus* is possible for you It is time to super charge your life with *Jesus*!

JANUARY 9

Build Yourselves Up in Prayer
Jude 20

But you beloved, building yourselves up in your most holy faith and praying in the Holy Spirit. As you pray, you are drawing closer to *Jesus* through the *Holy Spirit*. The Spirit intercedes to *Jesus* even when you do not know what to pray. He takes your requests to the *Father* so that He can answer your faithful prayers. Yes, your prayers will be heard, and your *Lord* will always listen. He bends down to hear you and respond. He hears every prayer!

Seek His face so that you can be transformed. Let Him lead you to new life. Let His desires become your desires. Let go of your past and let the *Lord* lead you to freedom. *Christ* has set you free! Submit to His way and see your life with a fresh faith. Your faith has made you well. You will be healed because you believed! There is healing and wholeness through *Jesus*. Draw to His Spirit and let your faith be bigger than your fear. He can do what seems impossible for you. He will surely do it. Do you really believe? Tell Him you believe and experience the power of the *Holy Spirit* and the truth from the words of your *Father* in Heaven and His *son, Jesus*. It's time to build yourselves up by more prayer. Pray, pray, pray!

JANUARY 10

Love is the Key that Opens the Heart
1 Corinthians 13:13

So now faith, hope, and love abide, these three, but the greatest of these is love. Love is the key that opens the heart. *Jesus* loves you. Do you love Him with all your heart? Do you believe He loves you no matter how many mistakes you have made? Be sure of His love for you. Abide in the love of *Jesus*. Make Him the first love of your life so that He can do great things through you.

Many will not understand, and many will not believe. Those who believe in *Jesus* and love Him will be filled with His Spirit. Yes, the Spirit of the living *God* will come alive inside of those who believe and trust. Are you believing and trusting the Spirit to guide you? Do you know that your life will be blessed abundantly by the power of the *Holy Spirit*? The same power that lives in *Jesus* lives in you. Love *Jesus* first, then activate the power of the *Holy Spirit* by letting Him lead you. Your life will be blessed beyond measure as you let the Spirit direct you. The love from the Spirit will refresh you and restore you completely. You will experience revival in your heart and soul as you let *Jesus* love you and the power of *Holy Spirit* renew you. Fall deeper in love with *Jesus* and feel how great His love is for you! His unconditional love is the greatest gift!

JANUARY 11

Follow Jesus to Freedom
John 21:19

Jesus said, "Follow me." He made His desires clear when He spoke these two words. He loves you so much that He wants you to follow Him. Are you following *Jesus*? Are you showing your love for Him by following Him? Are you continuing to trust and obey *Jesus*?

You show your love for *Jesus* when you obey His commands. Obey Him and follow Him to new life. He needs you to follow Him to freedom. He wants you to experience His amazing grace! There is grace upon grace in the arms of your *Lord* and *Savior*. Draw to Him completely with every ounce of your being. Let His love lavish you!

Every step you take toward *Jesus* is one step closer to love. His love will inspire you to love others. His joy will be yours as you keep drawing closer. Follow Him to find the joy you have been looking for. Your leap of faith with *Jesus* will lead you to new hope. Find your hope in *Jesus*!

JANUARY 12

Pray in One Accord
Acts 1:14

All these with one accord were devoting themselves to prayer. When we come together as one to pray with one heart, mind, and Spirit, all seeking the will of *God*, He is well pleased. He will answer us as we pray in agreement. He sees our hearts and knows our intentions. Our souls are connected to Him through our faithful prayers.

Are you ready to meet your *Lord* through prayer? Have you made time to pray with others so that you can praise Him? The *Lord* is well pleased when you meet and lift His name high. He knows your soul and wants to give you your heart's desire. Seek His will above your own and see how He will bless you. His face will shine down on those who exalt Him!

Many prayers have yet to be answered. Believe that He hears you when you pray. Keep praying and believing that it will be done for you. Seek others who can pray with you and lift your prayers up to the *Lord*. He is faithful to you. Are you faithful to Him? Keep the faith by continuing to trust and obey His call to pray in one accord. It's time to pray together as one!

JANUARY 13

Jesus is Faithful
1 Thessalonians 5:24

He who calls you is faithful; He will surely do it. Do you believe that *God* will do what He promises? Then go, and be blessed by His power, strength, love, grace and encouragement. Keep working for the *Lord* as He holds your hand. He will be your shield of protection. You do not have to fear when the *Lord* is with you. Why are you still so afraid?

Be a blessing and He will bless you. He is always faithful to you. Are you faithful to Him? Let Him show you His wonderful love for you. Let Him love you. It is your choice to love Him and let Him in your life. Only the *Lord* can and will be there for you always. He will never fail you so trust Him with all of your heart. How much of your heart are you willing to give Him?

Do not be afraid to give Him your whole heart and see how He will bless you. Your life will be different with the *Lord*. As you stand out for *Christ*, you will stand up with His power of freedom. With *Jesus*, the peace you have been longing for will flood your life and the joy you have been seeking will overwhelm you. All things are possible with *Jesus Christ*. Believe and receive all that is yours in *Christ*.

JANUARY 14

Live with United Hearts for Jesus
2 Thessalonians 1:3

Your faith is growing abundantly, and the love of every one of you for one another is increasing. As you live and work together in harmony, the *Lord* is well pleased. He sees your united hearts and faithfulness and He is honored and glorified by you. When His people come together and love one another, *Jesus* is lifted up. His Spirit comes alive in those who continue drawing to Him by faith and good works.

Let His love shine on you and cover you with hope. Feel His joy leap inside you as you continue working for His will and good pleasure. He will bless you as you continue blessing others. Never fear, because the *Lord* is very near to you, faithful one. He will meet your every need and supply you with the riches of His kingdom as you continue working faithfully. Not all have your faith or will understand, but the *Lord* is faithful, and He will surely do it! Come to *Jesus* with everything you have and be encouraged knowing that He will never leave you. He won the victory for you and now you must keep fighting your good fight of faith with Him. You never have to walk alone. He is right beside you and holding your hand to freedom!

JANUARY 15

Be Transformed
Romans 12:2

Do not be conformed to this world, but be transformed by the renewal of your mind. Let your mind be made new in His image. He is alive in you, dear one. Each day you draw closer to Him brings you closer to His love. Let His Spirit do His work in you so that you can come alive with the love of *Jesus* in your heart, mind, body, and soul.

Your mind will be filled with joy as you think about the gifts from *Jesus*. Dwell on these pure and true things that come from Him, so that your mind will be renewed in Him. Seek His way for your life. His way is the best way all the time! You will find *Jesus* when you seek Him. Your body is a temple that He wants to fill with righteousness so that He can use you to further His message of hope. He is waiting for you to come alive with the fire of the *Holy Spirit*. His living Spirit lives inside all who believe. His Spirit comes alive in all who are made new in *Christ* by being fully surrendered in their heart and completely transformed in their mind. You can have this if you so choose. Say yes to *Jesus* and experience an abundant life of everlasting joy and peace. There is still hope. That hope is yours if you believe in your heart that *Jesus* loves you and live connected to His love in your heart, mind, body, and soul!

JANUARY 16

Be Strong in Christ
2 Timothy 4:17

But the Lord stood by me and strengthened me. When you lean on Christ fully in your life, He will awaken you to new life. If you let him, the *Lord* will strengthen you. Are you seeking more power and energy in your life? Do you want to feel alive and free? Seek first the *Lord Jesus Christ* and you will be on the road to freedom with Him.

Take off the chains that bind you and let *Christ* set you free! He is the ticket to freedom and hope. *Jesus* will take you to new heights and give you new life in Him. Run to Him and throw off the shackles and chains of this world. He who is in you is greater than He who is in the world.

Love Him with all your heart, soul, body, and mind. He wants all of you so that He can mold you into a vessel to be used for His glory. Let Him in your life so that He can work it all out. You are trying to do it all by yourself and will never succeed alone. Put God in the center of your life and watch Him God-size your dreams! He can, and will, do more than you can ever dream or imagine! He is real and will do real things for you if you trust and obey Him first. What are you waiting for? It is time to let go and let *God* show up in your life!

JANUARY 17

Jesus is Your Perfect Peace
Isaiah 26:3

You keep him in perfect peace whose mind is stayed on you, because he trusts in you. You *Lord* are our perfect peace. When we trust you with all our heart and lean not on our own understanding, you show us the way. When we trust and obey, peace enters our heart and floods our soul. There is no better way to be full of joy than when we give our whole hearts to our *Lord Jesus*!

Let us surrender all to *Jesus* as He has given us all. He loves us unconditionally and abundantly. His love never ends as it creates new life in us by refreshing us and regenerating us completely. Yes, new life is ours in *Jesus Christ*! A life of promise and purpose exists for those who follow *Jesus*.

Choose *Jesus* and choose life. He is the only way to life everlasting. Your life can be full of hope as you strive to keep the peace by bringing the love of *Jesus* to those around you. Let His living Spirit touch you so that you can touch others with His power of love. His love is real and alive! Keep your mind focused on *Jesus* and experience a transformation of your heart, soul, body, and mind! It is real!

JANUARY 18

His Word Remains Forever
1 Peter 1:24-25

The grass withers, the flower falls, but the word of the Lord remains forever. Put your hope in the one true King, the living, eternal *Jesus Christ*. His word is truth and will never return void. Believe His word and live by it. The *Lord* gave us instruction, love, hope, and encouragement to help us. Choose to follow and abide in Him.

Call upon the counsel of the *Lord* and seek Him with all your heart. Know that He can do exceedingly more than you could ever ask or imagine. He wants the best for you and needs your whole heart to be engaged. Come closer to His love and experience the freedom He wants to give you! There is freedom and hope in the arms of your *Savior*!

Wait upon the *Lord* as He always comes through for you even when you do not understand. Have faith, even when you do not see. Have peace, even when you cannot change your circumstances the way you would like. Have hope, even when you cannot see all the details of your journey. *God* does all in His timing and in His way. Let go, and let His love lavish you from the top of your head to the tips of your toes. As you have believed, His grace has already saved you. Let that grace soak deep into your soul and be free!

JANUARY 19

New Life in Christ
Isaiah 43:19

Behold, I am doing a new thing. Now it springs forth, do you not perceive it? All things become new with *Christ* in the center. He is the one who brings life! if you will call upon the *Lord.* There is new life waiting for you around the corner from your heartache and pain, if you seek the *Lord* with all your heart and let him know your requests. He can give you more than you could ever dream or imagine!

Your dreams will come alive with *Christ* in the center. Put Him in the center of your life and He will transform you. Make *Christ* the one true king of your heart, once and for all. Let go of the chains that bind you and run your race with endurance and strength. He is with you every step of the way!

There is hope for you, faithful one. Your peace is just one step away, so keep on the path to freedom. Wake up to a new life with *Christ*. He takes all your chains that keep you imprisoned and gives you a full and abundant life in *Christ*! Know that His grace has saved you and is enough! Walk in His love and be lavished by His grace!

JANUARY 20

Jesus Cares for You
1 Peter 5:7

Casting all your anxieties on Him, because He cares for you. Give *Jesus* all your worries and your fears. Let His Spirit of peace come alive inside of you. Breathe in His Spirit, and breathe out His peace over your life. He has given you new life from the *Holy Spirit* which cannot be taken away from you. It is an eternal gift from *Jesus* to those who believe in Him.

Turn up the volume of His Spirit to hear Him and listen to the truth that flows from Him. Activate the *Holy Spirit* that already lives inside you by living surrendered and free. You are one step away from the freedom you desire. That peace flows from the living power of the *Holy Spirit* is yours. When you believed, *Jesus* has deposited His Spirit in you. Cling to the power and feel your worries fade away.

Leave your troubles behind you and come out of the darkness. Turn towards the light of hope that is found in *Jesus*. You do not need to be afraid any longer. It is time to let go and totally depend on *Jesus*. He is calling you to be awakened to His love as you bask in the glorious light of *Christ*! Wake up to new life today in *Jesus Christ*!

JANUARY 21

Seek the Higher Ways
Matthew 5:8

Blessed are the pure in heart, for they shall see God. Yes, *God* will show Himself to those who keep their minds and hearts on Him all the time. People who see *God* will be looking for Him. These people are in touch with His Spirit of truth and love Him with their whole hearts. They follow Him, by loving the *Lord* first and foremost. He will show Himself mighty to those who are walking closer with Him.

Are you wanting to see *God* move in your life? Are you searching for more of Him? Abandon self and serve Him with all your heart. Seek the higher ways of *Christ*. Look to the *Lord* and be lavished by His love for you. When you believe and choose to let Him in every part of your life, His grace and mercy will follow you. Even the parts that you are keeping to yourself need the touch of J*esus*! His touch brings healing and wholeness. His voice will lead the lost back home to Him. His love will comfort the empty and broken places of your heart and soul. His grace will welcome you home to His arms of compassion. Come back to your first love, or reach out and find Him for the first time! He yearns for you to come to life with Him! Yes, it is time to live the life you were made in *Christ* to live!

JANUARY 22

Love in Deed and Truth
1 John 3:18

Little children, let us not love in word or talk, but in deed and truth. Let us love like *Jesus* who saw people's needs and met them. As witnessed through His life on Earth and death on the cross, He always put others above himself. He died so that we could walk together in love and freedom! Let us truly live the life He has purposed for us.

Pour out your hearts in service to *Jesus*. Make Him the *Lord* of your life by trusting and obeying Him through it all. Only *Jesus* can show you the way to love. He is your friend, teacher, and role model. He will never let you down. He will meet your every need right where you are, so trust Him to do it!

Show kindness, be tenderhearted, and forgiving with your love since *Jesus* has forgiven you by His actions of love. He loved you so much that He paid it all for your freedom. As He was dying on the cross, He asked the *Father* to forgive the very ones who had put Him to death. Are you forgiving the ones who have come against you? Are you loving everyone with the love of *Jesus*? Try acting out of love and see how your life will not only be a witness for *Christ*, but be blessed with abundant hope, joy, and peace that is beyond all human understanding! It all starts and ends with the love of *Jesus*!

JANUARY 23

Jesus Always Shows Up for You
John 10:10

Jesus came that you may have life and have it abundantly. He wants you to have life through Him and to feel His great love for you. He has a purpose for you and yearns for you to find Him as He calls you to that purpose. His plans are for you to prosper and be filled with great joy. Are you seeking more joy in your life? Do you believe it is possible to find your joy in *Jesus*? Come to your *Savior* and you will find that joy and more! He gives you more when you allow Him to work in your life!

Jesus is the way, the truth, and the life. The only way to the *Father* is through His Son, *Jesus*. Keep *Jesus* in the center of your life to experience more life. It is possible to have all when you give Him your whole heart. Let go and let Him lead you to freedom and hope. With *Jesus* by your side, all your days will be full of joy. Even in the hard times, *Jesus* will show up to give you more power and strength just when you need Him.

There will be times where your faith grows stronger because you kept the faith and He strengthened you through your trial. Take His hand and walk in freedom. He is waiting to show you new life and it is possible to have this new life in *Christ*! Come to life with *Jesus*!

JANUARY 24

Jesus Breaks Down the Walls of Hostility
Ephesians 2:14

For He Himself is our peace, who had made us both one and has broken down in His flesh the dividing wall of hostility. Yes, the *Lord Jesus* is the way to peace through the walls of division that exist around us. He came to break down all that divides us and to give us hope again where there was none. When we live in harmony with our neighbor, by staying connected to His Spirit of unity through the bond of peace, He is well pleased.

The love of *Christ* will bring down these barriers. His love will give us a new purpose and the freedom to forgive and move forward. Are you struggling to forgive and forge ahead to this new life of peace? Have your burdens become too much to bear? Are you searching for hope during your hopelessness? Give it all to *Jesus*! Nothing is too big for Him to handle. He is your peace and anchor in the storm. When you trust in Him, He will meet all your needs. Only *Jesus* can give you a fresh start and a bigger purpose and calling. Trust Him to do what men say is impossible. Believe He can and will do all things for you because He is your perfect peace and He is the cord that ties together perfect love!

JANUARY 25

There is Power and Freedom in Christ
Galatians 5:1

For freedom, Christ has set us free; stand firm, therefore, and do not submit again to a yoke of slavery. We are free because Christ came to give us freedom from sin. He lives to give us hope! Why do we keep hiding behind our sins and refusing to let go of our chains that bind us? We have been forgiven and can walk freely with our living hope, *Jesus Christ*!

No more weight can hold us down when we put *Christ* in the center of our life. He takes every burden and frees us once and for all. Let us run our race with endurance by clinging to *Christ* and throwing off our chains of slavery that hold us back. Many will never break the chains because they are not living with the power of *Christ* or believing that He is the way to freedom. Others will try to convince us that we must work alone to be free. But *Christ* tells us that when we give Him all our cares and burdens, *He* will set us free! We are one step of faith away from freedom. We are one decision away from peace. We are one moment away from hope. We are one whisper away from His amazing grace. Listen to the whisper of His love and mercy and step out faithfully into a life of freedom with *Christ*! We are free indeed!

JANUARY 26

Give Him Your Whole Heart
Jeremiah 24:7

I will give them a heart to know that I am the Lord, and they shall be my people and I will be their God, for they shall return to me with their whole heart. Give the *Lord* your whole heart and return to your first love. He is waiting patiently for you to come back to Him. Have you left *Jesus*? Are you wandering away from the *Lord* again?

Come back to Him just as you are, and He will welcome you with open arms! There is nothing you could ever do to make Him love you less. He loves you just as you are, despite your sins and faults. His amazing grace is and always will be enough. His mercy is new every morning, just like the sunrise. Rise up to the one who never left you. Be strong in Him and let His love open the eyes of your heart in a fresh and brand new way.

When you give the *Lord* your whole heart, He will show you amazing things. He will manifest Himself to you as you listen and obey His promptings. Do you hear Him calling you? Are you ready to be blessed beyond measure by His powerful presence in your life? Let His love overwhelm you and His peace transform you. When you give Him your whole heart, His joy will be your joy forevermore! Find your joy in *Jesus*!

JANUARY 27

See with Spiritual Eyes
Matthew 13:16

Blessed are your eyes, for they see, and your ears, for they hear. When you keep your eyes open on *Jesus*, you will see what He wants you to see. There is much He wants to show you. Keep your focus on *Jesus Christ*. He is your joy and your strength when you are weak. He is your shield and song.

Listen to His voice calling you to hear what He has been trying to tell you. He is calling you to come to Him, so that He can show you the divine purpose He has for you. Most will not see or hear *Jesus* because they are too wrapped up in self. But you are blessed, because you believe, and He is ready to show you His glory! He knows your heart and sees inside your soul. He is well pleased with you, good and faithful servant.

Draw closer, and your life will become richer. His riches of glory are for those who seek and find Him with their whole hearts. Let His faith come into your life and grow beautifully inside of you. By faith, His grace has saved you. You are alive and new in *Christ*! Now, close your physical eyes and see with your new spiritual eyes. Tune out the noise and distractions of the world and hear His voice calling you into His arms. You are blessed indeed!

JANUARY 28

Pray Bravely and Boldly
Matthew 7:7

Ask and it will be given to you; seek, and you will find; knock, and it will be opened to you. Your prayers cannot be answered if you do not ask. Most unanswered prayers are the ones that have not been prayed. The *Lord* hears you when you pray. Seek Him and you will find Him and He will open the door to you as He hears you knocking. Keep praying, because *God* is faithful!

Find a place to meet the *Lord* and pour out your heart to Him. He wants you to pray without ceasing, believing that He will answer you. Your faithful prayers will be heard, so keep praying so that He can answer you! Do not lose faith when you pray. Remember *God's* timing is perfect. Wait upon Him, knowing that He can, and will, come through for you! Pray that brave prayer with bigger faith. He is waiting for you to believe that it will be possible. All things are possible with *God*! The small miracles have already happened for you. Dream big and pray that bravest prayer stirring in your heart. Today may be the day He answers you! Rejoice in hope that He will answer you. Be patient in your waiting and do not stop asking, seeking, and knocking!

JANUARY 29

Rush to the Light
1 John 1:5

God is light, and in Him there is no darkness at all. The light of *Christ* guides you into all truth when you follow Him into the light. Come out of the darkness and be filled with the power of the *Holy Spirit* guiding you into this light. *God* will never leave or forsake you. He is with you every step of the way! Do you see His light shining brightly? Can you feel the warmth of His power and love?

Rush to the light and be awakened to new hope. As you follow *Christ* to freedom, you will experience a peace like never before. This peace will surround you and cover you completely. At the same time, you will have feelings of joy rushing through you. Hope, peace, and joy all wrapped up for you through the grace of *God*! All this is yours, as one gift, in *Jesus Christ*!

Come boldly to His throne of grace. Run to the one who loves you and has given it all for you. Your salvation is possible through *Jesus Christ*. All you have to do is say yes to Him. Be a child of light and run away from the darkness of sin and shame into the arms of your *Lord* and *Savior*. In Him, there is no darkness at all!

JANUARY 30

Wings Like Eagles
Isaiah 40:31

They who wait for the Lord shall renew their strength; they shall mount up with wings like eagles; run and not be weary; they shall walk and not faint. Wait upon the *Lord* and be patient. He knows what you need and will surely answer your cries for help. Draw closer to Him and feel His Spirit lifting you up so you can live with endurance and strength. You are stronger with the *Lord's* guidance and protection. Keep Him close and run away from your worry and doubt. Do you believe in His living power? Are you willing to let go and let Him transform you? Take off your old self and let Him make you new. He will take what once was broken in you and heal you completely. He can and will do what seems impossible for you. He is waiting for you to totally trust Him for all your needs.

The *Lord* is your safe haven and shelter. Remember that He is there for you whenever you need Him. Call upon Him and be renewed in your Spirit so that you can soar with wings like eagles above all your problems and circumstances. Every fear will fade away as you find more peace with *Jesus.* Your joy will be immeasurable, and your hope will be unstoppable. Everything is possible in the mighty name of *Jesus Christ*!

JANUARY 31

Grace Upon Grace
Isaiah 12:2

Behold, God is my salvation; I will trust, and will not be afraid; for the Lord God is my strength and my song and he has become my salvation. God has given you grace upon grace so that you can experience true freedom. Take His grace and extend it to others so that they may know the love of *Jesus*. By your love and grace, they will know that He lives. Give a little grace and it becomes easier to give more abundantly.

Jesus is the way to life. Do not be afraid to trust Him more. Put Him in the center so that He can do His work through you. You can be that one person who makes a big difference in the life of someone who needs to know the love of *Jesus*. One day every knee will bow to His power and glory. He wants all His people to know and love Him today. Bring His love to those in need by loving them as *Jesus* loves you.

You are a living witness to the power of His Spirit when you see others with spiritual eyes of grace. By grace you have been saved. By *God's* great grace, the shackles of sin are shattered, and your chains are broken. Trust Him more for all you need, and experience hope and salvation through your *Lord* and *Savior, Jesus Christ*!

PRAYER TO JESUS

Dear *Lord*,

I will be still and know that you are *God*. You will be exalted among nations, you will be exalted in the earth! All that you want for me is to be close to you so that I can feel your love in all the moments of life. You are ready to show me great and mighty things if I will just listen and draw nearer to you and choose to accept your grace upon grace.

I am weak, but you are strong. You show your glory through my weakness. I believe all things are possible with you and I know that you are the one who is with me through it all. You show me your power and glory and I am amazed at your presence in my life more each day!

I see your wonder, power, and magnificence everywhere through your eyes of grace. Thank you for showering me with your love and overpowering me with your Spirit! I will follow you to freedom and know that I am saved by your love and made new through your Spirit. I will rejoice and give glory to *God* in the highest!

In *Jesus* name,

Amen.

DELIGHT YOURSELF
in the Lord,
AND HE WILL GIVE
you the desires
of your heart.
PSALM 37:4

FEBRUARY 1

Direct Your Heart to His Love
2 Thessalonians 3:5

May the Lord direct your hearts to the love of God and the steadfastness of Christ. You are His and He loves you so much. Direct your whole heart to Him and stand firm on His promises for you. He has answered your prayers, faithful one, time and time again and He will surely do it again! Keep believing even when you do not see. Your hope is alive through *Jesus Christ*!

God loved you so much that He gave His Son to die for you so that when you believe, you would receive eternal life. Repent, believe and share this good news that there is new life in *Christ*. The kingdom is at hand and your *Savior, Jesus* wants you to remain steadfast. He hopes that you talk of the hope that is in you because of your salvation. You will find joy when you find your hope in Him.

Find *Jesus* today in a new way so that He can deposit His Spirit within you. Once you have the Spirit, He lives in you but needs you to start using His power by turning your life over to the direction and promptings of the *Holy Spirit*. The Spirit inside you is so real and can be active when you activate Him. Draw to the love of *God*, the steadfastness of *Christ* and the power of the *Holy Spirit* and discover new life! It is real! It is real! It is real!

FEBRUARY 2

Let Go of Fear
2 Timothy 1:7

God gave us not a spirit of fear, but of power, and love and self-control. Do not be afraid, but be filled with more love and power of the *Holy Spirit* from the living *God* who loves you so much. He knows your every fear and your every desire. He wants you to trust Him with all of your heart so that He can take you through the hard times. Do not fear, but keep trusting the *Lord* in all that you do.

He will give you the self-control you need to persevere just when you need help. He is your strength and will never fail you as you run your race. He loves you so much! Only the *Lord* can bring you to a higher place. Do you hear Him calling you in the night? Go where He leads you with open arms and you do not have to look back. Look forward to freedom!

All good things will come to those who patiently wait upon the *Lord*. He wants to give you everything your heart desires. He is waiting for you to ask believing that it is possible with the *Lord*. All things are possible to those who believe! Yes, good is waiting for you around the corner from your pain. Hang on to *Jesus* and let Him meet your every need and desire. He is ready to give you your heart's desire! Are you ready?

FEBRUARY 3

Jesus is the Answer to Every Question
Romans 5:1

Therefore, since we have been justified by faith, we have peace with God through our Lord Jesus Christ. By His grace, we have been saved from the wrath of *God* for our sins. Our faith will bring us to a real relationship with Him. When we seek a deeper relationship with our *Lord*, we will experience a peace that is beyond our understanding and that will endure forever. We have eternal peace with *God* through our *Lord Jesus Christ*!

Our hope will come alive as we cling to *Jesus*: our source of eternal hope. He is waiting to bless our lives with more of His hope and peace. Only *Jesus* can bless us with all that we are seeking. He is the answer to every question!

Give Him all your anxieties, worries, and troubles, and He will relieve your stress and calm your soul. Your fear will go away when you surrender it all to *Jesus*. He promises to never leave or forsake you. He poured His blood out on the cross at Calvary for you because He loves you and wants you to live eternally with Him. Make the best decision of your life and trust Him today! If you are already a believer, increase your faith by surrendering everything to your Savior! His love for you is real and endures forever! *Amen*!

FEBRUARY 4

The Lord is Always Faithful
Psalm 117:2

For great is his steadfast love toward us, and the faithfulness of the Lord endures forever. Praise the Lord! He will be there for you even when your eyes cannot see. He lights up your night to show you the way. Keep believing and go where He sends you. Follow His voice to freedom and joy. Only the *Lord* can take you there. Let go and let *God* work in your life. Trust Him with all the details, even when you do not understand or see the end of the road. The *Lord* is always faithful!

God will take you to new places. He will be right there with you as you keep the faith. Never fear when the *Lord* is near to you. Let your faith be bigger than your fear. The *Lord* will be your shelter He will hold your hand and comfort you like no other can. The *Lord* is always faithful! Do you hear His voice calling you in the night? Are you ready to be blessed by His love and guided by His power? Faithfully, go where He leads you, and know that He will surely do what He promises. Believe His word to you. He has a greater plan and a future for you! His love is real, so get closer and come to life with the mighty power of the *Lord*. He wants to do mighty things in, and for, you, so His glory will shine through you! The *Lord* is always faithful!

FEBRUARY 5

Set Your Mind on the Spirit
Romans 8:6

For to set the mind on the flesh is death, but to set the mind on the Spirit is life and peace. Set your mind on things above that come from the Spirit of the *Lord*. The way to life is only found through *Jesus*. He is waiting for you to direct your focus to Him. Look to the one who gave it all on Calvary for you. He died on the cross so that you could have life everlasting! He poured out His blood for your redemption!

Believe in *Jesus* and love Him with all of your heart. His death brought you closer than ever before. His suffering gave you a second chance. Take that chance and walk in freedom with *Jesus*. Let His Spirit work in you so that you can stay connected to Him. Let His grace cover you completely and give you peace!

Perfect peace is possible through *Jesus Christ*. Let His peace become your peace. Feel the warmth of His strong hand upon you. He is your sanctuary and your living hope. Draw closer and live connected to the power of *Christ* in you! Through His stripes you are completely healed! Hallelujah!

FEBRUARY 6

Abide in the Love of Jesus
1 John 2:6

Whoever says he abides in Him ought to walk in the same way in which He walked. Abide in the love of *Jesus* and you will want to walk with Him. Can you feel His love calling you into a deeper relationship? Are you ready to be blessed by *Jesus* in a brand new way? Are you wanting more of His Spirit in your life?

He loves you so much! He needs you to be His hands and feet so that He can do His work through you. There is much work to do for *Jesus* and He has chosen you to do it. *Jesus* will be your strength so that you can persevere. He lifts you to greater heights and gives you extra strength in challenging times. Trust Him in all times. Only *Jesus* can be your rock and refuge from the storm. Only *Jesus* knows the deep desires of your heart and longing of your soul.

Run to your Savior and find rest in Him. The rest that *Jesus* gives is refreshing and restoring. He gives you new life in that weary body. He energizes you in a brand new way. Only *Jesus* can renew your life and make it beautiful. He makes beauty out of ashes!

FEBRUARY 7

God Will Fight Your Battles
1 John 4:4

He who is in you is greater than he who is in the world. The Spirit of the living *God* is alive in you and will direct your heart and mind. The living power of the Spirit is strong in you. Believe that you can conquer all with *God* when you have this power working mightily in you. He will fight your battles and help you. Why do you keep fighting alone? *God* is your strong tower and He has covered you with protection from harm.

Many will not believe and will choose the world and its ways. They will believe that they can conquer all through the world. But you know the truth. The flesh and evil influences will lead you into temptation and sin. The Spirit will give you life. This life is possible when you let the Spirit lead you into all truth.

Be filled with the Spirit. Let the Spirit lead you. Host the presence of this Spirit in your life and you will be showered with buckets of joy and produce baskets of fruit for His glory! He who is in you is greater! Believe and receive the *Holy Spirit*!

FEBRUARY 8

Trust Your Good Shepherd
1 Peter 2:25

For you were straying like sheep, but now have returned to the Shepherd and Overseer of your souls. The Good Shepherd will rescue, lead, direct, guide, and help you. He wants you to follow Him so that He can protect you from harm. He is searching far and wide for those who will abide in Him. The *Lord* will never lead you astray or abandon you. Look up and you will find Him. Lift your eyes to the hills to find your help.

The Overseer of your soul is calling you. Can you hear Him? Do you know that He loves you unconditionally? Are you ready to receive all that He wants to give you? Let Him be the one you look to for your strength as you run your race. He will strengthen you and bless your life with buckets of joy. His presence will overshadow you with peace.

Come back if you have strayed. You have been searching everywhere else for your joy and peace. But your hope is found in *Jesus Christ* alone. Stop running aimlessly without *Jesus*. You will be lost without your Shepherd. It is time to trust the one who gives you everything you need!

FEBRUARY 9

Power in the Gospel
Romans 1:16

For I am not ashamed of the gospel, for it is the power of God for salvation to everyone who believes. The good news of the gospel brings hope and life. Proclaim its message to those around us so that they can know the truth. There is freedom in the gospel message. There is much power in the word of *God*. It brings salvation and freedom to those who hear its message and believe!

We are not ashamed of the truth found in the word of our *Lord*. We can live with the joy of the *Lord* as we listen to His truth and obey Him. Let us trust and obey our *God* with all our heart so that He will make our paths straight. Let us lean securely on Him and not our own understanding. Let us faithfully follow Him to all truth.

The *Lord* is waiting for us to share His message of hope. He wants us to go spread the good news of the gospel message. He desires that we live out the message by living like *Jesus* through our faithful obedience and our unconditional love to others. We are His beloved children, born with a *God*-given destiny. Let us surrender all in faith to Him and follow Him to sweet freedom. In Him we will find our true destiny!

FEBRUARY 10

The Lord Brings Us Through the Fire
Romans 13:12

Let us cast off the works of darkness and put on the armor of light. This armor from the *Lord* will protect you from the world and its ways of darkness that will try to tempt you and make you turn away from righteousness. But you are strong in the *Lord* with His light shining in and through you. You have His living Spirit inside you, shining brightly. Let the *Lord* continue His good in you by strengthening you for what lies ahead. When you face the fire, know that He is right there with you bringing you through it. Yes, only the *Lord* can bring us through the fire!

Let go of your past fears, and let *God* lead you to freedom. Your future of peace awaits you now. Live moment by moment with your mind on the pure and lovely things that come from the *Lord*. Draw closer to the *Holy Spirit* and the light of His love.

Every day is an opportunity to love as *God* has loved you. Make the most of your days by trusting Him more each day. Everyday can be a good day, when you get real with *God* by seeking a real relationship with Him. Let Him in your life and open your heart completely to His love. When you let Him work in your life, His joy will be your joy. Do it today, because today is the day that the *Lord* has made for you! Let us rejoice and be glad in it!

FEBRUARY 11

Stay Connected to the Power Source
2 Timothy 3:16

All Scripture is breathed out by God and profitable for teaching, for reproof, for correction, and for training in righteousness. The word of the Lord is truth and is alive and real. The *Lord* works inside us to bring us life if we obey His commands and abide by His truth found in Scripture. The word brings us hope as we read about the love of *Jesus* in its pages. His love helps us grow closer to Him so that we can love others. We show our love to Him by obeying His commands meant for our good and His glory in our lives.

Let us live connected to His Spirit of truth and love. We have just enough grace when we have the love of *Jesus*! He loved us so much that He forgave us of our sins. He gives us a second chance. He yearns for us to give others that same grace. Let us live by grace through our faith in *Jesus Christ*, our living hope. He is our only true hope and anchor in this ever- changing world.

When we are living connected to the power source of Jesus, we are redeemed and made new in His image. His power is life-giving and life-saving! Only *Jesus* can save us! Turn to Him and let His grace wash over you because it is by His grace that you have been saved!

FEBRUARY 12

Grace is Enough
Titus 2:11

For the grace of God has appeared, bringing salvation for all people. Our *Father* loved us so much that He gave His only Son so that whoever believed in Him would have this gift of grace. Remember this promise and come back to His arms of grace. Let Him hold you up and bring you back to Him. You once believed with your whole heart, but now are running away from His love. Turn back to His love and let *Jesus* lavish you with His grace.

His grace is enough. Take it and let His Spirit of freedom and truth come alive in you. By faith you have been saved. Your faith will please the *Lord* and your works done in faith will be a blessing. Be all that you were made to be in *Christ*. You can stop trying to please man when you strive to please your *Lord Jesus*.

He loves you unconditionally through it all. Come back to the one who loved you even before you were born. Yes, He does love you and wants the best for you. He holds your future in His hands. Experience His perfect love that casts out fear and doubt by trusting Him with all your heart. Cry out to the one who weeps and rejoices with you. He knows your every dream and desire. Praise Him for giving you salvation and for being your living hope! *Amen*!

FEBRUARY 13

Let Your Cup Overflow with Jesus
Isaiah 59:19

For He will come like a rushing stream, which the wind of the Lord drives. The Spirit of the *Lord* has come in a mighty way like the rushing of the wind that moves all around us. He is all powerful and all knowing. He moves in ways that cannot be explained. His power and might will strengthen you and fill you with hope again. Are you still searching for hope in the temporal things of this world? Let go, shift your focus to *Jesus* and feel His Spirit come alive in you!

The Spirit of the living *God* will come alive if you make Him the center of your life. Try turning to JESUS and let go of everything that hinders you from knowing Him better. You have free will to decide how to live. Start living connected to *Jesus* and His power source and you will be energized in a fresh, new way.

You will feel the everlasting joy of *Jesus* fill your heart, body, mind and soul when you let Him in. Do not turn aside from this opportunity to make your life a living fountain of joy in *Jesus*. His living water will flow through you as you seek Him more and more. The fountain of life you are seeking to refresh you never runs dry. Pour out your heart to *Jesus* and let His joy fill your cup to overflowing!

FEBRUARY 14

Abide for a More Abundant Life
John 15:9

As the Father has loved me, so I have loved you. Abide in my love. His love is so real for you. He loves you so much and wants a real and deeper relationship with you. In order to have that close and real relationship, He needs you to abide in Him. Show your love for the *Savior* by abiding in Him. Abiding is following *Jesus* with your whole heart and faithfully serving Him where He calls you. Abiding also means staying connected to Him: your power source.

When you serve by faith, you will start growing fruit from your good works. *Jesus* wants to grow more fruit in you. He wants you to have baskets of glory. To have this bountiful harvest for Him, you must grow closer and continue abiding faithfully in His love. As you bear much fruit for *Jesus*, you will be blessed beyond measure! Others will see your works and give glory to *Jesus*! This is how Jesus wants you to live; striving to bear much fruit for Him!

Let your faith take you to new places. Let others see the love of *Jesus* through you. His love is so real. Abide in *Jesus Christ* and you will have an abundant life filled with the joy of *Jesus*! His joy is so real and true!

FEBRUARY 15

Ask and You Shall Receive
John 16:24

Until now you have asked nothing in my name. Ask, and you will receive, that your joy may be full. When you ask with great faith in the name of *Jesus*, you will receive. He is wanting to bless your life with more joy. So what are you waiting for? Ask in His name believing you will receive all that *Jesus* has for you.

Have faith in the beauty of what *Jesus* can give you. Believe that He is ready to bless you. Ask and get ready for a changed life when you are connected to *Jesus*! Yes, your life will be different with *Jesus* in the center because it is the best place to be! Draw close where *Jesus* can hold you the tightest!

Stay close and receive your greatest blessings. Be still and pray knowing that He will bless your life with the greatest joy ever! Have the time of your life as you see *Jesus* answering your prayers. It is time to believe in the beauty of your dreams! Dream big and pray bigger and bolder! What are your boldest prayers? Pray in the name and in the power of *Jesus* and see your prayers answered in ways you could never have imagined!

FEBRUARY 16

The Same Spirit that Lives in You, Lives in Jesus
John 20:22

And when He had said this, He breathed on them and said to them, "Receive the Holy Spirit." When you believe, *Jesus* gives you the *Holy Spirit*. Believe to receive this gift. Let His Spirit fill you and guide you to all truth and peace. You have a friend and an advocate who will direct your path and help you always. The Spirit is real. Receive the *Holy Spirit!*

The same Spirit that lives in you, lives in *Jesus*. This Spirit raised Him from the dead so that you can be forgiven and freed from your sins. Leave your past behind and turn to the cross of salvation. Be filled with the Spirit and find your hope in *Jesus*. He has given you His Spirit so that you can have joy. Receive the *Holy Spirit*!

The Spirit gives you life. Choose to activate this Spirit inside of you and listen to the voice of the Spirit. Live in the Spirit to have life. Say yes to the Spirit and see how your life will be full. Keep believing that there is more for you. You can have a life filled with hope. Your faith and His power will set you free! Receive the *Holy Spirit*!

FEBRUARY 17

Bloom Eternally in Jesus
John 11:40

Jesus said to her, "Did I not tell you if you believed you would see the glory of God?" He shows His glory when we believe. There is much joy waiting to be seen when we believe. Are you ready to experience the joy of *Jesus*? His joy is complete in those who follow Him by faith. Let your faith take you higher and fill you with the joy of *Jesus*!

Every day will be brighter with *Jesus*. All your hopes will come alive with Him. All your fears will vanish. Those who abide in *Jesus* will find a changed life of peace and joy. They will come alive with His powerful Spirit!

You can be one of His children of light if you so desire. Just confess with your mouth and believe in your heart that *Jesus* died for you and come to His cross of mercy and grace. Believe in *Jesus* who was raised from the dead and repent of your sins. Keep close to *Jesus* and let Him cover you completely with His grace. Abide in the truth and the only way to life, *Jesus Christ,* so that your joy will be complete. Keep abiding and you will bloom eternally in *Jesus*!

FEBRUARY 18

Fill Up Your Soul with the Living Water of Jesus
John 4:14

The water that I will give him will become in him a spring of water welling up to eternal life." Are you looking to fill your thirsty soul? Do you know that you can satisfy this thirst with the living water from *Jesus*? He gives you water that will refresh and revive you. These springs of life from *Jesus* will flow eternally in you. He meets your needs and desires completely. Are you ready to receive all that *Jesus* has for you? Are you ready to come to life?

Come to His fountain of life and drink of His water that never leaves you thirsty. He knows your every want and desire. He wants to fill so you have all that you need. The *Lord* supplies all your needs. Do you pray believing that He will meet your very need? Have you asked the *Lord* for that which you desire?

Pray in faith that *God* will and can supply everything that He knows you need. He does fulfill the desires of your heart when you are seeking His will to delight in Him! Drink of His living water and you will never be thirsty again!

FEBRUARY 19

Find it All in Jesus
Psalm 100:4

Enter His gates with thanksgiving, and his courts with praise! Give thanks to Him; bless His name! The *Lord* will meet you there. He is waiting for you to come and meet Him. He has been searching for you. Come just as you are and worship Him. Praise Him for His love and grace that He freely gives you. He has sacrificed so much for you!

All good things come to those who wait upon the *Lord* and trust Him with all their heart. His will for you will be established in His time. Believe that He will surely do it. He makes a way where there is no way. His promises for you are true and real. Start trusting Him and see that everything is possible for you, if you believe!

Your faith will take you to places you could never imagine. You will be filled with His peace and hope as you journey with the *Lord* and seek Him with your whole heart. Start today by saying yes to *Jesus*. His blessings are bountiful to those who accept all that He has to offer. Come to *Jesus* and find everything you need!

FEBRUARY 20

Reap the Rewards of Your Labor
Matthew 24:13

But the one who endures to the end will be saved. Keep working hard and do not give up, for your work will be rewarded. The *Lord* gives you the endurance and strength that you need to succeed. He will help you overcome that obstacle. Finish the race you have been given and persevere with the strength of the *Lord*!

Draw to the *Lord* for your power and rise above it all. As you turn to *Jesus*, you will soar higher. He will infuse you with His strength. You will be victorious because your faith in *Jesus Christ* will become bigger than your fear!

Wait upon the *Lord* and He will surely do it. Keep believing and trusting Him for big things to happen for you. He is waiting for you to ask Him for more. He is ready to bless you as you trust Him. Keep on going with your feet planted firmly in the soil of His love. Let His love grow deeper roots in you so that you can bear good fruit in the fertile soil of His grace and mercy. It is time to reap the rewards of your great faith and diligent work for the *Lord*! You will endure with *Jesus Christ*!

FEBRUARY 21

Bask in the Glory of the Lord
Matthew 25:23

His master said to him, "Well done, good and faithful servant. You have been faithful over a little; I will set you over much. Enter into the joy of your master." When you seek the *Lord* and His will and walk faithfully with Him, He shows Himself to you in mighty ways. You will find Him when you seek Him. He is ready to give you more as you seek Him more. Are you seeking Him? Are you asking Him to open the door for you? Are you searching for Him with your whole heart?

Turn to *Jesus* and seek His will. Ask Him and it will be given to you. The *Lord* will open the door wide for the opportunities He has for you! Believe that He can do it! Yes, He has put a new song in your heart to sing. He has given you a fresh fire in your soul. He has revived you as you have turned to Him. Only the *Lord* can revive you in a new way! He has created something brand new in you. You are alive and made new in *Christ*!

Experience all that He wants to give you today. Spend today basking in His presence. Love Him and praise Him like never before. He loves you so much and will satisfy and sustain you when you trust Him first. Delight in the *Lord* and He will give you the desires of your heart!

FEBRUARY 22

Let His Favor Shine Upon You
Psalm 84:11

For the Lord is a sun and a shield; the Lord bestows favor and honor. No good thing does He withhold from those who walk uprightly. The *Lord* will cover us with protection from harm and evil. He will keep us from temptation when we seek Him. He pours His blessing upon those who seek Him and walk with Him. His favor shines brightly on those who keep walking and living faithfully. Let us keep the faith by seeking Him with our whole hearts. He is waiting to bless us abundantly. We will see this blessing in our lives as we keep trusting Him even when others do not.

Hold up His shield of faith and let His favor cover you! Grab on tight to *Jesus* as He takes you through that storm. He is always there for you! He never leaves or forsakes you. Keep believing in His power and glory! He is a real force in the lives of those who will take His *Holy Spirit*. The power of the *Lord* is real. It is a power that we can have when we believe.

Keep on believing and keep on trusting. Let your faith be bigger than your fear! It is time to put your faith first and come to life with the power of the *Holy Spirit*!

FEBRUARY 23

Glorious Praises in the Arms of Jesus
Psalm 66:1

Shout for joy to God, all the earth; sing the glory of His name; give to Him glorious praise! How great is our *Lord* and *Savior*! He is so worthy of all our honor and praise! He has heard our prayers and is answering them! His mighty hand is upon us! Do you see Him? Can you feel His power and love? He is pouring buckets of love over us. He is showering us with blessings.

The *Lord* is so good. He loves us and is there for us all the time. He wants His people to turn toward Him and listen. He wants us to work together as one so that many can know this great love. He needs us to come together and shine for Him. As we do, we will bring others to know this peace. We will be glorifying Him as we sparkle and lead others into the arms of *Jesus*.

Our unity for *Christ* will shine forth as we come together. Our love will bring others to know His great and powerful love! Keep believing and working towards the prize of the upward calling of *Jesus Christ* Keep sharing your story of hope. Keep fighting the good fight of the faith. Keep loving *Jesus* first. As you do all these things, you will be a blessing and be blessed beyond measure. A double portion blessing is waiting for you!

FEBRUARY 24

Wait Upon the Lord
Psalm 130:6

My soul waits for the Lord more than watchmen for the morning, more than watchmen for the morning. Wait upon the *Lord*. He will keep His promises to you. His timing is always perfect, even when you cannot understand. Believe that He knows the best for you. A thousand years is like a day to the *Lord*, so be still and wait. Yes, wait for your answer to come in His timing and in His will, just at the right time. Have you asked your *Lord* for the deep desire of your heart? Would this be something He would want for you? Would it please Him to give it to you? If so, ask and you shall receive. Seek and you shall find *Jesus*. Delight in the *Lord* and He will give you the desires of your heart according to His will for you.

There is peace waiting for you down the path with *Jesus*. Your heart and soul will be calm when you are one with *Jesus Christ*. He takes away all your fears and wipes away all your tears. He truly lights up your life when you let Him. Keep on the lighted path with *Jesus*. Follow Him to a place of peace. Come out of the dark places and into the light of *Christ*. Your life will never be the same when you experience this true light. It is time to trust *Jesus*, your Prince of Peace!

FEBRUARY 25

Jesus is the Way to Peace
Colossians 3:15

And let the peace of Christ rule in your hearts, to which indeed you were called in one body. And be thankful. Jesus is peace and will give you peace. Put your trust in Him and let Him be your peace. He is waiting for you to surrender all to Him. Give Him your worries and your fears. He will take them away and give you peace. Yes, only *Jesus* can comfort you and bring you real peace.

Eagerly give all to Him and see how you will find peace beyond understanding. Put others before yourself and see how giving brings you peace. *Jesus* gave you all when He died on the cross for you. His sacrifice has made you whole again. It is for freedom that *Christ* has set you free. He loves you so much that He wants to give you freedom and peace.

He delights in you and wants the best for you. Take and receive all that is yours in *Christ*. He has so much that He wants to give you. It is yours when you, by faith, trust and obey Him.

Follow *Jesus* to the place of peace that He has for you. Submit to Him and let His peace cover you completely. Surrender all to your *Lord* and *Savior*. Faithfully serve Him and love Him well so it will be well with your soul! *Jesus* is peace and the way to peace is *Jesus*!

FEBRUARY 26

Live Weightless
Galatians 5:25

If we live by the Spirit, let us also keep in step with the Spirit. We are filled with the *Holy Spirit* when we believe in *Jesus* and give our hearts to the *Lord.* He gives us His gift of the Spirit when we believe in Him. Let us live with the *Holy Spirit* active and present in our lives.

In order to live by the Spirit, we must fully engage Him by surrendering all and walking with Him. *Jesus* wants us to live a life full of peace and joy. When we ask Him to guide us and our every thought, we will experience new life through Him. Only *Jesus* can give us this new life. Let us honor Him by connecting our heart to His through our trust. When we put our full weight down on Him, we will find our strength in Him. His Spirit will lift us up so that we feel weightless and free! The *Holy Spirit* will lead us into all truth and righteousness. He will direct our paths and make the way straight for us.

Arise and rejoice for the *Lord* has given us a gift that we need! He has put new life in us through the *Holy Spirit*: our friend and advocate. As we take this gift and activate Him in our life, we will be filled with the power of life. We will be one with the *Father*, the *Son,* and the *Holy Spirit*! Thanks be to *God* for this amazing gift that He gives us!

FEBRUARY 27

Get Lost in Jesus
1 Corinthians 15:58

Therefore, my beloved brothers, be steadfast, immovable, always abounding in the work of the Lord, knowing that in the Lord, your labor is not in vain. Read and listen to the word of the *Lord* found in the pages of the Bible. His word stands as truth for you to follow. Be steadfast in your faith and follow His guide to living an abundant life!

He has called you to work for Him and asks that you share His good news of great joy with this broken and lost world. Get lost in His word in prayer, not in the lies and temptations of the world. His way is the only way to abundant life! The ways of the world lead to a dead end. Only the *Lord* can bring you everlasting life and peace. Chose *Jesus* and you will find life!

Call upon the *Lord* to show you the way He wants you to go. Return to *Jesus*, your first love. He wants your whole heart so that He can transform you. His way is the way you have been searching for!

Stand firm in your faith knowing and believing that *Jesus Christ* can, and will, do the impossible for you! Just believe and your life will be filled with His great joy! His treasures are yours if you will faithfully follow Him where He has called you! Now, it's time to go!

FEBRUARY 28

Hearts Healed by Love
1 Corinthians 13:13

So now faith, hope, and love abide, these three: but the greatest of these is love. Yes, love conquers souls and opens hearts. The world needs more love. *Jesus* came to show love to those around Him. He fed, healed, ministered, performed miracles, and just loved those in need. Even when He was rejected, betrayed, persecuted, and crucified, He forgave and loved.

He loves us so much and wants us to love one another as He has loved us. The world needs *Jesus* and His everlasting love. Hearts can be healed with love. Greater good can happen when loving hearts work together as one. *Jesus* wants His people to come together in peace and unity. He hopes for a world where brothers and sisters can love even when they do not agree. Revival is possible when hearts are transformed by the love of *Jesus*!

Let us do our part to bring love through our faith in *Jesus* knowing that all things are possible when He is in the center of our life. With *Jesus*, the weak can be strong and the faint can be lifted up. The hopeless will find hope again. Loving *Jesus* is the key to opening hearts. Love Him today with an open heart and be revived and renewed in *Jesus Christ*!

PRAYER TO JESUS

Dear *Lord*,

Thank you for always being with me. I will not fear because you are near. You always have the best plans for me, so I will trust you even when I do not understand all the details. Therefore, I will not be anxious about tomorrow, for tomorrow will be anxious for itself. There are many days when I can only make it because of your strength. My days are filled with peace because you are with me. Thank you for helping me through all my days and comforting me through all my nights.

Your love can move mountains and I know you will do it again! You are always faithful even when my faith is weak. I will live in faith and not in fear. My days are in your hands. Thank you for guiding me to all truth through the *Holy Spirit* who lives in me. I will let the Spirit lead me moment by moment as I live fearless and free!

In *Jesus* name,

Amen.

I CAN DO
all things
THROUGH HIM
who gives me
strength.
PHILIPPIANS 4:13

MARCH 1

Let His Desire Be Yours
Isaiah 64:4

From of old no one has heard or perceived by ear, no eye has seen a God besides you, who acts for those who wait for Him. Our *God* acts for you, when you let Him work in your life. He loves you and holds you close to His heart! Wait on the *Lord* and you will rise up with wings like eagles. You will run and not get weary. You will walk and not faint.

He comforts you through the hard times. He rejoices with you during the triumphs. He knows you and loves you so much! You are so special to Him. Take heart, for you are His beloved who He cherishes. Only the *Lord* will never fail you. He purposes to know you and every desire of your heart. Let the desires of your heart be His desires for you. The more you know Him, the more you will know what He desires for you.

Listen to Him calling you. Hear His words of truth that He pours into you. Let His love cover you. Only *God* can give you a peace that surpasses all understanding when you let Him in your life and fully trust Him with your heart. He is the hope and light through the darkness. Do not wait another day to find your *God*. Surrender all to Him and your life will be guaranteed to change. *God* will act when you say yes to Him. He is your best yes!

MARCH 2

Let His Joy Shine in You
Isaiah 60:1

Arise, shine for your light has come, and the glory of the Lord has risen upon you. Wake from your slumber and arise! The light of the world has shined upon you. The light from *Jesus* is bright and His glory shines upon those who are His. Come to the *Lord* and see that He has made all things new!

He has brought light to the dark places and hope through the gray clouds of doubt. He brings rays of sunshine to a cloudy day and rain drops to cleanse the dry, parched days. The *Lord* refreshes you when you let Him fill you full. What a joy it is to be in the presence of the *Lord* and know His love!

He loves sinners because He is a forgiving *God.* He loves when you come to Him and repent and ask for Him to fill you with His Spirit. He yearns for you to serve Him and His kingdom. His plan for you is made beautiful when you follow Him. Follow your *Redeemer* to a life of greater peace and joy than you can even imagine.

Do not wait another day to come to *Jesus*! He has great works designed for you. Come and find your fountain of living water from *Jesus* and be refreshed by His love. You will bubble over with greater joy when you drink of His pure living water!

MARCH 3

Be Encouraged
Romans 1:12

We may be mutually encouraged by each other's faith, both yours and mine. Our faith grows stronger when we keep trusting the *Lord*. We can do all things through *Christ* who strengthens us. Our faith deepens as we begin to see the *Lord's* hand in our lives. As we work together with other believers, we are encouraged to keep walking faithfully.

Let us encourage each other and build one another up just as the *Lord* desires. He wants us to work together for His good. He desires what is best for us. He yearns for us to follow Him as He leads us. All good things come from the *Lord* who gives to us generously. Many will come to *Jesus* for the first time as they feel His love and learn of His amazing grace. They will be drawn to His marvelous light as they hear the good news of salvation. We can spread the love of *Christ* by our faithful service and encouragement to those around us.

Let us go through the open door that the *Lord* has provided. He gives us direction when we seek Him and His way. He is waiting to bless us as we let go and let Him work through us. The closer we get to His love, the stronger we will be as the power of the *Holy Spirit* energizes and empowers us to do what we are called to do for *Christ*.

MARCH 4

A Season for Everything
Ecclesiastes 3:1

For everything there is a season, and a time for every matter under heaven. The *Lord* orders everything in His time. He is the great I Am. He makes everything beautiful in its time! He is all knowing and all loving. He watches over us and knows what we need before we even ask Him. His love for us is everlasting and amazing. His plan is perfectly made just for us!

Let us look to Him for answers and direction. We will hear His voice calling us if we will listen as we read His word and pray. He confirms His plans for us as we draw closer to Him each day. We hear Him as we see His hand in our life through circumstances and people. He faithfully answers prayers and opens doors for us to confirm the way we should go.

Let us look to the *Lord*, the author of our faith, and trust Him to lead us. We need to stop trying to control our lives alone and start following the *Lord*, fully surrendered. His way is the only way to life.

Let us draw closer and feel His love warming the cold places of our heart and soul. He will start a heavenly fire inside of us that will light up our life! When we let Him love us, our hearts and soul will be glowing with His Holy fire!

MARCH 5

Many Who Hear Will Believe
Acts 4:4

But many of those who had heard the word believed. Yes, many believed after they heard the good news that *Christ* had come to love and save them! They simply heard and believed! In the same way, we need to help spread the gospel message so that others may hear and believe.

Let us do our part to help spread His kingdom message of love and salvation. We have been gifted for our calling so that we can do the works that the *Lord* has given each of us to do. When we work to spread His message, we are sharing the hope that comes from the *Lord*. As we work alongside other believers, we are shining His bright light into the dark places.

The light of the world has come to bring love and joy to the world! He cares for us deeply and watches over us completely. We are called to share this message with others. We are created to love one another as *Christ* has loved us.

Let us not waste another day without His presence. Let us share His hope and spread His love. He is with us every step of the way from the beginning to the end!

MARCH 6

Believe to Receive
Psalm 138:3

On the day I called, you answered me; my strength of soul you increased. Yes, call upon the *Lord* and He will answer you. He will increase the strength of your soul when you let Him be the anchor of your soul. Stay connected to Him and hold on firmly. He will never let you go!

The *Lord* defends you and watches over you. He has created you in His image and loves every part of you. Make Him the love of your life and let Him love you. He will not force himself upon you but will wait patiently for you. As you trust Him completely, He will love you richly and deeply. His love is enriching and encouraging. Every moment spent in His presence will strengthen you. Ask for more of Him, His Spirit, and His presence in your life. Lean on Him and His love for you. Feel His joy overwhelm you and His love lift you up.

Bask in His glorious presence day after day and come alive with the power of His Spirit! He will fill your cup to overflowing when you let Him. Ask for more of your *Lord,* and give Him your heart. He is the only one who can transform your heart and revive your soul! Believe to receive all that is yours in *Christ Jesus*!

MARCH 7

Lean on the Lord
Psalm 121:1-2

We lift our eyes to the hills. From where does our help come? Our help comes from the Lord who made heaven and earth. The *Lord* is your help. He is your refuge and your strength. Look to Him all you who are weary, and He will give you rest. Give Him your burdens, and He will take them from you. He knows your struggles and your pain. He hears you crying and will wipe away every tear, if you let Him.

Come to the *Lord* and find your rest in Him. Pray to your Heavenly *Father* in the name of His Son *Jesus* for what you need, and He will surely answer you! Our *Lord* is able and will work all things out for good. You may not see how things can ever work out for good, but your *Lord* will act, and your faith will grow and be strengthened through these struggles. Your trials will turn into triumphs!

Trust in the *Lord* with all your heart. Lean not on your own understanding. He is ready and able to give you your heart's desire as you delight in Him. Take your requests to the *Lord* and keep believing. He will surely do it! Don't wait another day to find your Life in *Jesus Christ*! There is still hope! Your hope is found in the one who hopes you will lean on Him, your *Lord Jesus*. He is waiting for you. Look to Him first and foremost!

MARCH 8

Gentle Whispers of Love
1 John 3:24

Whoever keeps His commandments abides in God, and God in him. And by this we know that He abides in us, by the Spirit whom He has given us. As we love our *Lord*, we want to obey Him. As we love and obey, we start trusting Him in all things. Our faith grows deeper as we keep trusting and obeying.

As we continue abiding in Him in all things, the Spirit inside of us comes alive. Our hearts come closer to Him as we remain connected to Him. He touches our soul with His gentle whispers of love. Oh, how wonderful to be in His presence!

We are connected to the *Lord* in Spirit as He has given us His Spirit. He has put His seal of the Spirit on all who believe. He wants us to remain in Him and activate the Spirit inside of us by letting the Spirit lead us. He will lead if we will follow. Let us follow faithfully with passion and determination. His plans for us are to prosper and be filled with joy! When we abide in Him, we will surely succeed! Keep *Jesus* close to your heart and listen to the Spirit inside of you. Even if you do not understand, know that all things will work for good for those who love the *Lord* and are called according to His purpose. Never give up! He is right there cheering you on one step at a time! Rejoice, for the *Lord* will never give up on you!

MARCH 9

The Lord is Patient with You
2 Peter 3:9

The Lord is not slow to fulfill His promise as some count slowness, but is patient towards you, not wishing that any should perish, but that all should reach repentance. Yes, the *Lord* promises good to those who love Him and keep His commandments! He will keep His promises and will never fail you. He yearns for all to repent and ask for forgiveness and healing.

Have you come to the *Lord* in repentance to seek His forgiveness? He is patiently waiting for you. He will give His amazing grace to you and His mercy will never end as it is new each morning! Come just as you are to your *Lord* and *Savior*. No sin is too big for your *God*. He sacrificed His Son so that you could experience complete forgiveness and freedom from sin! He will wipe away every tear and wash away every stain of sin. He hears you calling Him. He sees your heart as no one else can. He will answer you if you call upon Him. He loves you deeply and He needs your faithful heart.

Serve Him faithfully and love Him passionately. Open the eyes of your heart to His love and grace as His grace is sufficient for you! Give grace today and discover the blessings found through the saving grace of *Jesus Christ!*

MARCH 10

Abandon Your Fears
1 Peter 5:7

Cast all your anxieties on Him, because He cares for you. Give all your worries and fears to the *Lord.* He will take them from you, if you release them to Him. He is eagerly waiting for you to release all to Him. He lives so that you can live freely with His Spirit inside of you. Vow to live freely by giving all to your *Lord* and *Savior.* Make Him the first love of your life, because He loved you first.

He knew you before you were born as He created you perfectly in His image in your mother's womb. He wants you to love Him deeply like He loves you. Trust Him with all your heart to give you all that you need. Rely on His love to restore your soul. Allow Him to renew your mind. Count on Him to be there for you always. He will never let you down.

He promises good to all those who love and trust Him. He will show you the best way if you follow Him. Abandon all your fears and follow the *Lord* to a life filled with more peace, joy, and love than you can ever hope for or imagine! Your cup will run over when you put your hope in *Jesus* and make Him your first love. Do it and be blessed beyond measure by your *Lord* and *Savior!*

MARCH 11

Walk in the Light
1 John 1:7

But if we walk in the light, as He is in the light, we have fellowship with one another, and the blood of Jesus His Son cleanses us from all sin. Jesus Christ is our light of hope! He brings the light to the darkness. He wants to light up our world. See His light and follow Him. He is found by all who seek Him. His blood has already redeemed sinners like us. Come to Him and seek freedom from sin.

He wants all of us to come together in fellowship and find freedom and hope. Let us walk in the light of *Jesus* in fellowship with one another so that we can live in unity and peace. Let us love one another and share our love generously. Let us be the people who walk in the light because we let *Jesus* direct our paths and guide our thoughts and our actions.

We miss out on opportunities to be blessed and to bless others when we live in our own power and control. But with *Jesus* in control, we will live fulfilled, joyful, and satisfied. The more we rely on *Jesus*, the more we will see Him. As we give up our control to *Jesus*, we will be living in the power of the *Holy Spirit* and not our own strength. Keep walking in the light and find the hope you have been searching for in *Jesus Christ*!

MARCH 12

Faith First
Hebrews 11:1

Now faith is the assurance of things hoped for, the conviction of things not seen. The *Lord* desires that you hold on to Him and your faith at all times. There are times when you may not see what you hope for, but as you keep walking by faith, know that your *Lord* will be with you each step of the way. Yes, He will make your paths straight as you keep faithfully trusting Him. He will be there for you as you make Him the *Lord* of your life.

Continue loving and living in the truth of what you believe. The *Lord* has come to give you life everlasting! He has rescued you from your doubt, worry, and fear as He has come near. The *Lord Jesus* has come to be your hope! Let His hope cover you and take away all your distress and despair. Let His love rescue you, so that all your pain will turn to gain. You have gained a friend in *Jesus*. He wants to know you better. He desires to spend time with you. He longs to be the love of your life! Let Him in and let your faith come alive. Only His love can transform you so that you can love more and live freely. Come, just as you are and trust Him with all your heart again. Let your soul come alive with His redeeming love. Fill your heart and soul with *Jesus,* and you will never be the same faithful one! Believe!

MARCH 13

Revive Us Again
Psalm 85:6

Will you not revive us again, that your people may rejoice in you? Yes, you will do just that, *Lord*! We believe that you will revive us again! We know that you want us to be restored and made new. You have invited us to come to you with everything that is in us. We will find you as we seek you. Thank you for inviting us in so that we may know you and your redeeming love for us! Our sins are washed clean by the blood of your Son, *Jesus*. We will be forgiven, if we will ask. We will be free from the chains that bind us, if we will repent.

You have loved us so much that you gave us your Son. We are redeemed by His blood and have been given life by His resurrection power! What a joy to know that we can live surrendered and free because we are loved by you! Your grace is enough!

We praise you for joining the hearts of your people as we come united to seek revival in all our hearts. Show us your face, *Lord*. Touch us with the love of *Jesus*. Give us the power of the *Holy Spirit* as we surrender all to you. We are coming to you united in your love, *Lord*. We are drawn to the hope that is ours in *Christ*, the light of the world. We are alive by the power of the *Holy Spirit*. We believe that we will all be revived again!

MARCH 14

Rest in the Shadow of the Almighty
Psalm 91:1

He who dwells in the shelter of the Most High will abide in the shadow of the Almighty. Only the shelter of the *Lord* will be a safe place for you from these storms. He is your refuge and hiding place always. Dwell with Him always, because *God* alone will, and can, do the impossible! Everything is possible for our *Lord*! If He wills it, it will be done.

Make your shelter in His shadow and rest in His presence daily. Do not let a day go by without thanking Him for His mighty presence in your life. Surrender all to Him and be filled with more joy and peace than you ever thought possible. All your fears and your anxieties will disappear as you cling to the *Lord Almighty*. Nothing can stop the living power of the *Lord* at work in your life. He will protect and keep you safe in the shelter of His arms. You will see miracles and wonders all around you. Your world will light up in His beautiful living colors. Your life will be marked by His grace and beauty.

Give Him your whole heart. Open your soul to His love and power by completely trusting Him. Make Him the *Lord* of your life once and for all! Nothing will, or can, separate you from His love. Take His love and rest in the shadow of your *Lord Almighty* starting today!

MARCH 15

Faith Built on the Solid Rock Jesus
Psalm 73:28

But for me, it is good to be near God; I have made the Lord God my refuge, that I may tell of all your works. The *Lord* is near to all who call upon Him. He is eagerly awaiting our invitation to let Him in our lives. He is our refuge of hope. He is our strength in all times. Let us call upon the *Lord* to help us and revive us.

Let us continue to seek Him with all our heart and soul. As we continue trusting Him, we will see Him working out all things for our good. We will want to be obedient. We will strive to live side by side with others who are working faithfully for the Lord. We will see the works that can only be completed through our faith. Our faith will be built upon the solid rock: *Jesus Christ*. Only *Jesus* can fill us with everlasting life. We are made whole through Him as we repent and seek forgiveness. Let us turn away from our past sins and turn towards the light of *Christ*. He has made us new in Him! Never again will we wonder or fear with *Jesus* near! We are sure of His love and redemption for us. We are certain that we will find life through Him. The closer we get to Him, the closer we get to His amazing grace and love for us. Come closer, and come alive in *Jesus Christ our Lord*!

MARCH 16

Put on His Love
Psalm 95:6

Oh come, let us worship and bow down; let us kneel before the Lord, our Maker! Let us rejoice for the *Lord* is listening to His people, and He will hear our cries for help. He will answer our prayers. Do we believe?

Yes, we serve an all knowing and all powerful *God* who loves us so deeply. He wants good for all His children. He wants us to totally depend and rely on Him. He yearns for us to abide in Him so that He can do His work through us. He has much work for us to do to bring hope to those around us. Let us see with new eyes and follow the *Lord* to our destiny with Him. He wants to bless our lives and answer our prayers. Do we believe?

His love is overwhelming and abundantly rich. He fills the desires of our heart and soul when we let Him in our lives. He will capture our heart and bring us more joy the more we abide in Him. Let us continue abiding and working for the glory of *God* and not for our own glory. The work we do for Him is more fulfilling and satisfying than we can ever dream or imagine! Do we believe? Let us put on love and let *God* work through us. As we do, He will fill us and give us new life! Only *God* can do that! He is able, and He will do it! Yes, *Lord*, we believe!

MARCH 17

No One Will Ever Come Close to Loving You Like Jesus
Psalm 85:10

Steadfast love and faithfulness meet; righteousness and peace kiss each other. He will be the one who will show you love. Let His love direct your actions and your desires. He will direct your hearts closer to His love if you will let Him. *Christ* is devoted to you. His love for you will never waver. He is always constant and reliable. He works within you to bring you hope and joy. He lives inside of you so that you can experience His light and the warmth of His love.

Jesus is the answer and the hope. Through Him you have eternal life. He came to give you life! He laid down His life for you so that you could know how much He loves you. The glory of *God* is revealed through His life and His death. See the glory of the *Lord* and bask in it eternally through your faith in the faithful one. Not all have faith, but the *Lord* is surely faithful! He will certainly do it!

Your fears will vanish, and your hope will become real in *Jesus Christ.* The power of the *Holy Spirit* will guide you. Let His power and truth direct your hearts to His. Seek *Jesus* first and you will be satisfied completely. No one or nothing can fully satisfy and fill you except *Jesus*!

MARCH 18

Wake Up to Jesus
1 Timothy 4:10

We have our hope set on the living God who is Savior of all people, especially of those who believe. Yes, our hope is found in our *Lord* and *Savior*! He is the one who never leaves nor forsakes us! As we believe and trust Him more, we feel the power of His living Spirit fall on us in a fresh new way. A fresh wind and fire of the *Holy Spirit* will surround us. We will come alive as we surrender control and draw closer to *Jesus*. Only through our surrender will we be made new in Him! The *Holy Spirit* will direct our hearts to a fresh new way of living, fully connected to love. As we connect to the power, we will find life everlasting! We will find hope beyond hope. We will live freely with grace from grace.

Let us wake up with *Jesus Christ* filling our every thought and our every desire. Let Him be the one we desire above all else because He desires us above all! Every good and perfect gift He gives comes from the *Father of Lights*. The only way to receive all from the *Father* is through the *Son*. Come to *Jesus* and live freely. He has sacrificed all for us on the cross. Salvation was bought for us as *Jesus* became the sacrificial lamb for us. Through His blood our wounds are healed, and our sins are forgiven. We are forgiven, hopeful, and free, so let us live that way!

MARCH 19

The Lord Will Provide
Matthew 21:22

And whatever you ask in prayer, you will receive if you have faith. Do you believe this? When you truly believe, you will see great and mighty things. The *Lord* will provide all that you need. He works in you. He even gives you an extra portion of blessing as you give generously. When you give from your heart, the double-portion blessing you receive from the *Lord* is immeasurable!

Try trusting Him for all that you need. Seek Him and His righteousness first and all good things will be added to you. Your faith will be built on the solid rock of *Jesus*. His word will comfort you, encourage you, strengthen you, and guide you. Never will you want the same way when you totally rely on *God.* The *Lord* loves to give to His children graciously and generously. Ask Him. He will surely provide all you need in His will. Your desires will become His desires. Your mind will be renewed as you give your heart and soul to your *Savior*. Try loving your *Lord* first. Try seeking Him with all your heart and soul. He will become your all in all if you let Him give you every good and perfect gift that He has for you!

MARCH 20

Continue Praying
Colossians 4:2

Continue steadfastly in prayer, being watchful in it with thanksgiving. Yes, keep praying for *God* to answer the deep cry of your heart. Do not stop praying fervently and continually with a thankful heart. Your *Lord* is listening to you. He knows what you need before you even ask Him. It is so encouraging to know that He desires all good for you and knows the desires of your heart.

Keep praying, believing that you will receive what you ask with a thankful heart. *God* bends down to listen to you and gives generously. Continue praying to the one who never lets you down. Open your heart to the one who has given you so much grace and love. He has saved you, because He loves you! Be hopeful and eager to receive by faith. Your faith will become your joy because *Jesus* lives inside of you. See His light and turn your heart toward *Jesus*. Tell others about the light of the world. There is nothing more beautiful than one who is blind to truth finally opening his eyes to the light and the love of *Jesus*! The blind will see and the lost will be found in *Jesus Christ*

Jesus is the answer. He is the only way to the *Father*. Let the warmth of His light cover you and comfort you today. He is your *Savior* forevermore!

MARCH 21

Immeasurable Blessings
Ephesians 3:20

Now to him who is able to do far more abundantly than all that we ask or think, according to the power at work within us. Yes, the *Lord* works in you for His will to be done on earth as it is in heaven. He needs workers for His kingdom right now. It is *God* who calls you and *God* who will use you as He desires, if you will choose to go in His direction. Choose to follow and you will find life.

He wants you to take and eat His daily bread, so you will be nourished. He will strengthen you to work. Drink His living water and you will be filled with eternal life. Come to His fountain of life and let Him pour His Spirit over you. Grow in the grace and knowledge of our *Lord, Jesus Christ.* He gives you all you need to do the work He has called you. If the *Father* wills it, it will be done. Let Him do His good work in you. He needs all your heart to accomplish all that needs to be done through you. You have a preordained job to do for His kingdom. He has assigned you a task if you will listen, trust, and obey. The blessings you will receive as you work for His glory are immeasurable! Taste and see that the *Lord* is good all the time! Come to *Jesus Christ* fully surrendered and ready to receive your assignment with joy!

MARCH 22

The Real Answer is Jesus
Ephesians 4:4

There is one body and one Spirit, just as you were called to one hope that belongs to your call. Our one hope is *Jesus Christ*! Let us come together in one accord as one body and one Spirit to pray for peace and unity. Let us come together in faith knowing that only *Jesus* can heal us. As we draw closer to *Jesus*, we will feel the power of the *Holy Spirit* working in our lives and in our community. The power and the healing are real!

It is time for all of us to put aside our divisions and differences and see others in need right before our very eyes. There is loss and heartache all around us. It is time for us to heal together and comfort one another as *Jesus* loves and comforts us. Let us focus on those who need comfort and prayer instead of our own selfish desires. There are lost and lonely people all around us who do not know the love of *Jesus*. We are called to love our neighbors as *Jesus* has loved us. The struggles we are facing are real, so we must turn to the real answer to be healed! The real answer is *Jesus Christ*. The key to reviving our hearts and our souls is in the power of the *Holy Spirit* given to us through *Jesus Christ*. *Jesus* is calling us! Let us follow Him as one heart, soul, and Spirit!

MARCH 23

Let His Love Settle in Your Soul
1 Thessalonians 5:11

Therefore, encourage one another and build one another up, just as you are already doing. Your encouragement and love brings hope to those in need. Your positive attitude and spirit of joy brings joy to others. Your uplifting spirit lifts the spirits of those who are struggling. We all need to be encouraged so that we can continue to press on. You can be the one who helps build up the body of *Christ* by your love and your actions. You can be the peacemaker who helps bring peace.

You are indeed called to encourage and love those in need. Will you answer the call? Will you shine the light of *Christ*? Will you love like He loves you? Yes, you will, because you know you are loved by *God*. His love conquers all! His love helps you see clearly. His love gives you hope. His love settles on your soul and gives you peace. You can love because you are loved.

Jesus commands us to love one another. His love will lift spirits and warm hearts. Continue loving and living freely in the Spirit of the living God. His *Spirit* will transform your heart and your soul so that you can give love to those in need who the *Lord* puts in your path to love. Love and find your destiny in *Jesus Christ*!

MARCH 24

Let the Lord Fight for You
Joshua 1:9

Be strong and courageous. Do not be frightened, and do not be dismayed, for the Lord your God is with you wherever you go. Your *Lord* will fight your battles if you let go of control and let Him. He will never leave or forsake you. Just when you think you cannot go another step, the *Lord* steps in and takes you the extra mile. You can do all things through *Christ* who strengthens you!

Let *Jesus* lead you. Let Him take over. When you are filled with the power of the *Holy Spirit* and the truth of the word of *God*, you will have all you need. Be filled with His power and His truth and you will find the joy you have been searching for! Yes, joy is yours if you choose *Jesus*! Let His grace and mercy cover you, precious one. He is waiting with open arms for you to come and be comforted by Him. Lean on the *Lord* and give Him your heart. Open the eyes of your heart to His wonder and light. He is the hope that will fill the dark places.

Let His light and His love transform and revive you now. It is time to be a faithful follower of *Jesus Christ*. You will find everything you need when you rest in His presence and let Him help and comfort you. He is your strength when you are weak. He is the treasure that you seek.

MARCH 25

Live by Faith
Galatians 2:20

I have been crucified with Christ. It is no longer I who live, but Christ who lives in me. And the life I now live in the flesh I live by faith in the Son of God who loved me and gave himself for me. By faith, you live because you know that *Jesus* sacrificed all for you. By faith, you are brought to a right relationship with *God* the *Father* through *Jesus Christ*. You can know the *Father* through His *Son*. Believe in *Jesus* and be justified by faith not by works of the law. You were crucified with *Christ* on the cross. His grace saved you and gave you new life!

The life you now live in the flesh, you live by faith in the one who sacrificed all out of His great love for you. He loves you so much that He gave His only *Son*. He has given you His Spirit by faith as you believe. As you truly believe, your faith will be counted as righteousness in the eyes of *God*. He sees into your soul and knows the desires of your heart. Draw to Him by your faith and trust in His power to do great and mighty things in your life.

The righteous shall live by faith. You have received the promised Spirit through faith in *Jesus*. The law has not given you the Spirit. *Jesus* gives the Spirit freely to those who believe in Him. It is time to be led by the Spirit through your faith in *Jesus Christ*.

MARCH 26

Believe to Receive
Jeremiah 1:5

Before I formed you in the womb, I knew you. You were made in His image and created out of His great love for you. He loves you so much! Never stop believing that He loves you and wants the very best for you. He sees your potential and your calling for His glory. He is patiently waiting for you to come to Him. The *Lord* knows how everything will work out for your good in His timing. Be still and listen to Him. As you wait and fix your eyes on *Jesus*, He will show you great ways you can live connected to His Spirit. It is time to breathe in the Spirit that He gives you. His Spirit is life giving and full of peace.

When you choose to live in the Spirit, you will find that the *Holy Spirit* will be your comforter and your friend. He lives inside you to direct and guide you, only if you let Him. Be Spirit led and Spirit-filled and find that joy you have been searching for. *Jesus* has given you your gift. Have you unwrapped it to find all that you need? *Jesus* knows the deep cry of your heart. He wants to help you and comfort you. Together, you will be victorious. Together, you will be fearless. Pray that you will surrender all to your comforter. Pray that you will live filled with the Spirit. Believe to receive all that is yours in *Christ Jesus*!

MARCH 27

The Great Rewarder of Faith
2 Corinthians 5:7

For we walk by faith, not by sight. Believe in the things you hope for without seeing. Trust that the *Lord* will answer your prayers. He hears you and bends down to answer you. Lift up your eyes and focus on what you know that the *Lord* has promised you, and believe! Your faith will grow as you keep trusting and obeying His voice and His word. He will show you great and mighty things that you have not known.

Take that leap of faith into the deep waters with *God*. You are not alone when you are connected to Him. Keep walking by faith because one great day when you are together in your heavenly dwelling, you will see and your faith will be your eyes! He has prepared a place for you at His heavenly banquet. Right now, He needs you to do His work He while you are waiting. He has put His Spirit inside you as a guarantee so that you can live abundantly. With the eyes of a believer, you will find joy on earth with the Spirit dwelling in you. As you believe and faithfully serve Him by serving others, your *Lord* will be well pleased. Your great reward, faithful one, will be to spend eternity in heaven with *Jesus* who is sitting at the right hand of the *Father*. What a promise from our *Lord*!

MARCH 28

Hold Nothing Back
Psalm 18:3

I call upon the Lord, who is worthy to be praised, and I am saved from my enemies. Call on His name and believe that He came to die for you to live. Through *Jesus Christ*, you are forgiven and free! He gives you grace and His grace is sufficient for you. Those who believe in Him will receive all because *Jesus* holds nothing back for those that He loves. Come to *Jesus* and come to life because His power reigns! He needs you to be engaged in His love and take your cup from Him so that He can fill it. He will fill it so full that your joy will overflow abundantly. He loves to give, so be ready to receive all that is yours in *Jesus Christ.*

His light shines down on you as you come closer and live with His peace. Do you feel the difference as you walk in the light? He shines His path of light down on you so that you can see where to go. His light becomes brighter in the darkness, so come out of the darkness and turn to the light of hope found in *Jesus*. He has given you hope so cling to Him and come out of hiding. He needs you and wants you to help Him carry the gospel of peace to the lost. Your faith will come alive as you take steps with *Jesus*. Be a faithful follower and find your refuge and salvation in *Christ* alone!

MARCH 29

Spark of Hope
1 Corinthians 1:31

Let the one who boasts, boast in the Lord.
Yes, let us not boast about ourselves, but boast about
Jesus and His abundant loving kindness towards all.
Let us tell about how much He loves all of us. Let us
be His hands and feet to spread hope around us,
because He is our hope. He is worthy of our honor
and our praise! He gives us His amazing grace even
when we do not deserve it. We can be full of hope
when we focus on *Jesus* and live faithfully. He is the
one who will fire us up to live fearless and free. Let
us be freed in His love and grace!

Be strong and courageous and draw to His
love. Even if we do not understand what we see
around us, our faith will be our strength when it is
grounded in *Christ*. There is hopelessness all around
us and *Jesus* sees this lost hope. He yearns for His
children to come to Him full of faith so that He can
start a fire inside of us. This spark of hope will ignite
a fire in each of us. We can be that one spark that
lights another flame and another flame and another
flame until the whole world is full of His great light!
Be a peacemaker and a fire starter. It all begins and
ends with *Jesus*. He is the beginning and the end.
Come to *Jesus* and put your full faith and complete
trust in Him!

MARCH 30

Brotherly Affection
Romans 12:10-11

Love one another with brotherly affection. Outdo one another in showing honor. Do not be slothful in zeal, be fervent in Spirit, serve the Lord. Revival will come to us when we seek to live in the Spirit with a hunger for spiritual things and desire to zealously live connected to *Christ*. Let us search our own hearts and live in brotherly love. Let us honor the *Lord* and listen to what He is calling us to do. We can each make a difference in the body of *Christ* by seeking His will at all turns. Let us draw closer to the peace and unity He desires for us by living in His will and not our way. Let us serve the *Lord* faithfully by always seeking Him first. He hears us calling Him and will respond to our prayers. Do we hear Him calling us? Are we listening?

There is no other way that leads to life everlasting. Only the *Lord* can save us. Keep fighting the good fight of faith and keep loving with the love of *Christ*. Our joy will be complete in Him when we answer the call of the *Holy Spirit* and walk in obedience. He will bless our life with more of His presence and majesty when we host His presence in our daily lives. Start today by living in the Spirit and loving one another unconditionally with the love of *Christ*!

MARCH 31

A Time for Everything
Ecclesiastes 3:11

He has made everything beautiful in its time. There is a time for everything in *God's* timing. He is the one who makes beauty from ashes. He is the one who takes what is bad and turns it around for good. The plots and schemes of man meant for our harm will be transformed to good in His time.

Jesus will save the lost so that they can find salvation. He will bring hope to the hopeless. The power of the *Holy Spirit* will bring peace and joy to those who choose to live by the Spirit. Let us find that peace that awaits us in the midst of the storm. Let us live in *Christ* fully connected to Him. He will change the direction of the storm to bring refuge to us in His time. Let us lean on *God* as we put our trust in Him and seek shelter in Him. Salvation's tide is rising as we all seek His face.

We can be sure and believe that our *God* can do anything! He will take away our fears and put a new song in our hearts to sing praises of thanksgiving with joy! It is time to pray in faith even when we do not see. It is time to open our eyes to the wonder that awaits us. It is time to come together as one and pray. It is time to believe again with unswerving faith!

PRAYER TO JESUS

Dear *Lord*,

Oh how I love you and thank you for being my *God* who works wonders; you have made known your might among the people. You are mighty to serve and oh how I want to serve you more. You have stood by me and strengthened me for the work you have called for me and I am able to all things through you!

I see the many wonders you have shown me, and I am overwhelmed by all of them. How great are your works. Everything is made beautiful in its time. I see you making beauty out of ashes time and time again as you are the *God* of glory!

You are always faithful to me and I am eternally grateful for your faithfulness. Thank you for showing me your glory as I see your hand everywhere! Your hand saves and sustains.

I am walking freely and fearless today as I remember all that you have done for me. My heart is full of joy and my soul is at peace in your presence. I will praise you all the days of my life!

In *Jesus* Name,

Amen.

HE IS NOT HERE,
for he has
RISEN,
as he said.
COME,
see the place
where he lay.
MATTHEW 28:6

APRIL 1

Fervent Prayer
James 5:16

The prayer of a righteous person has great power as it is working. Keep praying and do not stop believing that *God* hears your prayers. He bends down to hear you as you pray. He listens, and He answers in His will and in His timing for you. Believe in the power of prayer. Keep praying even when you feel like you have prayed the same prayer over and over.

Keep up your faithful prayers and believe that they will be answered. Continue pursuing righteousness and *God* will answer in His will and in His timing! Keep on lifting your prayers up to Him because He wants to pour His blessings upon you. You may think you know what is best for you, but *God* ultimately knows. He knows everything. He knows how it will all work out, and He will work it all out for His glory. Are you asking and expecting *God* to answer you? Are you continuing to pray even when you cannot see the way? Are you believing in the power of prayer? Remember that nothing is impossible for *God*! Ask and you shall receive. Pray continually and meet *God* regularly. He loves hearing you pray. Your relationship with Him is strengthened as you constantly communicate with Him by prayer. Start praying with a new freedom and power today!

APRIL 2

Keep Your Heart Real
James 4:10

Humble yourselves before the Lord, and He will exalt you. Listen and do not be boastful or arrogant for the *Lord* does not honor those who act with selfish pride. He honors those who with humility seek Him and care for others more than they care for themselves. He loves to see a cheerful giver who gives out of love. He rejoices when His people come together to work for the common good with one heart, soul, and mind centered on Him.

Are you loving other people more than yourself? Are you serving Him by meeting needs of those around you? Are you giving glory to *God* for what He is doing for you and in you? Are you praising the *Lord* for the mighty things He has done? He will exalt those who come humbly before Him and act faithfully for Him. He loves to see your humility and kindness towards others. Feel His love poured over you for what you have been able to do by His power and strength from the *Holy Spirit*. Find your joy in the one who has given so much to you. He has showered you with buckets of joy! He has covered you with mountains of grace! Keep your heart real by seeking Him with your whole heart. Keep His grace close by believing that you are forgiven and free. And believe that He will exalt you!

APRIL 3

Lifter of Your Soul
Psalm 33:20

Our soul waits for the Lord, He is our help and our shield. He watches over you with His watchful eye always wanting the best for you. He knows you need Him and He will lift you up when you let Him. Remember to wait upon Him and let Him show you the way. He is the way to victory. He is the true hope that you have been searching all over to find.

Be still and sit in His presence. Hear Him calling you in the stillness of your soul. Keep Him in the center of your life and know that He is the lifter of your soul and the King of your heart. Tune into His frequency of love and be swept away in His strong arms!

The *Lord* will be your shield of faith and the strength of your mind, body, and soul. Let Him in and get lost in His great love for you. Again and again He has called you to come to Him just as you are. You have turned away because you feel unworthy and unforgiven. You are lost in your past sins and cannot escape. Remember *Jesus* has given you grace and you are forgiven and free if you let go and give *Jesus* your heart. Let *Jesus* break every chain and break free to your new life with *Jesus Christ*!

APRIL 4

Let the Lord Fight Your Battles
1 Timothy 6:12

Fight the good fight of the faith. Your faith will hold you up and make you stronger. *God* sees your struggle and He knows your pain. He wants you to turn to Him and believe that He can do what you need. He is your strength when you are weak. He is your hope when you feel hopeless. He is your shield of faith when you just cannot seem to go one more step.

Believe that your *Lord* will answer your prayers prayed in faith. He loves your faithfulness and wants the best for you. He sees your future and longs for you to trust Him to show you the way. There are days when you will need to fight harder. He will see you through all these times because He is a good *Father* and yearns to give you all that your heart desires. Trust Him to guide you into all truth. Let Him lead you by the hand across the way to freedom!

Are you still holding on to the past or are you prayerfully hoping for things to turn around for your good and His glory? He wants you to stop fighting in vain and fight the good fight of faith with Him! He has secured the victory for you. Do you not see it? Look a little closer and listen for that still small voice of *God* so that you can hear Him. He will speak when His servant is listening! Be still and know He is *God*!

APRIL 5

Come to the Light
Psalm 27:1

The Lord is my light and my salvation; whom shall I fear? The Lord is the stronghold of my life; of whom shall I be afraid? His light is shining through to you so that you will be able to shine with Him in your life. He is making a way for you out of the darkness and into His great light!

Do you see the light? Are you forging ahead with Him? Keep going as He is waiting and has never left you. You are the one who has left Him. You are pushing Him out to pursue your own ways without the *Lord*. Darkness has come into your life and you are now afraid. Fear has crept into your life and stopped you from doing what you know He wants you to do. You are continuing to pursue your own dreams without Him.

Pursue Jesus and come to the light. Find your strength in the *Lord*. Stop listening to the voices who tell you to go on alone because those voices are not from *Jesus*. Grab Him and do not let go! Feel the power of His Spirit within you! Cling to His promises and find your freedom in *Christ* today!

APRIL 6

Hiding Place
Psalm 32:7

You are a hiding place for me; you preserve me from trouble; you surround me with shouts of deliverance. You give us a place of refuge when we need to be delivered. You bring us comfort when we are struggling and love when we need it the most. You wrap your arms around us and keep us safe. You shelter us from the storms and remind us that we are safe with you.

Lord, you have always kept your word and you have never failed us! We are so thankful for you and your love that you pour over us. We are glad that we know you will never leave us. You are faithful even when we waiver in our faith. You are our sanctuary of strength and hope when we are weak and hopeless. Because with you, we will never have to face another day alone! We will shout from the rooftops with joy as we have found everything we need in you! Never again will we face anything alone and afraid because we have you in our life. You are showering us with great blessings of love and grace. You are encouraging us to go the distance with you. With you, we can finish the race set before us with a new strength and faith. Let us run with greater endurance fixing our eyes on *Jesus*, our *Savior* and *Redeemer*! He is waiting for us to finish strong!

APRIL 7

Live Fully Engaged
And Connected to Christ
1 Peter 2:9

But you are a chosen race, a royal priesthood, a holy nation, a people for His own possession, that you may proclaim the excellencies of Him who called you out of darkness into His marvelous light. He has called you out to be His own; a disciple to work and serve as you have been called and a witness for Christ to proclaim the hope and the salvation that is found in trusting Him.

Jesus came into this world so that our sins would be erased. He suffered much so that we could be redeemed. In Him, we find truth and hope in the darkness. He is our light and in Him and through Him, we have life everlasting!

You are precious and chosen to be examples to the flock of God. Eagerly and with joy, shepherd the flock that is among you. Keep loving others earnestly since love covers a multitude of sins. Keep walking by faith and giving your best as you serve others with kindness and goodness. Humble yourself under the mighty hand of God knowing that He opposes the proud but gives grace to the humble. When the Lord returns in all His glory, you will receive the unfading crown of glory. Clothe yourself with humility and stand firm in the true grace of God!

APRIL 8

Keeper of Our Heart
Psalm 51:10

Create in me a clean heart, O God, and renew a right spirit within me. We need to lay aside all that is hindering us and come to your cross of salvation with hearts and minds that want to know and serve you better. We need a fresh filling of your Spirit today. Help us to focus on your love and grace that you have given to us. We have not always listened or followed you, but you continually shower us with abundant love and amazing grace.

Search us and show us what is not pleasing to you. Give us the courage and the strength to change what you want in us so that you can do your complete work in us. We want to fulfill the ministry you have given us. We aim to please you *Lord,* but we struggle with our sins at times. Purify our thoughts and transform our minds to focus more intensely on you. Pour your Spirit of peace upon us so that we can overcome the challenges and temptations we face.

We are made whole through the blood of the Lamb who is the Overseer of our soul and Keeper of our heart. We are alive through *Christ* and can have the reward of great hope and joy today as well as the marvelous eternal reward we will receive in Heaven someday! Let us keep pressing on to glory with *Christ Jesus* every day!

APRIL 9

God is Your Sanctuary
Psalm 46:1

God is our refuge and strength, a very present help in trouble. He is your hiding place when you need to escape. He is your comfort when you just feel like you cannot go on. He is your encourager when you need to finish strong. He is there when you have lost all hope. He is your light and your salvation. Why are you so afraid? Why are you looking everywhere else except to *God*? He is looking for you.

Look to the *Lord* for all that you need to face your fears and wipe away your tears. He is constantly there for you. He has never left you, yet you have left Him. Come back to your first love and make Him your sanctuary. He will comfort you with His peace and will shower you with an abundance of joy!

Seek all that you need from your *Father* of lights! In Him there is no need to be frightened. In Him there is a way through it all! Give up fighting alone and let *God* fight for you. Be encouraged and empowered by His *Holy Spirit!* Be strong and press on!

APRIL 10

The Most Powerful Love
Psalm 31:16

Make your face shine on your servants; save me in your steadfast love! Thank you for shining down on us as we look up to you. We can feel the warmth of your love and the power of your mercy upon us. We know that our many blessings have come from you and we are grateful for every one of them. Abundant blessings are ours as we keep on trusting and obeying you!

You reward the faithful and pour down your love and blessings on those who walk in obedience. Help us to continue walking this way so that you can pour out your grace and mercy upon us. As we obey, we reciprocate our love for you and show that we are following you with our whole hearts. We are sure that you see our faithfulness and are pleased with our actions. We will not stop believing and acting by faith!

When we trust you, we will experience new freedom and wholeness. Your powerful love for us is overwhelming and everlasting and will hold us up. Let us love and trust you like never before! Let us engage our hearts and souls into a place of complete trust with you in the center. Let us trust you with our whole hearts now, so that we can walk in your Spirit of love and peace today!

APRIL 11

Live Fully Engaged and Connected to Christ
Psalm 26:3

For your steadfast love is before my eyes, and I walk in your faithfulness. Lord, we know you love us so much and want us to live in harmony. But we are still fighting and not always walking in your faithfulness. When we take our eyes off you and focus our attention on all our problems instead of your love and grace, we do not see your glory right before us. You are showing us the path to freedom through complete surrender to *Jesus Christ*, but we are not taking your path. Your ways are higher and better, but we keep blinders on to what you want to do in us and through us. We want our ways and our timing because we are selfish and impatient. But you tell us to seek you with all our heart and wait upon you. Help us to give you our whole heart starting today. Fully engaged and connected to you is the only way to live! You will help us because your love is steadfast and true. You are faithful even when we waiver in our faith. We will begin a new chapter in our lives with you in every sentence. Without you, we will fail. With you, we will soar with wings like eagles experiencing a renewed peace while waiting patiently for our eternal reward in Heaven!

APRIL 12

Speak in Love
Psalm 19:14

Let the words of my mouth and the meditation of my heart be acceptable in your sight. There are many words we can say and many choices that we can make about what we will say. We are in control of our tongues and how we speak to others. You, *Lord,* know our thoughts and our hearts. We cannot hide from you because you know us inside and out. Let our thoughts and words be honorable and acceptable to you.

You are the one who gives us your words of life. You are our great Redeemer and mighty *God.* You make a way for us when there is not a way. You give us hope when we feel lost and hopeless. You set our feet on higher ground with you because you want the very best for us!

We will try harder to live in love and walk in freedom. We will give you all our hearts so that you can show us the way to act that is pleasing to you. We are showing others *Jesus* when we act and speak in truth and love. Let us not get caught in the fray but make every effort to keep the unity of the Spirit in the bond of peace. Let our words bring hope where there is no hope. Let our thoughts be directed to *Jesus* so that we can be salt and light to a broken and hurting world!

APRIL 13

Heartfelt Prayers
1 Thessalonians 5:16-18

Rejoice always, pray without ceasing, give thanks in all circumstances. God's will for you is to keep praying, believing that He hears you and will answer your faithful prayers! Rejoice knowing that *God* knows your every need. Keep praying even when you do not see the answers immediately, because He will never fail you. *God* is always faithful to you when you are faithful to Him.

God loves your heart and beautiful heartfelt prayers. He embraces and comforts you just when you need it most. Keep praying and be ready to receive blessings He has to give you, faithful one. He showers His love over you one moment at a time. His love grows deeper when you grow stronger in Him.

God will surprise you with grace just when you need it most. Thank Him in all circumstances, even when you do not understand. His ways are higher, and His plans are greater. He may be redirecting you to trust Him more and calling you to come closer to His love. Never doubt that He knows the way it will all turn out when you turn to Him. He also knows the way it will turn out if you turn away from Him. Will you trust *God* and continue praying? Redirect your attention and refocus on *God* and you will be bountifully blessed!

APRIL 14

He Will Fulfill the Desires of Your Heart
Psalm 20:4

May He grant your heart's desire and fulfill all your plans! The *Lord* wants to see that grin on your face as He does the impossible for you! He yearns for you to trust Him to do more. Are you believing that your *Lord* can do what is impossible for man? Are you letting Him lead you on that path to victory? Are you letting go so that He can do mighty things through you and for you?

Stay connected to *Jesus* and start seeing miracles happen to you and around you. He is opening doors for you to walk through if you just let Him lead you. There is a way that leads to life with *Jesus* and He is the door you need to walk through. Talk to *Jesus* and tell Him that you believe He can do the impossible for you. Let Him lead you and show you the way. Delight in Him and let Him fulfill your heart's desires and all His great plans for you!

Jesus is delighted to know that you have let go of self and are letting Him lead you to freedom! Give *Jesus* the wheel, so He can steer you down the right path. Your faithfulness and obedience will be rewarded. Keep going with *Jesus* and do not give up because *Jesus* never gives up on you!

APRIL 15

Jesus is the Light of Life
John 8:12

"I am the light of the world. Whoever follows me will not walk in darkness, but will have the light of life." You will be given all the peace you want if you will turn to *Christ* always. Other people may frustrate, hurt, or condemn you to try to make you fall, but you can get back up when you keep your eyes focused on *Jesus*, the Prince of Peace. Yes, *Jesus Christ* is the way to life! Only *Jesus*!

This world will try to distract you from *Jesus*, your first love. You will be tempted to turn away from what you know is true and right when you get caught up in the sins you see around you. Do not go there as darkness exists where there is sin. The light is not found in those places and people.

Turn to the light of *Jesus* who encourages you to be your best always. He wants you to experience peace beyond understanding. He yearns for you to discover the truth in His word and the life in His Spirit. Living by the Spirit is the way to life but living by the flesh is the way to death. Stay connected to the Spirit and discover that His peace will permeate your heart, mind, body, and soul. Rest in His perfect peace today. Turn to the *Lord* and let His Spirit of Truth and His peace rule in your heart!

APRIL 16

Fullness of Joy
Psalm 16:11

You make known to me the path of life; in your presence there is fullness of joy; at your right hand are pleasures forevermore. We know that there is joy when we trust in you to lead us. Your path will lead us to a full life of pure joy, so we will extend our hand to yours to let you show us the way. We will stop going alone and will trust you to help us whenever we need you and wherever you call us to go. You never lead us astray.

You always show us the way we should go, and we will follow you. All our days are filled with hope when they are filled with you. Thank you for guiding us through this life. Only you can direct our hearts in a way that leads to life. Eternal life is found in you and through you. We are grateful for each day we can spend in your presence!

Every day is better than the day before when it is spent with you. You want our hearts and our minds directed towards you. You desire our souls to be connected to your Spirit. We are made whole when we are made new in you. We will stand on your promises, power, and plans for us. Thank you for loving us through it all!

APRIL 17

Extend Grace
Ephesians 4:32

Be kind to one another, tenderhearted, forgiving one another, as God in Christ forgave you. Let *God* do His work in you so that you can see what He can do through you. The *Lord* loves to show off His glory in your life so let Him shine through you as you seek Him in all that you do. Many will see *Jesus* because you have put Him first in your life. Many will know the love of the *Lord* because of your kindness and tender heart. As you lend a helping hand to those in need, people around you will feel His unlimited grace and abounding peace. His peace will cover all who need comfort and His grace will open the eyes of those bound by sin.

Open your eyes to see His glory and lift up your prayers to the most *Holy Lord* who is constantly lifting you up. Seek to be different and stand out for your *Lord* and *Savior* who stood up for you at Calvary. His blood has washed away your sins forever. He expects you to take His grace and pour it over the very ones who have hurt you or betrayed you. Why are you still so angry, bitter, unforgiving and, taking offense for wrongs done to you? *Jesus Christ* has forgiven you! Extend grace and discover that only through the grace of *Jesus* you will find your freedom and give honor to your *Lord*!

APRIL 18

The Lord Always Provides
Philippians 4:19

And my God will supply every need of yours according to His riches in glory in Christ Jesus. Can you hear Him telling you to trust Him to meet all your needs? He loves you so much that He promises to meet every need of yours. He knows what you need even before you ask, and He will meet every need according to His will. Trust Him. Listen and obey His commands so that you can find His will for you.

There are days when you will need His extra measure of love in your life. There are moments when *God* will lovingly hold you closer. There are seasons of life where you will cling to the hope that is in you to get through to the next season. He is there for you through it all. The *Lord* never leaves your side; you are the one who has left Him!

Find your rest in *Jesus* and stop trying to do everything by yourself. Your flesh and heart will fail, but *Jesus Christ* will never fail you. He is with you through every heartache and every fall as He heals and restores all. He makes all things new! Take off your old self and put on your new self in *Christ*. He is ready to supply all your hopes, dreams, wishes, passions, and pursuits of peace and joy. Come to the powerful Spirit of *Jesus* and be made new today!

APRIL 19

Work for the Lord
Colossians 3:23

Whatever you do, work heartily, as for the Lord and not for men. He will be with you as you work with all your heart. Your efforts carried out in faith and love for *Jesus* will be rewarded. Keep pressing on towards the victory found in *Jesus*. Work at it with all your might as working for the *Lord* and not for men. As you continue working, you will feel His presence all the way to victory!

Do not be discouraged by the long journey ahead of you but be encouraged knowing that the *Lord* will give you exactly what you need each step of the way. He is waiting to bless you with much as you give Him much. Turn towards His light and feel the warmth of His love and grace. He loves you so much and cares about you so deeply.

Does the road seem long and the journey impossible? Have you given up because the road has many turns, bumps, and detours? Do not focus on the potholes that surround you, but look to *Jesus*, your road warrior, to lead you through these challenging times. Look to Him and find the direction He wants to take you. Remember that He has a purpose and a plan just for you. Complete your assignment and discover the joy you will feel on the journey!

APRIL 20

Jesus is Your Power Source
2 Timothy 4:3

For the time is coming when people will not endure sound teaching, but having itching ears they will accumulate for themselves teachers to suit their own passions. Jesus is the way to peace and He is your perfect peace. When the world tries to tell you to look to temporal things of this world for peace, do not believe it. Only *Jesus* can give you peace that lasts forever!

You will find His peace even in the storms of life. When everything around you is falling apart, turn to the one who puts everything back together for you. He comforts you with His powerful love as you cling to Him. Walk on pathway of peace with your *Savior, Jesus Christ,* and feel His Spirit of love filling you with hope again. Yes, there is hope with *Jesus* in all seasons of your life. Be ready in and out of season to tell of the hope that is in you because *Jesus* lives in you! He is your living hope and because He lives, you can face tomorrow with a smile on your face and joy in your heart. The joy of the *Lord* is real not because of what you do alone, but because of *Jesus* living in and with you. You never have to walk alone when you are connected to *Jesus Christ*, your real power source! Stay connected and feel the energy of His love give you a new life of peace, hope, and joy!

APRIL 21

He is Risen Indeed!
Luke 24:6

He is not there, but has risen! Because He lives, you can live! There is promise and hope of greater purpose through *Jesus Christ*! You can live victoriously when you live connected to your *Lord* and *Savior*. Through His death, He gives you life!

What do you do with the Risen *Jesus*? You believe in Him with all your heart. Believe that He loves you and wants you to live closely connected to Him. As you hold Him close, rejoice in Him knowing that He can and will show you His glory in mighty ways. There is nothing greater than the joy of *Jesus* in a heart that believes and praises our *Savior*!

Go tell the good news of the Risen *Jesus*! There is a gospel message waiting to be heard by many who do not know or believe. There is grace upon grace available to those who believe. We all need the love and grace of *Jesus*!

Finally, live in a relationship with the Risen *Jesus*! He wants to know you and spend time with you. As you read His word, pray, journal, and think about *Jesus*, and your friendship with Him will grow deeper. You will experience new life and be renewed and revived! Spend time with *Jesus* by loving Him and praising Him and your joy will be full. His joy will be your joy. Find your joy in *Jesus*!

APRIL 22

Grace and Truth Through Jesus Christ
John 1:17

For the law was given through Moses; grace and truth through Jesus Christ. We were given these laws to guide us, but we were given grace to save us. Yes, grace was given to us so that we would walk freely in the love that our *Savior* has for us. He loved us so much that He gave Himself as a living sacrifice for us so that we would be completely forgiven for our sins. Our salvation is a result of the outpouring of the love of our Savior through the pouring out of His blood on the cross. It is by grace that we have been saved. It is for freedom that *Christ* has set us free! He wants us to walk in His freedom of truth so that we will want to live in truth. There is so much more freedom available to us each moment we trust Him more. Peace will wash over us as we let His love flow through us. Grace upon grace will restore us and His hope will revive us.

If you want to have a changed heart for *Christ*, begin by accepting His unconditional love for you. Then walk in His love by taking the grace He gives to you. Your reward is eternal life in heaven as well as manifestations of His glory seen in your life today. Miracles are waiting for you. Begin with the miracle of a changed heart for *Christ* by giving Him your whole heart today!

APRIL 23

Your Strongest Defense
Jeremiah 1:19

They will fight against you, but they shall not prevail against you, for I am with you; to deliver you. So keep the faith and keep the *Lord* by your side as you face this battle. The *Lord* goes before and behind you to hem you in safely into His arms of protection. He will not leave your side when you face those who come against you. Never fear, because the *Lord* is always near to you and He wants you to lean on Him and His power. *God* does not force you to lean on Him, but He promises help to you if you choose His help. Yes, He is your strongest defense against attack. The truth always prevails over evil because *God* is truth and He is greater and more powerful than anyone or anything. *God* will turn what was meant for harm against you into something good in His timing. Have faith and lean on Him more than you ever have before!

Trust Him and rely on His strength. Get your power from the *Holy Spirit* who will fill you with peace if you let Him lead you. Stop letting the distractions of the world keep you from the peace that is in you. Greater is He who is in you than he who is in the world! Victory is closer when *God* is active in your life filling every thought, action, word, and desire. Let go and let *God* lead you to freedom!

APRIL 24

Be Ready
Matthew 24:44

Therefore, you must be ready for the Son of Man is coming at an hour you do not expect. Be faithful to Him and do what you know is right and true. He sees inside your soul and touches you with His love. Are you showing Him your love by striving to grow stronger in your faith each day? Is your faith bigger than your fears? Let go of all your fears and follow *Jesus* to freedom by faithfully trusting Him in all situations. He can and will bring you through it all if you let Him.

Some will deny Him and His power. Others will scoff at you for believing and trusting with all your heart even when it does not make sense. Expect others to persecute you for relying on *God* as your refuge and strength. But you know the truth. The *Lord* is your living hope even in the middle of the storm. Your dependence on *God* is the solid foundation on which you stand. He will never fail you and you are determined to stand on that truth because of your great faith in the one who never lets you down! Be ready by continuing work in the faith. The world will tell you it is all about you, but the truth is that you are third. Put *Jesus* first, others second, and then yourself third. This is the way to live ready for His return. Well done, good and faithful servant!

APRIL 25

Wings of Comfort
1 John 3:20

God is greater than our heart, and He knows everything. He understands all our actions and motives and loves us anyway. He sees inside our souls and knows our thoughts and He gives us grace anyway. *God* is forgiving and faithful to us through it all. He is there for us through every storm, heartache, and disappointment. He helps get us through anything that comes our way because He is greater!

Are you struggling with your feelings and trying to make sense of it all? Are you having a hard time seeing a way out? Are you turning towards *God* or away from Him? Only *God* can help you through it all. He is the one who has made a way for you when there was no way. He is your strength and your shield of protection. He has set you free, so run to Him and let Him cover you with His wings of comfort. *God* is always there for you. He created you in His image and knitted every part of you in your mother's womb. You are His child whom He created out of great love. Reciprocate this love by engaging in a relationship with your *Lord* through abiding in Him. Make Him first in your life and see how He will mold you and awaken you to new life. Remember, He knows everything because He is greater than our heart!

APRIL 26

His Armor Cannot be Penetrated
Isaiah 52:12

The Lord will go before you; and the God of Israel will be your rear guard. When you let Him into your life, the *Lord* will lead you and will protect you from behind. He hems you in and brings you safely through it all. Never fear when you have the *Lord* with you!

Some will try to harm or threaten you, but you have your armor of *God* on that cannot be penetrated. He fights your battles and always wins, no matter what comes your way. Believe that He will prevail over your enemies. You will see if you believe. A thousand years is like a day to your *Lord*. He does it all in His timing. Be patient and wait upon the *Lord*!

Be strong and brave, faithful one. He is your strength when you are weak and your song of hope when you feel hopeless. Keep trusting and believing, because your victory is available through your *Lord, Jesus Christ.* Never doubt His faith and love for you! Cling to His gift of grace and hold on tight for the best journey of your life with your protector and friend, *Jesus Christ*!

APRIL 27

Taste and See that the Lord is Good
Isaiah 45:22

Turn to me and be saved, all the ends of the earth! For I am God, and there is no other. Our *Lord* is faithful and true. He is waiting for you to come to Him with all your heart. Can you feel Him? Can you hear Him calling your name? He has been right there beside you all along. Taste and see that the *Lord* is good! There is no other like Him. He is mighty to save all who come to Him. Let go of your fears and come to Him just as you are.

His amazing grace is for you too, because He loves you abundantly and unconditionally. Yes, He loves you! There is nothing you can do to make Him love you less. You were made for *Jesus Christ*! You were created by *God* to live in a real relationship with Him. Are you living with Him and experiencing His love freely?

Don't miss the secret to an abundant life of joy, peace, and hope. The secret to this life is *Jesus*! Yes, *Jesus Christ* is the answer to every question. He is the one who will help you. No matter what you are facing, *Jesus* can make a difference for you when you keep Him in the center of your life! Do it today and experience the joy of *Jesus*!

APRIL 28

Nothing is Impossible with God
Psalm 57:10

For your steadfast love is great to the heavens, your faithfulness to the clouds. You shower us with so much love that we are made whole and new again in you. We are so thankful and praise you for your faithfulness that never ends. Yes, even when we doubt or waiver in our faith, you never once leave us. You are a good *Father* who always gives abundantly and loves unconditionally.

There are days when we just think what we hope for seems impossible. But you continue to show us that nothing is impossible with you. We just need to keep praying and believing for the impossible because everything is possible with *God*! Let us thank Him in advance for what He is going to do. Let us realize the beauty of our dreams. Let us continue praying for what we hope for and see our dreams come to life with *God*.

Put *God* in the center of your life and you will find new hope again. Make Him the *Lord* of your life and you will find joy and peace again. Nothing is impossible with *God*. He desires to fulfill all your plans in His timing as He wills. Keep Him in the center and watch what He will do for you!

APRIL 29

Do Good
3 John 11

Beloved, do not imitate evil but imitate good. Whoever does good is from God, whoever does evil has not seen God. Do good so that *God* can see that you love Him and want to please Him. When you truly love Him, you will want to do what is honorable, true, pure, and just. Your love for *God* is seen through the way you treat His children. Are you seeking Him with your whole heart? Are you living in a way that people can see your love come to life? Are you doing good?

God will bless you as you work for His kingdom by loving and serving faithfully. Live out the purpose to which *God* has called you. Read and follow the truth from His words of life. Abide in His love so that you can grow deeper and stronger in relationship with Him. Keep praying for Him to show you how and where He needs you. Trust Him to give you the desires of your heart. The day will come for you when your faith will be your eyes. You will see what has been promised to you. Your dreams that *God* has placed in your heart will become reality. Until this day, faithfully fulfill the ministry you have been given. The *Lord* is calling you. Be still and listen to His voice and go where He needs you. Today is the day that the *Lord* has made. Rejoice and be glad in it!

APRIL 30

Alive to Hope
Isaiah 53:5

With His wounds we are healed. Yes, our living sacrifice, *Jesus*, suffered greatly for us so that we may be healed. His love for us came alive with every mark on His body. His stripes of pain gave us new life. He wanted us to have salvation, so He bore all our sins upon the cross. His pain brought us freedom!

Why are we looking everywhere else except to *Jesus* for redemption? He paid our debts by giving us His life. All our transgressions are wiped away through His act of love and sacrifice. The *Father* loved us so much that He gave us His Son so that all who believed would have everlasting life. Rest on this truth, believe, and come alive with the power of the living Spirit.

We are no longer slaves to sin, but we are alive to hope that lives inside us. Yes, *Jesus Christ* is our hope. Through Him, we live! His love has been poured upon us and we are free. Praise *God* for giving us *Jesus* because He loves us so much! Hallelujah, we are alive in *Christ*! Celebrate this truth today!

PRAYER TO JESUS

Dear *Lord*,

Thank you for pouring your love all over me. For you satisfy me in the morning with your steadfast love; that I may rejoice and be glad in all of my days. I am filled with great joy because of your love for me. I see the beauty of your love all around me and I feel whole again. Your love astounds me time and time again and I am ever so grateful!

Through your living sacrifice, you gave me grace. You have given me many second chances that I do not deserve. You have turned my disappointments into promises of hope. You have called me out of the darkness and into your marvelous light!

How can I thank you? By praising you in the storm knowing that you have it all in your hands. I am right in the center of your love and protection as a child of *God*. I am free to live because of the freedom you have given me. I will sing of your love and mercy all the days of my life! In you I will make my home forever and ever!

In *Jesus* Name,

Amen.

AND LET THE

peace of Christ

rule in your hearts,

to which indeed

YOU WERE CALLED

in one body.

And

be thankful

COLOSSIANS 3:15

MAY 1

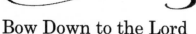

Bow Down to the Lord
Romans 14:11

"As I live," says the Lord, *"every knee shall bow to me and every tongue shall confess to God."* There will come a day when we all will be held accountable for our actions and judged by our *Lord* for what we have or have not done. Let us strive to do what is right for our *Lord* today. He knows our hearts and wants what is best for our souls. We cannot hide from Him.

Let us work for peace with all. Our *Lord* desires that we live peacefully with others even when we do not agree. He wants unity among His people even when there seems to be no way. With *God*, all things are possible!

It is time to abide in the *Lord*. Love well and please Him with your actions. It is possible to love your neighbor if you focus on the love given to you by your *Lord*. Bask in the love of the *Lord*. Feel the warmth and power of His love and His grace. Bow down to the *Lord* and pour out your heart to Him in prayer. Praise Him for the grace He gives to you. Come to His throne of grace and make *Jesus* the *Lord* of your life!

MAY 2

Stand Out for Jesus
Romans 8:18

For I consider that the sufferings of this present time are not worth comparing with the glory that is to be revealed to us. Joy will come as we see the glory of *God* that will be revealed as we continue seeking Him. All of our pain will dissolve, and we will feel His love grow deeper in us as we draw closer to Him. *God* wants to do something new in us. He is looking far and wide for hearts willing to turn to Him. The *Lord* yearns for us to give our weary souls to Him.

Help us to be different for you, *Lord.* We want to stand out to make a difference for you. We need your constant love and your encouragement during the days ahead. We are certain that we will see your glory through our struggles. We know that you are always with us. You have made a way for us when there was no way. Your way is always best, *Lord,* and we will follow you. Sweet freedom exists for us because we are connected to you. We are healed when we are in your presence. *Lord*, heal us and help us. We need you to show us your glory. We are seeking you with all our hearts. We are loving you with all our souls. We are ready to surrender all to you so that you can do something brand new in us! Do it, *Lord*! We will follow you to freedom!

MAY 3

Shadow of the Almighty
Psalm 118:6

The Lord is on my side; I will not fear. What can man do to me? The *Lord* is our refuge and strength. He is a very present help in trouble. Let us call upon Him to save us from our struggles. Let us turn to the *Lord* and not be afraid. He takes away our pain and heartache. He wipes away all our tears and holds them in His bottle because He cares so much for us.

Many will try to prevent us from following what is honorable, just, right, and true. But we will cling tighter to our *Lord*. He is the truth and the life. He is stronger than any temptation we face and will defeat any enemy. Let us remember that the power of our *God* is greater than anything or anyone!

Call upon the *Lord* and He will save you. Let Him be your strength when you are weak. He is ready to fight your battle and slay your giant. What giant are you facing now? Seek the *Lord* and give it all to Him now. When you release it all, your fears will disappear, and you will experience a peace beyond understanding! What can man do to you? Nothing, when you are in the shadow of the Almighty!

MAY 4

Take Up His Cross
Matthew 16:24

If anyone would come after me, let him deny himself and take up his cross and follow me. Jesus wants you to follow Him by making Him first in your life. When you come to the cross, repent and open your heart to *Jesus*, you open the door to a relationship with the *Father*. Through *Jesus*, you can have this deeper relationship with the *Father*. *Jesus* is the way, the truth, and the life. Follow Him to your new life!

The road to *Jesus* is through the cross of salvation. He has made a way for you when you choose Him. Come as you are and find the grace you are searching for through *Jesus*. He has all the grace you need. Follow Him to receive your amazing grace!

Let your hearts not be troubled. Believe in *Jesus* and let Him fill you with peace. His mercy and grace will be poured upon you as you have believed! Follow *Jesus* and you will have eyes to see the best in people, a heart that forgives the worst, a mind that forgets the bad, and a soul that never loses faith!

MAY 5

The Lord Hears and Answers
One Prayer at a Time
Psalm 86:12

I give thanks to you, O Lord my God, with my whole heart, and I will glorify your name forever. You are so wonderful to us! We love you and thank you for answering our prayers! You hear and answer one prayer at a time. We know that you are bending down to listen to us. We are so grateful that we serve such a mighty *God* who listens and answers our deepest desires! When the road gets tough, we know you are stronger for us. When the path seems unclear, you guide us the right way. When we do not understand, you give us your peace. When we choose to surrender control, we will be filled with joy and our doubts will disappear We will come alive with the power of the *Holy Spirit* working inside of us.

Our security is in you, *Lord*. Our hope rests in your loving arms. We are putting faith first and trusting you even if we cannot see. We are walking with you, *Lord*, one step at a time. Thank you for opening our eyes to see manifestations of your glory! Oh, how wonderful it is to be close to you! Once we connect our hearts and souls to yours, we will never be the same again! We are newly revived in you, *Lord*! We will glorify you forever!

MAY 6

Be a Peacemaker
Matthew 5:9

Blessed are the peacemakers, for they shall be called sons of God. If we bring peace to others instead of anger and bitterness, we honor the *Lord.* He longs for His people to walk peacefully together. *Jesus* shared this treasure with His disciples to encourage them and teach them. We can also know these blessings when we spread peace and let the peace of *Christ* rule in our hearts. Let us put away all bitterness and wrath and find that inner peace down deep in our soul that comes from *Jesus.* Only through *Jesus* can we find that peace. He is our peace. When we put Him first and let Him take over our lives, we can stop worrying because He will take the wheel for us. He will pilot us where we need to go.

As we make *Jesus* our peace, we are able to put others before ourselves knowing that it is better to give than to receive. We are at peace when we are not always striving to be first. *Jesus* takes first place and He makes it possible for us to live peacefully with others. As we trust Him more, we will rise above the problems and *Jesus* will pilot us above the clouds into His place of peace. He is waiting to bless our lives with the peace that transcends all understanding so that we can be a peacemaker. Blessed are the peacemakers!

MAY 7

Perfect Love Casts Out Fear
1 John 4:19

We love because He first loved us. He wants us to love one another as He has loved us. Love means loving all, even those who are unlovable. Love means opening our hearts to those who have offended us and giving them grace. *God* has given us unlimited grace so that we will extend grace out to others in our life.

When we love like *Jesus*, it is possible to love one another like He has commanded us. We can see others with His eyes and forgive again. We can reach out to those in need who are struggling to be loved and accepted. He asks that we love. He showed us unconditional love as He became our living sacrifice so that we could love and live in freedom!

Is your heart open to give and receive His perfect love that casts out all fear? Are you ready to experience a transformed heart and a renewed mind for *Jesus*? He is calling you to forget the past and move forward with Him to new life. There is hope through the love of *Jesus*. Receive His grace and love and move forward confidently as you love again with the powerful love of the Most High, *Jesus Christ*. His love will give you joy everlasting and take you higher with Him! What are you waiting for? Love as He has first loved you!

MAY 8

Power of Prayer
Psalm 66:19

But truly God has listened; He has attended to the voice of my prayer. Keep praying for He hears you and is responding. He bends down to hear you when you pray. He answers in His will and His timing, so never stop believing in the power of prayer. *God* will reward your faithfulness. By your faith, you will be healed!

Maybe you have not received because you have not asked. Ask so that your joy may be full! He has been ready to bless you abundantly. The prayers of a righteous person have great power and are working. Never stop praying and telling *God* what your heart desires. He is ready and able to bless you with all that you need.

When you think no one cares or listens to you, think again. *God* is the one who hears you and will never let you down. He cares deeply and wants the very best for you. Remember that He attends to the voice of your prayer. Keep praying faithful prayers and just see what He will do for you. He will meet your every need and will rescue you just when you need Him most. Keep seeking *God* and your life will be filled with bountiful blessings of joy through many answered prayers!

MAY 9

Heaven and Nature Sing of His Glory
Isaiah 55:12

For you shall go out in joy and be led forth in peace; the mountains and the hills before you shall break forth into singing, all the trees of the field shall clap their hands. The *Lord* shows you much joy and peace when you let Him lead you and show you the way you should go. All His great wonders and miracles are around you everywhere you look for them. When you seek Him with your whole heart, you will find Him and His peace and joy. Heaven and nature sing of His glory! There is peace and joy for you to see on earth! The *Lord* makes the trees thrive to show you that living for Him makes all things grow beautifully. He shows you His wonder and beauty in the mountains and the hills. Look up to the *Lord* of all creation and show Him your face. He is ready to bless you with much if you allow Him in your life. He has so much in store for you, faithful servant. He will give you more than you could ever dream or imagine! Trust Him to do it. Give Him your heart and let Him take you to places that you never thought possible. Anything and everything is possible with your *Lord*!

There is much waiting for you when you go where He is calling you. Do not be afraid or let your heart be troubled by what you see. Let your faith be bigger than your fear. Dream big and pray bigger!

MAY 10

Refuge of Hope
1 Corinthians 1:9

God is faithful, by whom you were called into the fellowship of His Son, Jesus Christ our Lord. God is always faithful to you. He has loved you so much from the beginning that He gave you His only begotten Son so that you could have life! He wants you to trust Him because His love for you is real.

He yearns for you to know Him and have a relationship with Him. Your faithful *God* has delivered you out of the barren wilderness and into the green pastures. He promises everlasting life to all who follow Him. Why would you not want peace on earth today and the promise of life with Him eternally? He will not force you to believe, and He still loves and forgives those that reject Him. But He weeps for those who have not seen the light of hope through Him. Yes, *Jesus* weeps for you and with you. His tears flow and His heart breaks for you. *Jesus* is your refuge of hope in this hopeless world. Do not let your heart be troubled or your soul be distressed. If you put your trust in *Jesus*, He will lift you up and protect you eternally. His peace is waiting for you. His joy is yours. His hope is eternal and real. Come to the living water of *Jesus* and drink this water that fulfills and nourishes you. You will be overflowing with new life and energized with new joy!

MAY 11

Call Upon His Name
Acts 2:21

And it shall come to pass that everyone who calls upon the name of the Lord shall be saved. Have you called upon His name? Are you seeking the *Lord's* will above your own? Have you surrendered your whole heart to your *Savior*? Your *Lord* and *Savior* is waiting for you to come to Him fully surrendered and ready to receive all His blessings. Make room for *Jesus Christ* to fill you. Keep seeking Him above all else. When you seek Him, you will find Him as you search for Him with all your heart and soul. Your *Lord* will bless you with much when you let go and let Him work in your life!

Your desires change to His desires for you when you live for *Christ*. Instead of wanting more for yourself, you discover that He gives you exactly what you need at the right time. You serve others because you want to serve, not because you feel obligated. *Jesus* shows you the purpose and the plan He has for you one step at a time as you trust and obey.

Your faith is secured in *Christ* and His love for you, not in the temporal things of this world. His grace and love will never end as it is new every morning! Feel His love and let His grace wash over you in a fresh way today! The *Lord* is your best portion, so live fully engaged and connected to Him!

MAY 12

Fulfill the Ministry
Colossians 4:17

See that you fulfill the ministry that you have received in the Lord. Seek His will for your life by hearing His voice calling you into service. The Lord has called you to a ministry chosen just for you. Pray that you will join Him in the work He has assigned to you. He delights in you and needs your hands and feet on earth to further His kingdom. Work for the *Lord* and not for men as the *Lord* rewards those who follow Him and make fishers of men.

When you are walking in your purpose, you will rejoice with the *Lord* when one who is lost is found. You will feel hope when the hopeless find hope. You will experience joy when a new believer repents and finds *Jesus*. Your eternal peace will come from *Jesus* and not in the things that are on this earth. You will seek your treasures in heaven as you seek to please *Jesus*. Seek first the kingdom of *God*, and all good things will be added to you. Walk in a manner worthy of the *Lord*, bearing good fruit in every good work as you increase your faith and knowledge of your *Lord, Jesus Christ.* Give thanks for the opportunity to serve in a way that is pleasing to Him. Let His peace be yours as you guard your hearts and your minds in *Christ Jesus* He is your peace!

MAY 13

His Glory Shines in the Darkness
Isaiah 40:5

And the glory of the Lord shall be revealed, and all flesh shall see it together, for the mouth of the Lord has spoken. Yes, the *Lord* has spoken and shown us His glory through giving us His Son, *Jesus Christ*. He came to this earth to live among us and then died for our sins. He died so that we may live! Our sins have been forgiven and we are freed by His great grace!

God's light has been revealed to all as His glory shines through the darkness. The blind will see Him when they open their heart to His beauty and wonder. The lost will be found and the hopeless will find hope through the light of the world, *Jesus Christ!* Many souls will be saved through *Jesus*, the *Savior* of the world! Much more glory will be seen day by day until He returns in all His glory.

Until that day, the *Lord* shows us much as we continue walking by faith. His fire burns brightly inside of us as we draw to His Spirit. We experience the best portion of *Jesus* when we let His Spirit come alive inside us. Let us activate the *Holy Spirit* by living connected to the one who loved us first. He gave us this gift so that we may know Him more deeply. Oh, how we love you, *Lord*! We are humbled and overwhelmed by your glory!

MAY 14

Your Love Lifts Us Higher
Isaiah 25:1

O Lord, you are my God; I will exalt you; I will praise your name, for you have done wonderful things, plans formed of old, faithful, and sure. You are the one we trust to protect and guide us. You have always laid out the best plans for us. When we seek you with our whole heart, we will find you and know the way we should go.

We look to you for help because we know you will be our strength and our comfort. When we are our weakest, you are our mighty, strong tower. Your love lifts us higher. Your peace surrounds us and quiets our soul. We find our comfort and rest in you, *Lord*, our rock of refuge and peace. We need you, *Lord,* because only you can get us through these difficult times. We praise you for being our all in all, *Lord*! Our hope is in you. We are not lost anymore because we have seen the light and are following it to find you. We are looking to your light. Our path is clearer with you lighting each step of the way. We know the way we should go, and we will stay on this well-lit path with you guiding us and cheering us on to victory. Together we are stronger and wiser. We can do all things through *Christ* who strengthens us. We believe that nothing is impossible with you *Lord* and that everything is possible to those who believe!

MAY 15

Arms of Grace
Colossians 1:13

He has delivered us from the domain of darkness and transferred us to the kingdom of His beloved Son. Yes, the *Lord* brings us out of the darkness of sin and carries us into the light of His beautiful Son. Let us rejoice in this truth! The *Lord* is so good to us all the time. The days of our life here on this earth are filled with joy as we have this hope that we will be forever with Him in eternity. As we turn away and run from evil into His arms of grace, we will find everything we need. *Jesus Christ* is our *Savior* and our hope. Come to the hope of glory. *Jesus* always provides all that we need.

We never have to worry when we are trusting in Him. He takes our fears and our pain. He brings us hope when we are hopeless. He gives us joy when we are feeling lost and alone. The hope and joy He brings us when we trust in Him is everlasting and so real. Only *Jesus* can bring us that kind of hope and joy!

As we trust, we will be free. As we let go and let *God* work in us, we will have all we need because He gives us all we need. Hear this good news and believe. Trust and obey. Be still and know that our *God* can and will do what is impossible with man because it is possible with *God*! Let us rest in His presence today and forevermore!

MAY 16

Have Faith in God
Mark 11:22

Have faith in God. Be free in *Christ.* Break the chains of slavery you are carrying around so that you can stand firm. Stay grounded in your faith and do what is right and true. You can do all things through *Christ* who strengthens you!

Drop the anchor of sin and anchor yourself to the one who is your true anchor. The *Lord* will never let you go when you let Him hold you up. He is your firm and stable foundation of hope. Cling to His promise to give you the freedom you are looking for. Only your faith in Him will get you through these hard times of loss. As you draw closer to love, your love for the *Lord* will grow deeper. The roots of love will grow more fruit in you so that you can share that love with your neighbor. Love the *Lord* your *God* with all your heart, soul, and mind. Make Him the first love of your life. All good things will flow from that love and you will be able to live freely and victoriously without fear or anxiety. When you cling tighter to His love, your whole world is filled with His wonder. You will see Him everywhere. He will speak to you and you will hear His voice. Stand firm in your faith and find that freedom in *Christ* alone!

MAY 17

Stand Up Together
Isaiah 50:8

Let us stand up together. Let us stand up and stand out for *Christ*. Let us stand firm in our faith for what is right and true. The *Lord* is the one who will help us! He has rescued us out of captivity into a place of comfort and peace. The *Lord* is the one who will help us and awaken us into all truth.

Believe that He loves you with an everlasting love. Fear the *Lord* and rely on Him to be your advocate. Behold, He has engraved you on the palms of His hands. Lift your eyes to see His glory. Open your ears to hear Him speaking to you. Turn your heart towards the one who has redeemed you and set you apart to work for His good purpose.

You will not be hungry or thirsty when you feast of His daily bread and drink of His living water. His bread and water flow continually. Taste and see that the *Lord* is good. He will renew your strength as you rise up with eagles' wings and fly freely above the fray. You will stand as you stand together with *Christ*. Seek the *Lord* first in all your ways and be renewed, revived, and restored!

MAY 18

Walk Obediently
Romans 14: 12

So, then each of us will give an account of himself to God. Our mighty *God* will be the one who will ask us why we did the things we did. Were we listening when we heard His voice calling us? Or did we turn our backs and keep walking totally in our selfish ways? Did we help others in need or did we keep serving ourselves?

He will praise us for our obedience to Him as we walk in our purpose. He knows our hearts. He will be our ultimate judge, not those around us. Let us honor the *Lord* our *God* in all that we do. He is the audience of one who we need to please always!

Keep pursuing Him and His amazing love. All good things come to those who love the *Lord* and work obediently according to His purpose. It is not too late to repent and ask for *God's* great mercy. He is the one who will forgive us and direct us back on His path of righteousness that leads to peace and joy.

Bow down and honor Him for He is a good and faithful *Father*. Love His son *Jesus* who has given His love so freely to us. He paid it all so that we could walk in freedom. He is the only true freedom maker! It is for freedom that *Christ* has set you free!

MAY 19

Come to the Light
2 Corinthians 4:6

For God who said, "Let light shine out of darkness," has shone in our hearts to give the light of the knowledge of the glory of God in the face of Jesus Christ. We have light in our hearts when we believe. Our hearts are alive by the fire of the Spirit given to us by *Jesus*. This fire will light up our lives when we keep looking to the *Lord* in all our ways and keep living in the Spirit.

We have been given a *Savior* who has come to rescue us. As we repent and draw to the *Lord* faithfully, we will see His glory through His signs and wonders all around us. He forgives and saves us from our dark places and brings us hope once again. Only the *Lord* can fill the dark places with light. He is the light of the world!

Let us come to *Jesus* and see His face welcoming us to a place of love, hope, and peace. He is the only daily bread that will nourish and sustain us. We will never go hungry when we eat of His living bread. He has come to bring life and wants to us to open the door to His love. We can find joy right here on earth if we stay close to *Jesus*! Our hearts and our souls will be revived and renewed by His power and mercy. Come to the light and come to life in *Jesus Christ!*

MAY 20

Peace in the Storm
Psalm 56:4

In God, whose word I praise, in God I trust; I shall not be afraid. What can flesh do to me? We are strong because our *God* is stronger! We can stand because our *God* is our rock and our fortress of refuge and hope. He is our strength when we are weak. He is our light in the darkness. He is our peace in the storm. He has come to bring us life everlasting. Through His death on the cross, we have been saved. Through His blood, we have been redeemed. He has taken our place on the cross and won the victory for us!

We do not need to fear because our *God* will fight for us. He will bring us through the hardest of times when we trust in Him and He will continue living in us when we give Him our whole heart. The truth found in His word is food for our souls. He nourishes us and speaks to us time after time through His living word. We can hear Him calling us when we draw near to Him and listen. Those who seek Him, will find Him! Let us seek the *Lord* and draw to Him more each day. He yearns to know us better. Let us praise our *Lord* for His promise to meet us in our darkest days and brightest moments. He walks with us and meets us where we are as we let Him in our heart and soul. We will not be afraid!

MAY 21

New Song of Hope
1 Timothy 6:18

They are to do good, to be rich in good works, to be generous, and ready to share. The *Lord* needs us to do good to all. He has good works for us to do. So, let us walk diligently in these works and be ready to share. There is much work to be done for the glory of the *Lord*! Do we have a burden for those in need? Are we continuing in the faith by sharing love and hope? Are we hearing the voice of *God* calling us out of our comfort zones and into His will?

Let us be still and know that He is *God* and that He will be with us all the time. He wants the best for us, so let us bring our best to Him. There are many who need the *Lord*. Let us continue the good work that He has assigned to us. Let us feel His abundant love holding us and encouraging us along the way as we work for His glory. He will always be our strength and our song so let us sing a new song of hope and joy for the *Lord*. Many are waiting to be blessed and we have been chosen to bring these blessings in the name of the *Father*, *Son,* and the *Holy Spirit*. It is time to lay aside every weight that holds us down and forge ahead faithfully with the power of the word and the spirit. As we continue faithfully working, we will grow closer to the *Lord* and He will infuse us with life. Come to *Jesus* and come to life!

MAY 22

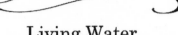

Living Water
Psalm 63:1

O God, you are my God; earnestly I seek you; my soul thirsts for you; my flesh faints for you, as in a dry and weary land where there is no water. You are our living water which has been poured out on us. We are completely refreshed and satisfied because we drink of this water that you give us. You quench our thirst fully with your water that never leaves us thirsty. We can share as we are enriched and nourished by you.

Thank you, *Lord,* for giving us the best portion. Thank you for loving us so deeply. Our love for you grows as we spend time hosting your presence in our lives. We wake up with you on our minds and in our hearts. We lay down to sleep with a smile on our face knowing that we are loved by you. We are alive with the fruit of the Spirit you yield in us as we drink of your living water. Love, joy, peace, patience, kindness, goodness, faithfulness, gentleness, and self-control are blooming. Your desires and passions have taken root in us as we have become one in Spirit with you, *Lord.* We are born again with hope, and we are made new in you, *Lord Jesus*! We praise you again and again for all your mercies upon us. We are free! We are fearless! We are alive! We are strong! We are loved!

MAY 23

Salvation is Nearer
Romans 13:11

Besides this you know the time, that the hour has come for you to wake from sleep. For salvation is nearer to us now than when we first believed. Yes, it is time for us to wake up and realize that we need *Jesus* like never before. There is evil in the world and life with *Jesus* is the only way to overcome the world. We are lost without Him. We are hopeless without our light of hope. Wake up and see the hope that only comes from *Jesus*!

He has made a way for us in this dark world. He has shown us that the way to joy is through trusting Him. When we trust Him and obey His calling for us, we will see rays of hope in our life through *Jesus Christ*. This light will shine in the darkest places and warm the hardest of hearts.

Let *Jesus* give you everything you need. As you put Him at the center of your life, He will give you all. Do not live another day without Him. He wants all of you right now. It is time to trust and obey. Do not delay another day in His presence. You will find *Jesus* when you seek Him with your whole heart. Wake up and seek Him today as salvation is nearer now than when you first believed!

MAY 24

Turn Towards His Light
Ephesians 5:13

But when anything is exposed by the light, it becomes visible. Jesus has come to give you life, but you must set your mind on Him and the *Holy Spirit* who bring life. Much peace will be yours when you trust and obey. Turn towards His light and turn away from the dark. You will be lavished with love when you come to your *Lord.*

His peace will settle inside you and heal the broken places of your heart. Only the *Lord* can bring you this lasting peace. His peace is beyond any human understanding or worldly view. Let the peace of *Christ* rule in your heart. Stop looking to other people or things to fill you. Look to the *Lord* and put Him above all else to find life. Place your trust in the one who will never leave or forsake you. His love will fill you with pure joy. His joy is lasting and fulfilling. His peace will endure until the end!

Jesus is the promise of life and peace for you. Put Him first and see how your heart and soul will come alive like never before! The light from Him inside you will light up your world and you will have life and peace!

MAY 25

True Friend in Jesus
Isaiah 44:22

I have blotted out your transgressions like a cloud and your sins like mist; return to me, for I have redeemed you. Only *Jesus* can wipe away your and completely forgive you. Come to Him, repent and be redeemed! Through His grace you have been saved. Look to Him and let His grace cover you. There will be trials and temptations in this world, but greater is He who lives in you than he who lives in this world. Do not be troubled, for *Jesus* has come to give you abundant life. He will set you free if you desire. You have a choice to believe and give your heart to your *Savior*. Choose *Jesus* first and you will find life and peace. You have a true friend in *Jesus*!

Make Him your friend by spending time with Him through prayer and His word. His treasures of truth will guide and comfort you. Your prayers to Him will encourage and strengthen you. His word and your prayers go together like two sides of one coin. They must exist together for your relationship to be enriched. He loves you more than anyone or anything else can or ever will. And to prove it, He died for you. Yes, He died for sinners like you so that you could walk in love, joy, and peace completely forgiven and free! What a gift you have been given! The only gift that will last forever!

MAY 26

See with Spiritual Eyes
Proverbs 15:3

The eyes of the Lord are in every place, keeping watch on the evil and the good. He sees all and knows all. The *Lord* knows our heart. He watches us as we do good to others and He is well pleased. He also knows when our intentions are not good, and we act in ways that are not pleasing to Him. Let us always desire to do good and listen to the *Holy Spirit* inside of us. Let us desire to please our *Heavenly Father* by choosing what is good and pure and righteous.

Lord, we need you to be our strength and our help in times of temptations. We know that you will always give us a way out when we seek you. Let us seek you first. Let us love you deeply and serve you intentionally. You promise good to all those who faithfully follow you and work to please you. We want to do what is pleasing to you, *Lord*! We will strive to be your children of light as we walk in the light of your promises. Help us, *Lord,* as we need you. We are helpless when we take our eyes off you and turn away. Let us shift our eyes to you, *Lord,* and see with spiritual eyes. Your blessings of love are greater than we can imagine. Oh, how we love you, *Lord,* and thank you for loving us and showing us the way to life!

MAY 27

Believe to Receive
John 11:25

Jesus said to her, "I am the resurrection and the life. Whoever believes in me, though he die, yet shall he live." When you believe, you shall have life through *Jesus Christ* He came so that you may live freely and abundantly. Believe wholeheartedly that He is your *Savior* and your King forever! Look to *Jesus* and find all that you need. He is able to give you everything when you are willing to receive.

Love Him with all your heart and your soul. Seek Him in all your ways. Rely on Him to bring you peace beyond understanding. His ways are best for you, so trust Him with all your heart. His love for you can and will conquer all!

Jesus knows the way you should go faithful, one. Keep believing and trusting Him to get you through it all. These days with *Jesus* are the best days yet for you. Your life will be enriched and fulfilled when you are living with His Spirit inside of you! Cast all your cares and fears upon the *Lord*! He will bring you through it all so that you may have life everlasting! Believe to receive all that *Jesus* wants for you!

MAY 28

Whispers of Love
John 10:7

So Jesus said to them, "Truly, truly, truly, I say to you, I am the door of the sheep." His sheep know His voice and enter the sheepfold through *Jesus*. He wants us to know His voice as we are His sheep. We can wander and be lost, or we can listen to His voice and follow Him. Only through *Jesus* can we find our way. We will get lost if we do not look to *Jesus*, our Good Shepherd.

As we follow the voice of *Jesus*, we will be able to find life through Him. We will be able to see good as we follow Him and do not go astray. As we stay connected to *Jesus*, we will find hope once again.

Our path and our purpose will be clearer as we follow Him. He will show us the way. He will give us the joy and peace we want! The voice of *Jesus* is loving and gentle. His whispers of love are so comforting. His kindness and patience towards us is rewarding and overwhelming.

Let us open our ears and hear Him calling us. Let us open our eyes to see His wonder and grace. Let us open our hearts to His everlasting love. Let us fall in love with our protector and keeper of our heart, *Jesus Christ*! He is the door to life so enter and be saved!

Fully Surrendered
Psalm 147:5

Great is our Lord; and abundant in power; His understanding is beyond measure. Yes, our *Lord* is all powerful and wonderful to us. He loves every part of us and wants all of us to come to Him fully surrendered and ready to receive His power. He desires for us to love Him with all our heart, soul, and mind for this is the first and greatest commandment. Love the *Lord*, and serve Him with joy!

Let us give Him all that He desires. Let us make Him the first love of our life. All good things will flow from a heart fully surrendered and connected to the *Lord*. He is true to His word for us. He has promised that if we believe, we will have life everlasting. He has given His *Son* as a true living sacrifice so that we can have a relationship with Him.

Through His blood shed, we are forgiven and free. Let us not forget the sacrifice for our freedom. Walk in this freedom and power. We have been given everything. Let us walk by faith connected to *Christ* and stop walking alone by ourselves. With *Christ*, we have life, so let us walk on the path to life with Him leading us every step of the way!

MAY 30

King of Your Heart
Psalm 145:9

The Lord is good to all, and His mercy is over all that He has made. Our Lord loves you. He is a good *Father* who has given you His saving grace. Only by His grace you have been saved. Your salvation rests in *Jesus*, the King of your heart.

Let *Jesus* remain with you and abide in you always. Once you say yes to His love and believe that He is your living sacrifice, you will have a heart filled with the love of *Jesus* flowing through you. His blood has been poured out for you so that you can live freely. Let go of your burdens and cast your cares upon the *Lord*. He has come so that you can be free!

The endless mercy of the *Lord* is for all. You do not have to earn His grace and mercy. All you have to do is believe! He is so good all the time! Every day will be a good day when you get real with *God*! Make the most with what you have been given by *God* and you will find the most life! Do not wait another day to find joy here on earth.

It's never too late with the *Lord*. The more you love Him, the more you will obey and trust Him and desire to do good. The desires of your heart will be His desires for you. Live fully engaged and fully connected to your *Lord* and *Savior, Jesus Christ*!

MAY 31

Wonderfully Made Out of Love
Psalm 139:14

I praise you, for I am fearfully and wonderfully made. Wonderful are your works; our soul knows it very well. We love that you love us so much that you know every part of us. We praise you for creating us so beautifully and wonderfully! You made us perfectly in your image and we are so blessed by your faithfulness to us!

We thank you for doing your mighty work in us so that we may see hope through you. We want to take your light into the dark places and bring this renewed hope to others in need. Help us to reach those in need. Open our eyes so that we may really see. Take the scales off our eyes so that we see dark places around us that need your light.

Our hope is found in you. It is not found in the temporary things of this world. Our joy is found in you. It is not found in others. Our peace is found in you. It is not found in ourselves. Give us more of you *Lord* so that we can have more hope, joy, and peace! We ask for more of you to fill us to overflowing and we want our cups to run over with you. Overshadow us with your blessings, *Lord,* as we are ready to receive!

PRAYER TO JESUS

Dear *Lord,*

My heart is heavy with many burdens and I do not know what to do. Fear is creeping up inside me because I am looking at all the problems in the world. You have told me in your word of truth to trust you and look to you for all that I need. Today, when I hear your voice, I will not harden my heart. I am ready to surrender my whole heart to you!

You have overcome the world for sinners like me, and I am promised salvation through you. The freedom I seek and the victory over sin is found only in you, *Jesus*! I pray that you will help me today to see the light. I have been in the dark and blinded by my own fears. I am ready to let my faith be bigger than my fears.

Nothing or no one can take away the hope that you have given me! You have called me out of the dark and into your great light. I am alive and made whole in you, *Lord.* Today is the day that you have given me, and I will live it to the fullest with joy! You have always stood by me and strengthened me when I have asked. I need you, *Lord*, so I will open my heart and trust you completely with my whole heart!

In *Jesus* name,

Amen.

TRUST IN THE LORD
with all your
HEART,
and do not lean
on your own
UNDERSTANDING.
PROVERBS 3:5

JUNE 1

Live by the Golden Rule
Matthew 7:12

So whatever you wish that others would do to you, do also to them. If we all would live by this Golden Rule, maybe we could all live in peace. If we could all love like *Jesus*, love would be the norm instead of hate. Let us live in love and show our love to others. Let us help someone in need who may not believe that anyone loves them. Let us show our love by our actions so that we can truly live a fulfilled life like *Jesus* wants for us!

Are you believing that good exists in our world today? Do you want to find peace? Are you eager to see *God* at work around you? All things are possible with *God*! You can be a point of peace and love that shines out to those around you and spreads His love to those in need. Make your life come alive with the power of the *Holy Spirit* by trusting Him completely and giving Him your whole heart!

People need to see love in action. We all need to feel peace and joy in this world today. The answer is *Jesus*. Make every effort to show others His amazing love by treating them with kindness, gentleness, and patience. Our actions will speak louder than words as we love like *Jesus* today!

JUNE 2

Make God Your Dwelling Place
Psalm 91:1

He who dwells in the shelter of the Most High, will abide in the shadow of the Almighty. Make *God* your dwelling place and rest in His presence. He will cover you with His wings of protection. Make the *Lord* your hiding place and your refuge. You are looking for help everywhere else but in the arms of *Jesus*.

Come to Him and let His Spirit cover you. Allow His presence in your life and stop quenching the Spirit by turning away. Lean into His love and power and keep pressing on. You can keep going with His strength and power even when the world comes against you. His shadow of protection will cover you completely.

Are you feeling anxious and worried? Do you think that there is no way out? Are you putting your faith first in all circumstances or still focusing on the problems? Be encouraged that *God* will see you through it all. He has already made a way for you. Lean into His Spirit and let Him guide you out to new life with the freedom you desire! All things are possible with the *Lord*! Do you believe?

JUNE 3

Let Your Light Shine
Matthew 5:16

Let your light shine before others, so that they may see your good works and give glory to your Father who is in heaven. Shine your light from *Jesus* onto others to encourage them and strengthen you. People need love and you can be that person who shines your love brightly upon them. As you shine, the glory of the *Lord* will shine upon you!

We all need the hope and love of our *Savior*. We all are drawn to the warmth and power of the light of *Christ*. As we work for *God's* greater purpose and glory, we are shining His light so that others may believe. We can meet a need in the life of someone else when we focus our attention and love outward. See how wonderful it is to love and be loved by our *Father* and His Son. There is no other place as peaceful than next to *Jesus*.

His peace is real and surpasses all understanding. His great love awakens us and refreshes us, and His awesome power energizes and revives us! Life is glorious when it is lived in the light of *Christ*! Come to the light and shine so you can have this perfect peace and everlasting joy! Then shine outward so that others may bask in His glory with you!

JUNE 4

Feel His Favor and Love
Psalm 5:12

For you bless the righteous, O Lord; you cover him with favor as with a shield. The *Lord* shields you from harm and protects you from trouble. He shines His light on you to infuse you with His power of Spirit and truth. He gives you all to protect and guide you, so take all that is yours in *Christ*.

Let His favor shine down on you and feel the warmth of His love. He lifts you up and comforts you. No good thing does He withhold to those who have surrendered to Him and are walking righteously. Have you looked to the *Lord* for your power and strength? Are you making Him the *Lord* of your life? Are you letting His shield of protection cover you? Are you walking in His light? Are you trusting Him through all your fiery trials so that He can build your faith?

Let Him in your life so that He can show you favor. He has many blessings that He is ready to give to you. It is up to you to invite Him in your life. He is waiting patiently for you to come to Him. Let Him infuse you with the power and strength that comes from His mighty hand. The hand of *God* saves and comforts. Take His hand and let Him lead you to freedom!

JUNE 5

Find Your Hope in Jesus
Colossians 1:27

Christ in you, the hope of glory. He is the one from whom you can draw your strength and your hope. He is the lifter of your head and the protector of your soul. No one can take away His love from you and His Spirit remains strong in you. Even when your flesh fails, and your body grows older, your spirit can be constantly restored and renewed within you. *Jesus* can awaken and revive you when you have Him present in your life!

Have you lost hope? Are you still looking for people to give you encouragement? Are you turning to things or circumstances to give you hope? Give your hand to *Jesus* and let Him lead you to a place of hope and peace. He will never leave you and He will be your constant source of hope! Every day can be a good day when you get real with *Jesus*.

Do you believe this? He is present and real, so turn towards Him and away from anything else preventing you from having a closer relationship with Him. *Jesus* loves you so much. He yearns for more of you. He sees into your soul and knows your desires. He hears your boldest prayers. He delights in you and cannot wait to bless you. Grow closer and live in His presence daily. Draw from His living water and come alive with His Spirit living inside of you!

JUNE 6

Soften Your Heart to Jesus
1 Peter 1:22

Love one another earnestly from a pure heart.
Keep your heart focused on *Jesus* and His love. Turn towards the love that He wants to give you, so that you can give it to others. There is so much heartache and sadness in the world today and only His love will conquer all. Love like *Jesus* and keep pursuing the pure love from Him.

Are you struggling and cannot see what *Jesus* is trying to show you? Are you searching for love from the world but can't seem to find it? Are you bitter because you have been hurt and offended? Is *Jesus* part of your thoughts or are you just consumed by your problems? Try loving with the love of *Jesus* and let Him love you. Give Him your whole heart. He is waiting on you to turn to His light and His love! He will soften your heart to others even when you think that it is impossible. Those that have hurt or betrayed you will not steal your joy, because you have peace with *Jesus*. A peace that passes all understanding will flow through you when your heart is connected to Him. Let Him take away your fears and He will add years of joy to your life! The love of *Christ* conquers all and no one can ever take away His Spirit that lives inside of you! Live by the Spirit and live in the love of *Jesus*!

JUNE 7

Look at Him in His Sanctuary
Psalm 96:6

Splendor and majesty are before Him; strength and beauty are in His sanctuary. Look around and see Him everywhere. He created all things beautiful in its time. There is a season for everything and a hope for all to see. Believe that you can have hope even in this storm you are facing!

Be still and know that He is *God.* Listen to Him calling you in the night and go where He leads you. He has been looking for you to come to Him and rest in His presence. There you will find refuge in His comfort and peace. His powerful strength will energize you again to a new life of renewed hope!

Are you ready to rest in His sanctuary? Are you hoping to see a way out of the challenge you are facing? Are you ready to surrender all to your *Lord* and *Savior*? Come to *Jesus*, the sustainer of your soul and King of your heart. He is the only way to find the perfect peace you seek. All other ways will not sustain you like *Jesus* can. Believe in the power and glory found in the arms of *Jesus* and be encouraged.

JUNE 8

Steadfast Love of the Lord
Psalm 100:5

For the Lord is good; His steadfast love endures forever, and His faithfulness to all generations. God is so faithful and His love for you never ends. Great is His faithfulness to you! His love for you endures forever. There is no place you can go that He is not there right beside you, loving you.

Do you believe that He loves you? Are you sure of His never-ending love for you? As sure as the sun shines brightly, warming the earth and all within it, the *Lord* will surely and continually love you and shine His love brightly upon you without ceasing.

His endless mercy and grace will fall upon you. Seek Him and repent so that you can feel this grace cover you completely. There is no sin too big for the *Lord* to forgive, but He asks that you repent and come to Him ready to change. Give Him your whole heart. You are saved by His grace. You are made new by the living sacrifice of *Jesus*. The blood of the lamb has taken away the sins of the world! That means your sins are washed by the blood of your *Savior, Jesus Christ*! There is victory in *Jesus*, so come accept His love and grace and find your freedom in the power of the *Most High*!

JUNE 9

His Mighty Hand Saves
Psalm 90:17

Let the favor of the Lord our God be upon us, and establish the work of our hands upon us; yes, establish the work of our hands! The *Lord* shields you from harm and protects you from trouble. He shines His light on you to infuse you with His power of Spirit and truth. He gives you all to protect and guide you, so take all that is yours in *Christ.*

Let His favor shine down on you and feel the warmth of His love. He lifts you up and comforts you. No good thing does He withhold to those who have surrendered to Him and are walking righteously. Have you looked to the *Lord* for your power and strength? Are you making Him the *Lord* of your life? Are you letting His shield of protection cover you? Are you walking in His light? Let Him in your life so that He can show you favor. He has many blessings that He is ready to give to you. Will you invite Him into your life? He is waiting patiently for you to come to Him. Let Him infuse you with power and strength that comes from His mighty hand. The hand of *God* saves and comforts. Take His hand and let Him lead you to freedom!

JUNE 10

Jesus is Your Perfect Peace
John 14:27

Jesus said, "Peace I leave with you, my peace I give to you. Not as the world gives do I give to you." *Jesus* is our peace. His peace is perfect and beyond understanding. He wants you to come to Him and lay your burdens at His feet. Come to Him, weary one, and you will find rest and peace. Cast all your cares upon Him, because He cares for you. Open your heart to His perfect love that casts out all fear.

Jesus is calling you to come find healing and rest in His arms. He is waiting to be your comforter and your refuge. You have a choice to come to Him. Surrender all and let Him fill you with His Spirit! He wants to pour His blessings upon you. Show Him your face and look to the *Lord* for all you need! *Jesus* is your real peace. *Jesus* is your real hope. *Jesus* is your real joy.

You need *Jesus* to have a life filled with peace, hope, and joy! The world will tell you otherwise, but the truth is that *Jesus* will give you all that you need. He is ready to restore and revive you. Ask and you shall receive all that is yours. As you knock, the door will be opened for you. Do not waste another day but come to *Jesus* fully surrendered and ready to be filled. You will be blessed beyond measure with His bountiful blessings!

JUNE 11

His Power Can Overcome the World
John 7:38

Whoever believes in me as the Scripture has said," Out of his heart will flow rivers of living water." Yes, living water flows from the believing heart. *God* will nourish us with His water that never leaves us thirsty. Our thirsty souls will be filled and satisfied!

The more we trust and obey Him, the more we will know Him. The *Lord* longs to show us the way and the truth that is found only in Him. Keep trusting and believing to find a life full of joy. Our cups will overflow with good from the *Lord* as we keep seeking Him. Take heart, *Jesus* has overcome the world and He will be with us always.

He will win the battle when we let Him fight for us. Only His power can overcome the lies and schemes of the enemy. As we cling to the *Lord* and trust Him to bring us through it all, we will find hope and victory. Our hope is *Jesus Christ* our *Lord*! Trust Him and let His power of truth take over our lives. The *Lord* is our refuge and strength in trouble. He is our rest when we are weary and weak. He is the joy of our heart and the hope of our soul! Let us find Him and love Him with all our heart and soul!

JUNE 12

The Lord Lifts You Up
Matthew 7:14

For the gate is narrow and the way is hard that leads to life, and those who find it are few. There is only one way to the *Father*. That way is through His *Son, Jesus Christ*. When we find *Jesus*, we will find life! The path is narrow and harder to follow, but the rewards are greater! Once we get on the path, we will see the light continually guiding us. Keep looking to the *Lord* for He will show you the way to go. His way is the only way. Believe this and get on the right path with *Jesus*. He will guide your every step.

Trust Him to be there for you because He will always be right by your side. He promises to never abandon or forsake you when you chose to live with Him. He is your refuge in trouble and your strength in the battle. He will never leave your side! It is so comforting to know that *Jesus* is for you. When the world is pulling you down, the *Lord* will lift you up! He keeps His promise because He loves you. He wants the very best for you, His beloved.

Turn your heart to the *Lord* and know that He will be your strength and your song. You have the victory in *Jesus Christ*! Come with Him on the narrow road that leads you to life and find *Jesus*!

JUNE 13

Be Humble and Kind
Philippians 2:3

Do nothing out of selfish ambition or vain conceit, but in humility consider others more significant than yourselves. Jesus was humble and kind to everyone as an example for how we are to live. He loved others more than He loved himself. He sacrificed His life for our freedoms and poured His mercy and grace over us. Let us forgive and give grace to others as we serve *Christ.* Let us seek out the lost, lonely, and hopeless and reach out and touch them with the love of *Jesus* and a humble heart. For it is *God* who works in us for His good pleasure. Let us shine as lights in the world so that others may find *Christ* through our acts of kindness. As we shine, we must stand firm in one Spirit, with one mind, with faith rooted and grounded in the living Spirit of *God*!

Let us continue the race set before us as we run with endurance to the finish line. We will run and not be weary as we trust in our *Lord, Jesus Christ,* each step of the way. Glory to *God* for shining His light in us and giving us hope each day. We are safe in His arms of love. Let us open our arms to spread the love of *Christ* to others! Press on towards the goal for the prize of the upward call of *God* in *Christ Jesus*!

JUNE 14

Bless the Lord
Psalm 103:1

Bless the Lord, O my soul, and all that is within me, bless his holy name! We love you and thank you for your many blessings in our lives! You have brought us out of our pit of despair and taken us out to a joyful place with you. We are made whole again with you transforming our thoughts and renewing our minds. Our heart is rejoicing because of your love for us!

Every day we spend with you is more wonderful than the day before! We are filled with your power each day as we turn to the Spirit and read your Word. Thank you for watching over us and letting us come alive with the power of the *Holy Spirit* directing our path. Your power is active and alive in us and we are clinging to hope from the promises found in your Word. Your word is sharper than a two-edged sword and will be our greatest weapon of defense. Help us continue on this path of righteousness with you. In you is everlasting life and overwhelming joy! Thank you for being our strength and our song all day long. We praise you for giving us rest through the night, so we can wake up with a fresh filling of your Spirit each morning. Joy does come in the morning. Bless the *Lord,* O my soul, and in all that is within me!

JUNE 15

Follow the Lord to Freedom
John 3:21

But whoever does what is true comes to the light, so that it may be clearly seen that his works have been carried out in God. Come to the light of *Christ* and carry out the plans He has for you. Make *Jesus* the source of your life by placing Him in the center of all that you do. Keep walking and working in the truth and the light and He will bless you greatly.

Are you looking to His light? Are you trusting Him with all your heart? He has made a way for you if you will just open your heart to His love and your eyes to His way. The ways of the *Lord* are higher, and His plans for you are greater. He has a perfect plan and purpose for you. Keep seeking Him through all your trials and joys. Activate the power and presence of the *Holy Spirit* by making the choice to let Him guide and direct you. You have a choice to follow the *Lord* to freedom. Do not waste another day apart from His presence. Pride and selfishness quench the presence of the *Holy Spirit* in your life and He cannot do His work in you. Try letting go of self and humbly turn towards the *Lord* so that He can exalt you! Today is the day for you to find that perfect peace you are seeking by connecting to the one and only true power source, *Jesus Christ*!

JUNE 16

Jesus is Life
John 3:16

For God so loved the world, that he gave his only Son, that whoever believes in him should not perish but have eternal life. Live the life that you were made to live by loving your *Savior*. Let Him shower you with love and fill you with hope again. There are many days that He is giving you on this earth so live it to the fullest. Start each day knowing that you are loved. Live each day connected to your power source.

You can keep going today because you have *Jesus*. He is with you always and never lets you down. He holds you up just when you need Him. He is your rock of refuge and strength who will weep with you when you weep. He is your joy who will rejoice with you when you rejoice. He is your hope always, so trust Him to be there for you and lead you wherever you go!

He knows the way so follow Him to freedom and peace. Do not be lead astray by anyone or anything else because *Jesus* is the true way to life! He is the way, the truth, and the life, and the only way to the *Father* is through Him! When you know the truth, He will set you free! Be set free and come alive with *Jesus* by your side!

JUNE 17

Listen to His Love as You Read His Word
James 1:21

Receive with meekness the implanted word, which is able to save your souls. Come to the *Lord* with humility and meekness as you search for answers or seek direction in your life. Turn to the truth in the scriptures and follow the *Lord* as He guides you. The word of the *Lord* is like a seed that continually grows inside of you changing you from the inside out. Your heart, mind, and soul will be transformed as you seek the truth and obey. Love the *Lord*, obey His commands, and remain in Him as you seek His wise counsel daily. The *Lord Jesus* changes everything as you become a new creation united with Him. When you become one of His believers, you are a follower. This means you do not just hear the truth of *Christ*, but you apply His truths to your life by doing what the word says. Do not merely listen to the word but do what the *Lord* says. Keep reading the truth as it brings comfort and joy. The *Lord* speaks to you through the pages of the Holy Bible so listen to His love and take heart for you are loved. Seek His counsel and let *Jesus* transform your thoughts, desires, will, relationships, and your purpose. Only the *Lord Jesus* can transform you from the inside out!

JUNE 18

Love One Another
John 13:34

A new commandment I give to you, "that you love one another; just as I have loved you, you also are to love one another." We love others because He first loved us. This powerful love of *Jesus* is working in us when we believe in Him and give our hearts to Him. We must activate this love by reaching out beyond ourselves to give this gift to others around us.

Feel the amazing love of the *Father* who gave us His Son *Jesus* to conquer all our sins. When we invite *Jesus* into our hearts, we are filled with His Spirit of love. This love is so powerful we are able to love the unlovable just like *Jesus* loves. We show this love by our actions and not just our speech. We live as a witness of this great love so that others will find *Jesus* through our love. Be the hands and feet of *Jesus* by spreading His joy to others as you love unconditionally. The blessings you will receive are greater than any treasure on earth. Seek the treasures in heaven and be filled with His bright light of hope. Give your heart to the one true King who will bring refreshing waterfalls of joy into your life today for you to splash on those around you. Be alive in *Christ* and love one another like He loves you!

JUNE 19

Have Faith
Hebrews 11:6

And without faith it is impossible to please him, for whoever would draw near to God must believe that He exists and that He rewards those who seek him. Have faith and lean on the *Lord* even when you do not see all the details. As you draw nearer to *God* and believe that He exists, your faith will grow stronger. *God* rewards those who seek Him in everything by faith. You must have faith to move mountains. Your faith will please *God* and bring you into His will and in touch with His desires for your life. Your purpose will be revealed as you seek the *Lord* and trust Him with all your heart.

Lean on the *Lord* and walk by faith to places He calls you even when you do not see. He will equip you with everything you need as you go. Believe that He is all you need, and He will show you great and mighty things that only He can do. His power will show up in your life as you live as a child of *God* with childlike faith. You will enter a spiritual bond with the *Father, Son,* and *Holy Spirit* as you live by faith.

Not all have this faith, but the *Lord* is faithful. He wants you to experience His peace by living a faith-filled life. It is your choice to believe and walk by faith. What are you waiting for?

JUNE 20

Spread the Love of Jesus
Jude 20

But you, beloved, building yourselves up in your most holy faith and praying in the Holy Spirit. We must persevere in our holy faith as we keep ourselves in the love of *God* with the *Holy Spirit* inside us. Even when we see division and strife in the body of believers, we keep praying in the *Holy Spirit* for unity and peace. It is true that we live in a world of chaos where people are following their own worldly passions by living selfishly in the flesh. *Jesus* weeps for us as He sees worldly sin reign over brotherly love. He cries with us when we are suffering in sin and not rejoicing in love.

Our *Lord, Jesus Christ,* is the way, the truth, and the life and He has already paid the price for our sins. Share His truth by sharing the gospel of salvation with those that *Jesus* puts in your life. The time is now to bring hope to our world by spreading the love of *Jesus.* Be the hands and feet of *Jesus,* by showing others the path that leads to eternal life. Build up your faith by spending time with the *Lord* in prayer and reading His word. Join with others who are living in the *Holy Spirit* so that you can be encouraged. He will give you the courage to boldly proclaim His love!

JUNE 21

Living Example of Christ
John 13:15

For I have given you an example, that you should do just as I have done to you. What has *Jesus* done? He has given you grace so that you can have freedom from your sins. He has loved you just as you are so that you could know His everlasting and unconditional love. He has continually met your needs so that you could know His living hope. He has comforted you so that you could feel His peace. He has walked with you so that you could feel His joy.

Are you living by His example? Will you forgive as *Jesus* has forgiven you? Will you put the needs of others before yourself? Will you search for joy and peace in the arms of your *Savior* instead of the temporary things of this world? Breathe Him in, worship and praise Him for being a living example for you to follow and serve. Keep the faith and pray in the Spirit as you continually seek His presence. He is alive in you and wants you to experience all that is yours by faith. It is your faith that will take you to greater heights. It is your obedience that will open doors. It is your love for *Jesus* that you give to others that will open hearts for *Jesus*. Do for others what *Jesus* has done for you. It is time to put feet to your faith and loving actions to your words!

JUNE 22

Fill the Deep Places of Your Heart
with Jesus
Psalm 143:8

Let me hear in the morning of your steadfast love, for in you I trust. Make us know the way we should go, for to you we lift our soul. *Lord*, we hear you calling us. We feel your love covering and comforting us. We will put our trust in you completely as you hold us. We see the way you want us to go when we walk by the Spirit with you in charge. Our soul longs for you. Our heart cries for you. Only you can fill the deep places in our heart and soul. We will trust that you will do that very thing right now in our brokenness. Renew our strength and resilience!

We are grateful that we are wonderfully and fearfully made in your image and in your power. We will make the most out of the time you have given us to faithfully love and serve you. Help us stay connected in heart and soul. Many things steal our attention and compete for our time. The attention and time we invest in you and your kingdom is eternal. We will trust and obey you until the end of time, for we earnestly love you first and foremost. We love you, *Lord,* and we give up all control and put you first. We are complete in you *Lord*, the lifter of our heart and soul!

JUNE 23

Unwavering Faith
Hebrews 10:23

Let us hold fast to the confession of our hope without wavering, for He who promised is faithful. He who is our hope will always remain faithful. Even when we doubt, the faith of the *Lord* will overwhelm us. He is greater than anything that is in the world. He can do more than we can ever dream or imagine because He is faithful. It is our unwavering faith that will keep us going. Even when we feel like we cannot go anymore, we can do it with the help of the *Lord*!

When we choose to act faithfully, the *Lord* can do His work through us. Our obedience will show the *Lord* we love Him, and He will manifest Himself to us. He loves to show His children His glory and magnificence! Look for His blessings and see the joy of the *Lord* in everything. Our mighty *God* is able. Our loving *God* is gentle and comforting. Our powerful *God* is faithful.

Give thanks to the *Lord* who will surely do it again and again. Praise the name of the one who is mighty to save. He has saved us from our sins and delivered our souls from the snares and toils that haunt us. He will rescue us from the depths of sorrow and hopelessness and will put a new song in our hearts to stay. Hold fast to the promises from the *Lord* and live abundantly in His amazing grace!

JUNE 24

Surrounded by a Great Cloud
of Witnesses
Hebrews 12:1

Therefore, since we are surrounded by so great a cloud of witnesses, let us lay aside every weight and sin which clings so closely, and let us run with endurance the race that is set before us. We have saints in heaven that are watching us and cheering us on every step of the way as we run the race marked for us. We have a *God* who loves us so much that He gave us His only Son that we may have everlasting life. Let us keep running with endurance and determination never forgetting that we are loved and supported by *God*. As we set aside our sins and sit at the cross with our *Savior*, our faith will be strengthened, and our hope will be real because of *Christ* who came so that we may live.

The way to live a full, abundant life is found when our eyes are fixed on the author and perfecter of our faith, *Jesus Christ*. Repent and return to the only one who gives abundant life. As we seek the *Lord* with our whole hearts, He will call us out of the dark and into His marvelous light. Let us keep fighting the good fight of faith as we are setting examples for *Christ* by our active faith. Let the *Lord* lavish His grace upon you so that you may lead others to know and love *Christ* more deeply!

JUNE 25

Let Jesus Hold You
Matthew 6:34

Therefore, do not be anxious about tomorrow, for tomorrow will be anxious for itself. Sufficient for the day its own trouble. Each day you draw closer to the *Lord* will be a day closer to His love. Each time you get more of His love, your anxiety and worry will melt away. When you trust Him, *Jesus* takes your worries and shows you hope. He turns your sorrows into joys and makes beauty from ashes. Do not let your worry and anxiety prevent you from living life to the fullest with *Jesus*. He is the way, the truth, and the life. Trust and obey Him and you will find the secret to a joy-filled life! Live one day at a time with *Jesus* guiding all your thoughts and guarding your heart. He desires to love you and know you more intimately. He wants to love you more deeply so turn aside from your fears and cling to His promises!

Look for Him first and everything else will fall into place. You will be able to say it is well with your soul when you lean on *Jesus* first and foremost. Your faith will grow stronger as you grow closer to Him through daily living with *Jesus*. Watch your worries vanish and your fears disappear as you fall into His arms. You are safe in His arms. Let *Jesus* hold you today, tomorrow, and always!

JUNE 26

Abide to Receive
John 15:7

If you abide in me and my words abide in you, ask whatever you wish, and it will be done for you. Abide in His love so that you can find Him. Your *Lord* is patiently waiting for you. His love is amazing and so real and when you abide in Him, you will feel His presence so powerfully. As you stay closely connected, ask the *Lord* for what you need, and He will surely answer you! Abide and ask to receive! *Jesus* is the vine, and when you stay connected to the vine, He will continue to give you all that you need. Apart from Him, you can do nothing! With Him, you can do everything! Do you see how much He loves you? Can you feel the power of His love and grace? He takes you in His arms and loves you no matter what you have done. He is doing a new thing in you as you keep abiding in Him!

Stay close to *Jesus* and you will bear the good fruit He wants in you. Keep abiding and you will see *Jesus* working in a new way in your life. Your life will be blessed with much fruit that comes from a life of abiding. You will experience His glory in the baskets of fruit that you will bear for *Jesus*. And His promise of truth that His joy will be your joy will come true for you! Abide today so that your joy will be full!

JUNE 27

Be a Beacon of Light
John 16:33

I have said these things to you, that in me you may have peace. In the world you will have tribulation. But take heart; I have overcome the world. Yes, *Jesus Christ* has overcome this world through His blood. He is the one who paid it all so that our sins would be wiped clean. We are forgiven and free and we have a fresh, new life in Him. Turn towards *Jesus* and feel His peace. Complete peace is found through our *Savior, Jesus Christ!*

The world will try to offer its peace to us. Some may be fooled by the world to believe in its way. But we who know *Jesus*, believe in the truth that He is the only way to peace. To live in *Christ* is to truly live in peace Let us turn away from all that hinders us and distracts us from *Jesus* and set our eyes upon Him. We must boldly come to Him and boldly proclaim His greatness to the world so that others may know this peace we know. The days are more desperate, and the nights are lonelier without Him. We can be a beacon of light shining brightly for others to see that there is still hope. The world is wanting a *Savior*. We can make a difference in our own community and in our own life by opening our eyes and fixing them on *Jesus Christ* and His wonderful peace.

JUNE 28

Character Through
Endurance in Sufferings
Romans 5:3-4

We rejoice in our sufferings, knowing that suffering produces endurance, and endurance produces character, and character produces hope. Rejoice in hope which can be found through the *Lord Jesus Christ*. He will bring you through it all as you continue in hope. Your faithful endurance is building character which builds hope. Even the smallest hope you see becomes bigger when your hope is found in *Christ*! Your faith will grow stronger. You will see that *God* has a greater purpose and calling for you as you walk by faith. For *God* can do far more abundantly than all you can ask or think according to the power of *Christ* at work within you. Believe that He is working mightily through you and in you to accomplish the plans He has for you. Seek the *Lord* and find your purpose in Him.

You are saved by grace. You will find joy in this grace through your trials and suffering. Believe this and keep on running the race set before you. Your path will be directed by the *Lord* who loves you and cares for you, His precious child. But you must choose His path, the narrow path that leads to life! Choose *Jesus Christ* and find your identity and your destiny! *Jesus* is life! Amen!

JUNE 29

Follow His Voice
John 10:27

My sheep hear my voice, and I know them, and they follow me. Do you love *Jesus*? Then feed, love, and tend to His sheep. People are lost and need to be found and loved like *Jesus* loved. You can give this love when you love Him by opening your heart and soul and listening. There are many who need you and your love. It is easy to complain and argue, but these attitudes quench the Spirit. Be a person who lives fully empowered by the Spirit. Choose to live with this power active in your life and let love conquer all your anxieties and fears. Cast all your cares upon *Jesus*. His love will encourage and enrich your life so much that you will want to love others and share the love of *Jesus*.

Take heart, because your faith will please *Jesus*. As you walk faithfully and serve Him, your life will be full of great joy and peace. People will be blessed by your faithfulness. They will see hope once again through your kindness and compassion. As you lean on *Jesus* daily, He will strengthen you and bless you with greater love. He loves you so much! If you love Him, you will obey His command to love others. Now, go feed His sheep with love that conquers all. He is well pleased by your love for His sheep!

JUNE 30

Receive Your Gift
Acts 2:38

Repent and be baptized every one of you in the name of Jesus Christ for the forgiveness of your sins, and you will receive the gift of the Holy Spirit. Come now and receive all that is yours when you believe. Your freedom from sin and your gift of the *Holy Spirit* are waiting. When you call upon His name and realize that you need *Jesus* in your life, He is there. He has been waiting there for you. Come now and do not delay for He has your peace and your joy wrapped up in His love. Unconditional love is found in *Jesus Christ*. You are fully forgiven and abundantly loved!

He is always there for you. Your surrender of self will bring you to a place of peace because you are able to let *Jesus* take the wheel. He determines the way you should go. He makes your path straight. All because He loves you and wants the best for you always!

Believe in Jesus and receive your inheritance. Your cup will overflow with joy and this joy of the *Lord* will be your strength. Your sins will be wiped away and new life will be found in *Jesus Christ*! You will have a new friend that will not abandon or forsake you! You will be transformed, renewed, and revived! Hallelujah!

PRAYER TO JESUS

Dear *Lord*,

Thank you for answering my prayers! I give you all the glory for working all things out for me as you have willed. I will boast about you, *Lord*, as you are so faithful and true. How great is your faithfulness to me! I know that all things will work out for my good and your glory as I have believed!

You are there for me whenever I need you, and I am so grateful. I am realizing that I need you every moment of my life. I am tired of trying to do things on my own because I will surely fail without you.

I feel so close to you as your powerful presence is so real to me as I hold you close to my heart. I am listening to you knowing that you have my best interest at heart. I am waiting upon you to lift me up when you choose. You have moved mountains for me and I believe you will do it again! I praise your holy name that is above all names!

In *Jesus* name,

Amen.

REJOICE IN HOPE,
be patient
in tribulation,
be constant
IN PRAYER.
ROMANS 12:12

JULY 1

He Will Do It Again
Matthew 8:26

Why are you afraid, O you of little faith? The Lord has protected you and held you up all this time. He has been right there for you. He has remained faithful when your faith wavered. He has called you out and set you apart. Do you not perceive how much He has done for you? Do you not see how mighty your *Lord* is?

He has moved those mountains for you before, and He will do it again! He made a way when there was no way, and He will do it again! He healed you when you needed healing, and He will do it again! He has broken down the walls in your life, and He will do it again! The *Lord* is always faithful!

Look up and let the *Holy Spirit* fill you anew and refresh you. Let His power shower you with joy. Open your heart to His love and allow Him to fill you with hope. Feel His peace settle in your soul. Take His grace and know you are forgiven. You have a second chance to live with the freedom and peace you desire because of His love and grace for you. Remember, He made a way when there was no way and He will do it again for you! Come to the cross of salvation and discover the most marvelous life with *Jesus Christ*!

JULY 2

Set Your Mind on the Spirit
Romans 8:6

For to set the mind on the flesh is death, but to set the mind on the Spirit is life and peace. If you set your mind on the Spirit of *God*, His Spirit will dwell in you. Be conformed to the image of the *Son* with this power of *Christ* renewing your heart and transforming your mind. *Jesus Christ* helps you as He intercedes for you on the throne at the right hand of *God*. *Jesus* takes your prayers to the *Father* as you are led by the Spirit as to what you need to pray.

Nothing will be impossible as *God* will answer in His will and in His timing. Keep praying earnestly, because *God* hears your prayers in the name of *Jesus,* and He will answer. His love is real and powerful and will cover you. Nothing can separate you from the love of your *Lord God.* Stand firm in the hope that He has called you and confess with your mouth that *Jesus* is *Lord.* Everyone who looks on the Son and believes in Him will have eternal life. *Jesus* is your daily bread and your living water. If anyone thirsts, direct them to *Christ* where they can drink of His refreshing living waters. If anyone is hungry, show them *Jesus* who will be their fresh, daily bread. Whoever comes to Him shall never hunger and whoever believes in Him shall never thirst!

JULY 3

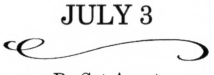

Be Set Apart
Romans 15:6

Together you may with one voice glorify the God and Father of our Lord Jesus Christ. Let the *God* of patient endurance and encouragement grant you to live in such harmony with one another in accord with *Christ Jesus* Welcome your brothers and sisters into the family of *God* so that together you may glorify His name. Praise Him among all nations with thankfulness in your heart.

Let your love be genuine. Rejoice in the hope that is yours through *Christ Jesus*. Seek to do the will of the *Lord* with joy as you continue walking in faith. The *Lord* has predestined you as He has called you to stand out and be set apart for His glory. You are a disciple of *God,* created and justified into the faith by the *Father*. He has chosen you to bring the good news of great joy found in salvation through *Christ Jesus*

Blessed are you whose lawless deeds are forgiven and whose sins are covered. Blessed are you whom the *Lord* will not count your sin. When you receive salvation through *Christ*, you are given the gift of grace through the redemption that is in *Christ Jesus*. This grace cannot be taken away Walk by faith knowing you are saved by your faith. *God* is faithful to you for eternity! He is the source of your life in *Christ Jesus*. Let us come together as one in *Christ*!

JULY 4

Blessed Are Those Who Believe
Who Have Not Seen
John 20:29

Blessed are those who have not seen and yet have believed. Faith is born in the hearts of those that can look beyond their circumstances and believe without seeing. Faith grows as we trust in the *Lord* knowing that He will do what He has promised to those that truly believe.

Faith is the assurance of things hoped for and conviction of things not seen. Let us walk by faith and not by sight, in obedience, as the *Lord* calls us. As we step up and stand firm in *Christ*, we will stand out as we have been called. We must fix our eyes on *Jesus*, the author and perfecter of our faith. For the joy that was set before Him, He endured the cross and is seated at the right hand of the throne of *God*. Knowing no sin, He was made sin and shame, so that we may have salvation. Through the cross, we can have a new covenant relationship with the *Father*. *God* is faithful. May your faith rest in the power of *God* and not in the wisdom of men. Be imitators of *Jesus* who gently and humbly loves everyone. Let us pursue the love of *Christ* and build each other up by acts of kindness and grace. Be steadfast in love and immovable in faith knowing that our *Lord* is always faithful!

JULY 5

Let Your Soul Wait for the Lord
Psalm 130:5

I wait for the Lord, my soul waits, and in His word, I hope. Be strong and wait for the *Lord* to answer you. He is attentively listening to you as you pray, and He will always answer. When you wait upon Him, you will rise and not grow weary. You can have greater strength when you seek the *Lord* and His power. Rise with the *Lord* and know that you are surrounded by His never-ending love!

Hope in His words of truth. Know that the *Lord* and His words are with you wherever you go. His word is life, and those who follow it are blessed beyond measure. There will come a day where your faith will become your sight and you will see what you have believed. Your prayers will be answered in a mighty way when you choose His way!

Are you listening to the *Lord*? Are you waiting for His answer as you continue praying? Have you looked to His word of life? Do you believe that He can do it all for you as you wait patiently for His timing? Keep praying, listening, waiting, and believing that He can do it all for you. Stand firm, keep your position of faith and remain strongly grounded in His words of wisdom and truth. Rise up and come to life with *Jesus Christ*!

JULY 6

His Sacrifice for Our Salvation
Psalm 141:2

Let my prayer be counted as incense before you, and the lifting up of my hands as the evening sacrifice! Yes, *Lord,* we come to you and lay our burdens down at your feet. We come with arms wide open to receive all that you are wanting to give us. You love us more than we deserve and have sacrificed all for us to have salvation. We give you thanks and praise for loving us. We know you hear our prayers when we ask in your will and in the name of *Jesus.* We lift our prayers up to you knowing we will receive what is best for us. We believe in the power of prayer! Our faith is strengthened through prayer and our hearts are full when we pray in the spirit. You are our living spirit, alive and active in us, as we trust in *Jesus* as our *Savior.*

Our relationship with you grows deeper, as we trust you more. We will trust you even when we do not understand or have the answers. You know what we need even before we ask. You will give us the desires of our hearts when we continue seeking you and your desires. Let us see with spiritual eyes and not only desire to see with our physical eyes. You are showing us your glory every day, and we do not want to miss a single blessing! We love you and praise you *Lord*!

JULY 7

Walk Debt Free
Psalm 119:175

Let my soul live and praise you, and let your rules help me. You will find life when *Jesus Christ* is *Lord* of your life. Your soul will be connected and activated to His when you let Him help you. When you follow His rules and commandments, you show Him your love. When you obey, your faith continues to grow. When you trust, your heart changes and you will find new life!

In Him, there is no darkness or fear. Take heart and do not be troubled, for *Jesus* has overcome the world. He has paid your debt so that you can walk in freedom. You are debt free when you make Him the *Lord* of your life. He has forgiven you, so walk in peace knowing your sins are gone in the eyes of your *Savior*. His grace has saved you!

Only *Jesus* can give you what you really need. Find comfort knowing that *Jesus* is your refuge and your strength. He is the way, the truth, and the life. *Jesus* is the only way to the *Father*. Come to *Jesus* and feel His arms holding you up securely. He will never let you down. He will intercede for you as you pray to the *Father* in His name. Call upon Him and let go of yourself. Hold on to *Jesus* as He is your anchor of hope now and forever. He is worthy of your honor and praise!

JULY 8

Trust Him in All Your Ways
1 John 3:24

Whoever keeps His commandments abides in God, and God in them. And by this we know that He abides in us, by the Spirit whom He has given us. As we love our *Lord*, we want to obey Him. As we love and obey, we start trusting Him in all things. Our faith grows deeper, as we keep trusting and obeying. As we continue abiding in Him, the Spirit inside of us comes alive. Our hearts come closer to Him, as we remain connected to Him. He touches our soul with His gentle whispers of love. Oh, how wonderful to be in His presence! We are connected to the *Lord* in Spirit. He has put His seal of the Spirit on all who believe. He wants us to remain in Him and activate the Spirit inside of us by letting the Spirit lead us. He will lead if we will follow.

Let us follow faithfully with passion and determination. His plans for us are to prosper and be filled with joy! When we abide in Him, we will surely succeed! Keep *Jesus* close to your heart and listen to the Spirit inside of you. Even if you do not understand, know that all things will work for good for those who love the *Lord*. Never give up, because He is right there cheering you on one step at a time. Rejoice, for the *Lord* will never give up on you!

JULY 9

Grace Upon Grace
John 1:16

For from His fullness, we have all received grace upon grace. He gives us great grace and mercy even when we don't deserve it. We are made whole because of Him. His grace covers our sins so that we can walk freely and fearlessly. But we must turn away from sin and repent. No sin is too great for the *Lord* to forgive!

When we come to the cross of salvation, He saves us and gives us new joy. We will experience all the fullness of *Christ* when we are engaged and encouraged by His Spirit. *Jesus* gives us the *Holy Spirit* as our encourager and friend. We can experience all that He has for us when we activate Him in our lives by choosing Him. We will have His spiritual power as we draw closer to His love.

He wants for us to have and experience new life. He desires good for all His children. We must repent and seek to do good. We must believe and faithfully follow Him as we serve. We will have new life as we are revived again as *Jesus Christ* and the power of the *Holy Spirit* come alive in us! Let us praise the *Father* above for giving us His word and His power!

JULY 10

God Hears Your Cries
Psalm 77:1

I cry aloud to God, aloud to God, and He will hear me. God hears our cries for help and will answer us. Believe that He cares and will answer. All we must do is call upon Him and ask in the name of *Jesus* and we will receive. If *God* wills it, it will be done for us. Let us never stop believing as we pray. Let us never stop praying. As we diligently and fervently pray and seek *God*, we will receive all that is ours in *Christ Jesus*

Let every knee bow to the *Lord* who gives generously. Let our hearts not be troubled because we know that our *God* will answer us! The *Lord* desires good for His children. He wants us to have continual joy. We must gravitate towards Him more deeply and lean upon Him more each day to increase our joy. The closer we get to the *Lord*, we will experience more of what he wants to give us.

As we keep trusting Him, we come alive! Our fire will keep burning brightly when we keep leaning on the *Lord* daily. Let us grow our faith by being obedient to Him. Let us find hope that comes from *Christ Jesus*! Keep believing and we will receive!

JULY 11

Planted by the Lord
Isaiah 61:3

They may be called oaks of righteousness, the planting of the Lord, that He may be glorified. We are planted by the *Lord* to minister to those around us. He plants us and gives us what we need to grow strong roots so that we can spread His love by our fruits. His love is the first fruit He gives us so that we may grow stronger with deeper roots. As we receive this love, we grow courage and can endure much. We find joy even in the hard times of our life because we are grounded in faith. Our peace grows as our roots grow deep in the *Lord*! Our goodness, patience, kindness, and gentleness come out in our actions of faithful service even in the hardest of conditions.

There will be sunshine, misting rain, and rainbows. But there will also be dark storm clouds, thunder, and lightning. We must receive *Jesus* to stay the course, in the good times and the bad times. Let us not be afraid or discouraged by what is in front of us. Let us cling to the *Lord* and let Him plant us where He desires. Only then will we be able to see the beauty all around us with our eyes like *Jesus*. His compassion will become reality and His burden will become ours. Only then will we be able to minister to those around us!

JULY 12

You Can Have the Same Power
Romans 8:11

If the Spirit of Him who raised Jesus from the dead dwells in you, He who raised Christ Jesus from the dead will also give life to your mortal bodies through His Spirit who dwells in you. The same power that rose *Jesus* lives in you and gives you life. When you believe, you receive the *Holy Spirit*. Activate it by allowing the *Holy Spirit* to be in control. Give up the fight to always be in control of all and let *Jesus* take over.

His gift of grace has already saved you. His gift of the Spirit will empower you. His love will nourish and comfort you. His joy will strengthen you. His hope will give you deeper faith. Look to the *Lord* and know that He is waiting to bless your life.

When you live by the Spirit, you will find life. As you live with the Spirit, you will be one of His children who is content and free to be you because the power of the living *Christ* gives you confidence. You cannot buy or bargain this power into your life. All you need to do is believe and receive. Yes, believe that *Jesus* rose from the dead to give you life. Believe in the power of the living Spirit and receive Him into your daily life by faith! Let the power of the living Spirit work in you as you faithfully walk daily in the word and the Spirit.

JULY 13

The Word is Sharper than a Two-Edged Sword
Isaiah 40:8

The grass withers, the flower fades, but the word of our God will stand forever. The word is the truth and is sharper than a two-edged sword. It gives us wisdom and knowledge that encourages us. Our *Lord* speaks to us through His word and He delivers us and makes our paths straight. His word will stand forever. Read it, listen to it, and obey it.

When we let our paths be directed by our *Lord*, we walk where He desires. Our actions show that we trust Him to guide us and show us the way we should go. Our obedience to His commands shows our love for our *Lord*. Our strength and power are renewed in Him as we make the *Lord* our priority. He gives us all that we need when we surrender all to *Jesus*. The *Holy Spirit* guides us into all truth. Our spirit-filled prayers connect us to the *Lord*. He hears our prayers and will answer us as we speak to Him. He speaks to us through the pages of His word. Let us open our hearts to hear Him as we open the pages of our Bibles. Let us ask the *Holy Spirit* to help us understand and apply the scriptures to our lives. We will receive all that He has for us when we seek His fresh word daily. Taste and eat His daily bread and see that the *Lord* is good all the time!

JULY 14

Answer the Call
Romans 1:12

We may be mutually encouraged by each other's faith, both yours and mine. Let us keep our hope through faith. Let us not be troubled and distressed by what we see, but let us be encouraged and comforted by what we believe will happen. The *Lord* does work everything out for good in His will and in His timing. His way is always best! We must continue walking and living by faith as faithful servants who have been set apart. The *Lord* needs us to do what He has called us to do when He calls us.

Let us draw closer to the *Lord* each day as we grow in our relationship with Him by reading truth in the word and praying in the Spirit. He wants us to grow deeper. He yearns for us to talk and listen to Him like we would a friend. Let us start by opening our heart and soul to Him completely. Let go of the control we have taken for ourselves and let the *Lord Jesus* take over. When we do this, we will have that peace and joy that we have been hoping to find.

Jesus Christ is our peace. *Jesus Christ* is our joy. Nothing or no one else even comes close! Draw closer to Him and experience revival and renewal like never before. Start today and do not delay. *Jesus* is calling us and is waiting for us to answer the call. Will you answer His call for you?

JULY 15

He Answers You
Jeremiah 1:19

They will fight against you, but they shall not prevail against you, for I am with you, declares the Lord, to deliver you. Call upon the *Lord*. He is waiting for you to come to Him with open arms and ask for Him to strengthen you. He is ready to bless your life with joy because He loves you. He does not want you to suffer anymore. Call upon Him and love Him with all your heart, soul, mind and strength. He will strengthen you. Are you struggling today because you just cannot see a way out? Are you looking for someone to rescue you? Are you hoping for a miracle? Look to the *Lord* and He will rescue you! Start praying in faith believing for that miracle, because all your hopes and dreams can come true with *Jesus*! He promises to bless you as you love Him and walk by faith. He desires for you to live righteously, always seeking to please Him.

Do not lose heart or be troubled because *Jesus* has come to save you! Start opening your heart to Him today by trusting Him more so that your faith can grow stronger. Aim to please the one and only *Jesus Christ*! You will find everything you are searching for in His arms of grace and comfort. Everything is possible with the *Lord*!

JULY 16

One Heart and Soul
Acts 4:32

Now the full number of those who believed were of one heart and soul. These believers were of one accord in prayer and fellowship. They had all things in common as they relied on the power of the *Holy Spirit* in all their ways. They worshipped in Spirit and in truth as they taught and read the word together. They were pursuing all good things together in one accord. Their souls were filled with faith as they looked to the *Lord* for nourishment and comfort.

We can be like these believers in the early church inside and outside the walls of our church as we all come together as the family of *God*. All are welcome to be included in this family with one heart, soul, and Spirit. As we come together as one to pray, the power of the *Holy Spirit* unites us. We will have all things in common as we ask *God* in unity to answer us. He will do great and mighty things for those who believe. As we seek truth from His word together as one, we will hear His voice like never before. A holy fire will unite our hearts and our souls and spread like a wildfire out of control. Let us be the people who are united and not divided. Let us aim to please our *Lord* and *Savior*! It is time to unite as one with one heart, soul, and Spirit!

JULY 17

Come to the Good Shepherd
John 10:27

My sheep hear my voice, and I know them, and they follow me. Are you hearing the voice of the Good Shepherd? Are you following Him? If you are in His sheepfold, He knows it and He knows you. Come through His door and find refuge. Seek Him and you will find shelter from that storm. His door is always open for you.

You who are weary will find your rest in Him. You who are weak will renew your strength in Him. You who are afraid will find peace in Him. Come to your *Lord* fully surrendered and ready to experience joy beyond measure. He brings the complete joy you have been searching your whole life to find. It is available to you when you say yes to His abundant and amazing love. Are you ready to say yes to new life?

Stop looking everywhere else for love and security and look to the *Lord.* He is the anchor of your heart and soul. When you are anchored to Him, you will truly be able to say it is well with your soul!

JULY 18

Let the Light of Christ Shine in You
2 Corinthians 4:6

For God said, "Let light shine out of darkness." The light of *Christ* is shining through you as you speak the truth and follow His light. As you act in faith, your witness is stronger. Even when they do not have the same faith, people can see the light of *Jesus* when they see you faithfully serving Him. Touch Him and feel the warmth and encouragement of His love. He is the one who has promised good to you always.

Speak of the truth found in the word and pray in the spirit with others. People need to be built up and not torn down. As you come together in one accord with the power of the *Holy Spirit*, you will feel the presence of the *Lord* in a mighty way. Yes, His presence is powerful and overwhelming! He will lift you up, carry you and your burdens, and give you hope once again. Trust Him in all your ways. Do not look to your own self interests, but come back to the *Lord*, your first love. Let His Spirit increase in you as you surrender all to Him. As He increases in you, a spark of His light will start a fire inside of you. Keep that fire burning in you, faithful one. More will find Him as they see the spark and the flame of the *Holy Spirit* who fills this place with fires of revival!

JULY 19

Love the Lord with all Your Heart and Soul
Deuteronomy 6:5

You shall love the Lord your God with all your heart and with all your soul and with all your might. The *Lord* loves you and yearns for your love in return. His love will enrich your heart and fill you with eternal joy. Your joy will be complete in Him when you give your whole heart to Him. Your soul will find rest when you put your total trust in the *Lord.* Your mind will be transformed and renewed when you seek Him in all your ways. Find your strength in the *Lord* your *God.* He will never leave or forsake you. He will not abandon you but will bring you to a place of peace with Him. Do not go alone but go with the *Lord.*

He is waiting for you to come to Him for complete healing. He is the one who will heal you. Trust Him to lead you out of the wilderness of your life. He is the one who will stand with you. Come to Him in your brokenness and in your pain and let Him restore you with His living water! He loves you so much and wants to rescue you. Love the *Lord* and see your desires become His. Feel His love showering you with all His good and perfect gifts from above. Blessed are the pure in heart who love the *Lord* with all their heart, soul, and mind!

JULY 20

Come and Pray Together
Matthew 18:19

Again, I say to you, if two of you agree on earth about anything they ask, it will be done for them by my Father in heaven. When you come together and pray in His will and in His name, the *Lord Jesus* hears you and intercedes for you to the *Father*. Ask together and it shall be given to you. Seek together and you shall find. Two or more coming together to pray will find the *Lord* in their midst. The presence of the *Lord* and the power of the *Holy Spirit* will be present in a mighty way.

Are you seeking the power and the presence of the *Lord*? Are you praying in the Spirit and truth? Have you joined with other believers as one heart, soul, and Spirit? The *Lord* will answer you and He hears you calling Him. He is greater than anything you are facing. Seek the *Lord* first and you will not be alone. Lean more closely upon Him. Continue praying and do not stop believing. The thing that you hope for is waiting for you. Your joy will be complete when you let go and let *God* work in you and through you. All good comes to those who wait upon Him. Your faith in your *Lord* will be your strength and your joy. When you need Him, the *Lord* is there. Right there, just when you need Him. He is the one who you can count on all the time!

JULY 21

The Lord Knows Your Heart
Psalm 1:6

For the Lord knows the way of the righteous, but the way of the wicked will perish. The *Lord* knows our heart. We cannot hide from Him. Let us continue drawing to Him and His righteousness so that we may be complete in Him. Let us see the evil around us and turn away from it. When we seek the *Lord* and His righteousness and love, all good things will be added to us. Our desires will be pleasing to the one who desires good for us. Let our hearts beat to please the *Lord,* our mighty *Redeemer,* with every step we take. He needs us to continue on the path with Him. When we leave the *Lord* and turn away from Him, everything in our life will be turned upside down. Our security and peace come from placing our trust in *Christ* alone. The world will tell us otherwise, but we know that *Christ* is our cornerstone. We are strong and secure with *Christ* as our foundation. Nothing can take away our joy when we cling to Him!

Let us trust in the *Lord* with all our hearts and lean not on human understanding. This mountain we are facing will be nothing compared to the hope we have in *Christ* who will help us. Everything is clearer when we cling to *Christ.* Let us keep walking in faith and make the most of our days.

JULY 22

Be Renewed By His Spirit
Ephesians 4:23

And to be renewed in the spirit of your minds.
What a promise we have right here in this truth! He
cannot renew us if we do not ask. Let us seek His will
and ask in the name of *Jesus* so that He may hear us
and that we may receive. He is waiting to hear our
requests. He longs for us to speak to Him.

He is the one who longs for a relationship
with us. We are the ones who can choose to follow
Him and His truth. Let us open our hearts to His great
love. Let us see Him everywhere we look. He
surrounds us with His great love and glory! Believe in
the name of *Jesus* that you have eternal life because
He has overcome the world. Our faith has brought us
victory and freedom because we are born into life
through *Jesus Christ* We live because He died for us!
What a wonderful sacrifice our *Father* made to give
us this hope through His only Son. We praise our
mighty *God* for giving us this confidence and this
hope so that we can go on living with His *Holy Spirit*
inside of us. We can live right now with His joy and
we will live eternally with joy in heaven. *Lord*, let
your glory fall on us! Let it rain down and flood our
souls with joy and our hearts with peace! Let it be
Lord!

JULY 23

Serve By Doing Good
3 John 11

Beloved, do not imitate evil but imitate good. Whoever does good is from God, whoever does evil has not seen God. The *Lord* is good, and all good things flow from the *Lord*. He loves you so much and wants the best for you. See to it that you honor Him by your good works done in faith. Stay away from evil and keep your heart connected to the love that flows from *Christ*.

Love one another, as love will conquer all. Comfort your fellow brother or sister like *Jesus* has comforted you. Be a friend who lays aside selfish interests for the needs of others. Give up control and fully surrender your heart to *Christ*. You can do more when you lay aside yourself and let *Jesus* work through you. You are His hands and feet. You are the one He has called to work for His greater purpose.

Listen to His voice and go serve. Many need a *Savior*. They need to hear the message of hope and truth through you. Be a messenger of peace and go tell your story that *God* has written on your heart. It is time to share, love, and care. The days are numbered and there is much work to be done, good and faithful servant! It's time to go!

JULY 24

Faith is the Key
Romans 5:1

Therefore, since we have been justified by faith, we have peace through God through our Lord Jesus Christ. The only way to *God* is through His Son, *Jesus*. We have access to a relationship with Him when we believe in *Jesus*. Our faith is the key to having this relationship with *Jesus* and our *Father*.

Do you have faith that endures because you know you have a *Father* in heaven who loves you? Do you believe that He sacrificed His perfect Son so that you could have His perfect peace? If so, why are you not giving Him your whole heart? Why are you so afraid to totally trust Him? Is your fear bigger than your faith?

Put faith first and let your faith be bigger than your fear! Stop letting the world and its ways pull you down because *Jesus* wants to pull you up with Him. He needs you to lean in closer and give Him your whole heart by letting go and surrendering all to Him. You can do it and will not regret a single moment that you live with *Jesus* in control. He is the author and perfecter of your faith. You are made whole in *Christ*, not in yourself. Let go and let *Jesus* give you life again!

JULY 25

The Lord Goes Before You
Deuteronomy 31:8

It is the Lord that goes before you. He will be with you; He will not leave or forsake you. Thank you, *Lord,* for creating us in your image and for giving us security in you and your great love. We praise you for being a loving and giving *Father* to us always! You never leave or forsake us, and we are made whole only in you. You made us to be strong and secure in you, *Lord*, so we will look to you and your love more every day.

Each day spent with you is better than the day before. You are a place of refuge and a point of peace for us to dwell in forever. We are alive with the power of the *Holy Spirit* because you live inside of us. We can face each day with an extra measure of hope only because of you, *Lord*! Every day is a great day when it is spent in your loving arms. We find our strength in you, our *Father of Light*. We look to your light for our power and know that only you can revive and refresh us completely. We are renewed in you, *Lord,* by your never-ending love and powerful Spirit. We can always find comfort in your promises to us and through our open communication with you through our prayers. Your love for us never ends! Thank you, *Father,* for knitting us so wonderful and beautiful in our mother's womb!

JULY 26

Breathe in His Love
Nahum 1:3

The Lord is slow to anger and great in power; and the Lord will by no means clear the guilty. The *Lord* is speaking to you, so open your heart and listen. He wants you to step away from sin and step into a life of righteousness. He knows your heart and sees you. You cannot hide from Him. He is waiting to bless your life, if you are willing to surrender and repent.

He is slow to anger and forgives you by His amazing grace. He is seeking those who will open their hearts and souls to His love by forgiving and loving others. He rewards those who walk in truth and integrity with His treasures from heaven. Be one who forgives and brings joy wherever you go!

Stop quenching the *Holy Spirit* with anger, bitterness, and hatred. Activate the *Holy Spirit* in your life by surrendering your heart to Him. Feel His love for you and love one another, as it conquers all and opens the door to the heart and soul. Feel His Spirit flowing through you like living water. Drink of this water that *Jesus* gives. He is the living water that quenches all. Breathe in His love and power and discover a brand new life of pure joy!

JULY 27

Let the Lord Strengthen You
2 Timothy 4:17

But the Lord stood by me and strengthened me so that through me the message might be fully proclaimed. Together with *Christ*, we can stand firm and stand up for what the *Lord* is wanting to do through us. He has called us and set us apart to share the message of hope that is found in *Jesus Christ.* He has kingdom work for us to do, and He promises to stand by us and strengthen us as we boldly proclaim the message that He put in our hearts.

When we seek His will above our own, we will discover all that is ours through *Christ,* our redeemer. He will show us the way we should go to fulfill all our heart's desires. The desires of our heart will become the desires of the *Lord* when we live abundantly in *Christ*. He put His Spirit in us so that we can have joy along the way here on earth. When we live faithfully, and in our *God* given purpose, we can experience a joy-filled life in *Jesus Christ*!

Let us stop asking why, but instead, ask how can we make a difference for *Christ*. Our eternal reward awaits us where our faith will be our sight. But until that glorious day, let us continue walking and working in faith one day at a time. Our faith in *God* alone helps us stand strong. Rejoice and praise the *Lord* because He is good all the time!

JULY 28

He Will Tell You Great Things
Jeremiah 33:3

Call to me and I will answer you, and will tell you great and hidden things that you have not known. Yes, our *Lord* will answer you when you call Him. Look for Him wherever you go. He surrounds you, but you do not see because you are distracted. Spend time listening and looking for the *Lord* as you watch, work, and wait upon Him.

Be still and know that He is *God*. Spend time getting to know Him and His will for you. The *Lord* Almighty can do more than you ever dreamed or imagined. His Spirit is in the wind that you feel flowing through you. The *Holy Spirit* is in you when you choose to make *Jesus* the *Lord* of your life. The *Holy Spirit* is alive in you when you choose to activate Him and seek Him daily for guidance and direction. He will help you always, so trust completely in the one who loves and cares for you unconditionally. His strength will be your song. The joy of the *Lord* will carry you to places you never thought possible. Today is the day to be strong and courageous because He is going to release the floodgates of His power upon all who will receive. The *Holy Spirit* will fall fresh on those who are ready to receive! Say yes to His power and let your heart and soul be revived and made new in *Jesus Christ*!

JULY 29

The Lord Will Be Faithful
2 Thessalonians 3:2-3

Not all have faith. But the Lord is faithful. The *Lord* will be faithful to you even if you do not understand why or see what you hope will happen. He is there for you in the best times and in the hard times of your life. Cling to your faithful *Lord*. All you need to do is love and trust Him above all else with your whole heart, mind, body, and soul. Keep believing and asking in faith through your prayers for what you need. Keep your hope alive as you continue trusting your *God* to do it. He knows your needs and desires before you even ask Him.

Be still, listen, and know that whatever happens the *Lord* is there for you and will fight your battles. He has not left you or forsaken you even now. When things in your life seem hopeless, His loving arms will carry you and lift your spirit. When it looks impossible, the *Lord* will show you more than you ever thought possible.

He that is within you is greater than He who is in the world! Show the world that *Christ* lives in you through your active faith. Bring the love of *Jesus* to those who need Him today. Keep your faith alive and keep walking in your purpose. Your joy will be found in *Jesus Christ*!

JULY 30

Crown of Glory
1 Thessalonians 4:13

But we do not want you to be uniformed brothers, about those who are asleep, that you may not grieve as others do who have no hope. Those that have died before us and have believed in *Jesus* and His resurrection are with *Jesus* in heaven. Our hope and our promise is that we who believe will see them again someday. We know that those who are with *Christ* in heaven have received the treasures of heaven and the crown of glory promised to them. They have finished their race and kept the faith. Now we are to keep fighting the good fight of faith so that we can find complete joy here on earth as we work for the glory of *God*. Our reward in heaven awaits us! Turn to Him for all you need and know that He will deliver you. He is your redeemer and your Savior. He died and suffered so that you could be free.

Why are you still struggling and not surrendering all? Why do you not believe and trust Him with your whole heart? Give Him all and do not hold on to any part if you want to experience the fullness of *Christ*. There is more when you live by the power of the *Holy Spirit* inside of you. More life and more joy are yours when you choose to surrender all and activate this power that is inside of you.

JULY 31

Seek the Things Above
Colossians 3:1

If then you have been raised with Christ, seek the things that are above, where Christ is seated at the right hand of God. The spiritual treasures of heaven are yours when you seek them in *Christ*. Look to the *Lord* and seek Him and His will for you. He has called you out of the dark and into His great light. You will see His glory when you rely on Him always!

Be of good courage and trust Him to show you the way. His strength will carry you and His love will enrich your life completely. Only the *Lord* can make you complete. His plan for you will never fail when you let go and let Him guide you. Surrender all your cares to the one who cares for you no matter what. Even if you fail, He will love you because He is your *Father*.

When the storms come, He will guide you through them and be your peace and give you rest for your weary soul. He will be your joy no matter what happens. Be certain of what you know. Be confident of His love for you. Be sure that you are forgiven and free. Turn away from sin and the desires of the flesh and turn to your *God* who will heal and redeem you. He loves you and is waiting for you to give Him your heart, soul, mind, and body. He will transform you from the inside out. Your joy will be found in *Jesus*.

PRAYER TO JESUS

Dear *Lord*,

I lift my soul up to you as I pray today. You gladden the soul of your servant, for to you, O *Lord*, do I lift up my soul. You make me feel alive as I draw closer to you. Your mighty power is active in me!

I want you to show me your will and your way. I am eager to follow you as you lead me where you want me to go. Your way is always best, so I will step aside and let you step into my life. I hear you calling me and I will obey you, *Lord*.

I am complete and made whole in you. My desires, passions, and purposes have changed now that I am yours, fully surrendered and ready to serve. You will lead me to the green pastures and still water that my soul seeks as I put my full faith and trust in you! I am yours, *Lord*, so use me as you will to advance your kingdom!

In *Jesus* name,

Amen,

For nothing WILL BE IMPOSSIBLE with God.

LUKE 1:37

AUGUST 1

God has Attended to the Voice of Your Prayer
Psalm 66:19

But truly God has listened; He has attended to the voice of my prayer. Yes, *God* has heard you and is rejoicing as you pray. He loves to hear your voice calling Him. He yearns to hear your requests and your desires. He has heard you and He will answer you.

He takes broken things and makes them whole again. He restores what was lost so that it may be found. He walks with you as you lift Him up higher. Be still and know that He is *God,* and He can do anything He pleases. He can do what seems impossible! Your *Lord* can accomplish all! Just believe as you pray!

The *Lord* is so good to you. He has rewarded your faith by answering the desires of your heart. The more you seek Him, the more your desires become His desires for you. Faithfully pursue the good things that He longs to give you. Earnestly pray to your *Lord* and *Savior*. Rest in the comfort of His presence with hope in your heart. Prayer will connect you with *Jesus*, so call upon Him in Spirit. He will intercede for you to the *Father*. The only way to the *Father* is through His *Son, Jesus*. Let Him put that smile back on your face and that joy back in your heart! He will surely do it!

AUGUST 2

Obey His Promptings
and Live in the Spirit
1 Thessalonians 2:12

Walk in a manner worthy of God, who calls you into His own kingdom and glory. Speak boldly with words of encouragement and truth so that others may hear the mystery of the gospel. Spread hope by sharing the truth found in the pages of the Bible. Find joy as you serve others before yourself. Love the *Lord* with all your heart and soul and spread the love of *Jesus* wherever you go.

Live connected to *Christ* and you will find life. He is the word and the word is life. He needs you to carry His message of love to the world. Start with those He puts in your path daily and listen to the *Holy Spirit* directing you to speak. Obey the prompting of the Spirit and act in faith. Your faith will make you bolder because you will want to please your *Lord* who has loved you even before you were born. He promises good to those who love Him and walk in obedience. *God* needs you and wants you. Do not wait another day to seek His purpose for you. When you call upon *Jesus* in prayer, seek Him through the pages of the Bible, and be still and listen, you will hear Him calling you to your purpose. You can live out your *God*-given purpose when you are fully engaged and connected to the one who gave you life.

AUGUST 3

He is Greater than the World
John 14:12

"Truly, truly, I say to you, whoever believes in me will also do the works that I do; and greater works than these will he do, because I am going to the Father." Keep drawing to *Jesus* and His love and turn away from the desires of the world. He is greater than anything the world offers. Look to *Jesus* for your strength to overcome. The *Lord* will strengthen you and protect you if you let Him. Take heart and come to the one who promises good to you. He rejoices when His. He loves to bless those who obey Him and His commandments. As you obey, you are showing your love for your *Savior*. Watch *Jesus* love you back with more love than you can ever imagine. He is love. When you love Him with your whole heart, you can love others fearlessly. There is no fear in love because perfect love casts out all fear!

Your love for *Jesus* will bring others to know Him. Your love for them will open their eyes to see *Jesus* through your kindness and compassion. The only way to love those who persecute you is to keep pressing into *Jesus* and His love. His love will transform you so that you can love and bless others. Love the *Lord* with all your heart, soul, and mind. Give His love to others and you will receive His everlasting love abundantly!

AUGUST 4

Humble Yourself Before God
1 Peter 5:6

Humble yourselves, therefore, under the mighty hand of God so that at the proper time He may exalt you, casting all your anxieties on Him, because He cares for you. Come to the *Lord* all who are weary, and you will find your rest. Believe that He can take away all your pain and all your heartache. Humble yourself before Him and trust that He can take your burdens. He wants to comfort you and protect you. Give Him your worries and He will take them all!

Let *God* be your shelter and hiding place. He cares for you and loves you with a never-ending love. Trust in the one who wants all of you. He made you in His image and knows and wants every part of you to surrender to Him. Your heart, body, mind, and soul are precious to Him. Cling to the *Lord* and give Him all. Let the *Holy Spirit* come and lead you into all truth. Stop running from the one who wants to help you. His mighty hand will rescue you and give you everything you are looking for. It is time to trust and obey. Surrender all to your *Father*. Trust that *Jesus* is your *Savior* who lives in you and delight in knowing that you have your friend, the *Holy Spirit* to lead you. Come to the fountain of life and start living with a new joy!

AUGUST 5

You are Free in the Spirit
Romans 8:2

For the law of the Spirit of life has set you free in Christ Jesus from the law of sin and death. Christ indeed has set you free and He is the one who has made you whole. His sacrifice was for your freedom so that you could have the Spirit living inside of you to guide you into all truth. The wages of sin were paid by *Jesus* on the cross for you. Look to your *Savior* with hope because He has given you salvation!

In *Jesus*, there is no more doubt about your standing with the *Father*. He gave His life so that you could enter a new relationship with *God*. Through this relationship, you are free to live under the law of the Spirit. You are no longer a prisoner to sin and death but are alive to grace and mercy from the living Spirit of the *Lord*!

Listen to this wonderful news! You are not a slave to your past. You are a child of light covered by the grace of *God* through *Christ Jesus*. Why do you keep going back to the sin that holds you captive? Why are you struggling with the flesh and not clinging to the Spirit? Do you see that you are free to live by the Spirit? Keep clinging to the cross of salvation and to the *Holy Spirit* and believe that you have been set free by *Jesus*!

AUGUST 6

Double Blessings
Romans 10:17

So faith comes from hearing, and hearing through the word of Christ. Are you believing what you hear about *Christ*? Do you know that His word is truth and those who follow it are children of *God*? Do you want to live righteously? Start by reading His word, listening to Him, and then trusting your *Lord* with all your heart. Surrender all to the one who gave it all for you and obey His commands born out of love. He loves you so much and wants what is best for you! Take to heart what you know to be true about the love and blessings of your *Lord*. He loves you so much and wants you to love Him. Hear that He loves you, child of faith. Keep believing in His promises for you and showing Him that you love Him by acting faithfully, not fearfully.

Count your blessings and not your troubles. Turn your worry list into a prayer list. Start believing that the *Lord* will answer your prayers and keep praying. He hears you when you pray and bends down to hear and touch you with His love and lavish you with His grace! His promises are real, so hope in the Lord and trust Him with all of your heart. In His presence are pleasures and treasures for you to enjoy today and eternally. Double blessings await you when your faith is placed in *Jesus Christ*!

AUGUST 7

Train Yourself for Godliness
1 Timothy 4:7-8

Train yourself for godliness; for while bodily training is of some value, godliness is of value in every way, as it holds promise for the present life and also for the life to come. Your life is full of choices. You get to choose how you will live on this earth. The *Lord* wants you to choose Him and seek godliness, purity, and righteousness by walking with Him and applying His truth. You can know Him more and train your soul by spending time with Him daily. Walk with Him through the word of life found in the Holy Bible. Pray to Him asking for His direction from the power of the *Holy Spirit*

Seek the things that are yours in *Jesus* as these treasures are lasting. The promise of a life filled with joy is right here for you as you trust Him more. The promise of eternal life with *Jesus* is yours if you believe. You are not alone when you are walking hand in hand with *Jesus*. He will strengthen you to go the extra mile. Your weakness will become His strength in you. Lean on *God* and strive for spiritual success. Your body will waste away, but your soul will never age with *Christ* in the center of your heart. You are young, alive, and free when you know your *Lord* and *Savior* and are empowered with your friend, the *Holy Spirit*!

AUGUST 8

Believe and You Will See
John 11:26

"And everyone who lives and believes in me shall never die. Do you believe this?" We must keep working as we are called. He is eager for us to keep persevering in the faith as we serve Him. We must not give up like those without faith who need to see in order to believe. We will keep working and believing without seeing as we have this hope in the depth of our souls that comes from our faith.

Jesus will show us greater things as we keep obeying Him. He will open our eyes and our hearts to the joy that comes only from Him. Our dreams will become reality when they are grounded in faith. With *Jesus*, we will not abandon in frustration what we have planted in faith. He will bring light to our plans and open our heart to more of His desires as we grow in faith. He will bring to completion the good work that He has begun in us. All we need to do is trust Him completely with our whole heart, listen to His voice calling us, and act in obedience according to His plan. Keep believing that He will surely do it. Keep working even when you do not see. Keep praying in faith knowing that our *God* can do the impossible. When the world says no, *God* says yes! Just believe and you will see!

AUGUST 9

Open Door to Joy
Romans 12:12

Rejoice in hope, be patient in tribulation, be constant in prayer. There is hope when you follow *Jesus*. He will be with you when you face the challenges of life. Only *Jesus* will get you through those tough days when you are weary and weak. He will be your strength and your living hope. Turn to Him and pray constantly knowing that He will answer you! Are you faithfully praying, believing that He will answer you? Do you see His hand of protection guiding you as you wait patiently and love Him passionately? Are you praying fervently believing that He will meet all your needs and deepest desires?

When the darkness of doubt and fear surrounds you, look up and see the light of *Christ* shining down on you. His rays of hope are lighting the way for you as you keep seeking and obeying *Jesus*. You will find peace as you keep faithfully trusting the *Lord* through it all. He knows the way you should go, so trust Him to take you through that open door that leads to joy. There is fullness of joy in His glorious presence. Open the door and let Him fill you with His Spirit so that you will come alive with the joy of the *Lord*! Continue praying earnestly and constantly believing that *Lord* hears you and will bless you abundantly!

AUGUST 10

Return to God with Your Whole Heart
Jeremiah 24:7

I will give them a heart to know that I am the Lord, and they shall be my people and I will be their God, for they shall return to me with their whole heart. The *Lord* wants us to give Him our whole heart. Let us give Him our whole heart with total surrender. We can trust in Him to guard our heart as He loves us with an everlasting love. When we surrender all to our *Lord* and *Savior*, the Spirit inside of us will come alive. We will be directed by His power when we host His presence in our lives daily and live with the power of the *Holy Spirit*. Our way will be clearer as He guides us each step of the way each and every day.

Let us start each day in prayer and thanksgiving as we give thanks to the *Lord* for His great love and Spirit in our lives. He has put His Spirit in us to guide and direct us to a life of freedom and wholeness. We are set apart and made whole because we have already been set free through our *Savior, Jesus Christ* Our victory has already been won and our hope rests in the promise of salvation. We are His people, and He is our one true *Lord* of all. He is *God* alone up on His throne. Bow down at His feet in prayer and stand up in awe and worship His Holy name!

AUGUST 11

Let the Lord Restore You
Joel 2:12-13

Return to me with all your heart, with fasting, with weeping, and with mourning, and rend your hearts and not your garments. Repent and come to the *Lord.* He has called you and wants you to come back to Him with your whole heart. He has forgiven you and has washed you clean. Cry out to Him to restore the things you have lost. Seek renewal and revival by total surrender of your heart.

Trust Him and He will make a way for you. Give Him all control over all in your life and you will find your joy. Keep loving Him and you will find hope. Keep seeking good and righteousness and you will find peace. Keep obeying Him and you will find truth.

He is your Savior and deliverer and will save and deliver you if you repent and come to Him. He wants to give you freedom and asks that you turn to Him and His light. His way is the way you should go. Stay on the path with Him and keep following Him where He leads you. Let Him love you completely as you obey Him. Rend your hearts and come to Jesus for restoration!

AUGUST 12

The Lord Will Provide All You Need
Jeremiah 29:12

Then you will call upon me and come and pray to me, and I will hear you. Call upon the *Lord* and come to Him in prayer so that He can answer you. He is waiting for you to seek Him by opening your heart to Him. Wait upon the *Lord* who will answer your cries and rejoice with you in your praises. Our *Lord* gives, so ask believing that it will be done for you in His will.

Worship Him and pray in spirit and in truth so that you are ready to receive all that the *Lord* is ready to give you. Only the *Lord* can provide all that you need. He will find you and restore you if you seek Him with your whole heart. He will pick you up when you fall and carry you in His loving arms.

His peace which is beyond human understanding will guard your hearts and minds in *Christ Jesus.* The *Lord* knows all the plans that He has for you. He will give you hope and a future and fulfill all His promises for you. The *Lord* will raise you up on eagles' wings and lift you higher above all the pain where you will find the joy of *Jesus*! You will be alive in *Christ* as you trust in Him and believe!

AUGUST 13

God Smiles with You
Isaiah 55:9

For as the heavens are higher than the earth, so are my ways higher than your ways and my thoughts than your thoughts. The *Lord* wants the best for his children. He longs for us to know Him better and to hunger and thirst for more of His goodness. His ways are higher than our ways and His thoughts are higher than our thoughts. The *Lord* hears our prayers from heaven as He bends down to listen to us cry out to Him. He smiles when we praise Him with grateful hearts for His miracles and answered prayers.

The *Lord* loves us so much that He yearns for us to come to Him in faith believing that He can accomplish much through us. He knows us intimately as He created each one of us in His image. He wants us to fulfill the purpose He has given each of us. He sees the potential in us and knows the desires of our hearts. When our desires line up with His, we can accomplish much to the glory of the *Lord*. Everything is possible to those that believe. The *Lord* is compassionate and kind. He reaches for us with His outstretched arms from heaven to lift us up when we fall. We do not need to fear, because He is right there beside us always. Seek the *Lord* with all your heart and lean not on your own understanding. You will go out in joy and be led in peace as you trust Him more.

AUGUST 14

Work Heartily for the Lord
Colossians 3:23-24

Whatever you do, work heartily, as for the Lord and not for men, knowing that from the Lord you will receive the inheritance as your reward. Be a servant for the *Lord* and whatever you do, work for the *Lord*. He honors your hard work for Him and will bless and reward those who follow Him and obey His commands. Seek first the kingdom of *God*, and all good things will be added to you. You will find peace when you live out your *God*-given purpose. Continue your calling to serve Him with compassion, kindness, humility, patience, and meekness.

Continue steadfastly in prayer and be thankful in advance for the answers you will receive when you pray expectantly. Pray that the *Lord* will give you opportunities and a willing heart to share the gospel of peace and truth to those that He chooses for you.

Make the best use of your time as you live each day on earth. Let the *Holy Spirit* guide your days and direct your path. He will show you many wonders and miracles as you trust Him and surrender all. As you work and honor the *Lord* first in all you do, you will be a laborer for *Christ*. Blessed are the laborers who will hear the *Lord* proclaim to them, "Well done, my good and faithful servant!" Live, love, and work for the glory of the *Lord*!

AUGUST 15

Touch Others with Your Love
1 Peter 4:8

Above all, keep loving one another earnestly, since love covers a multitude of sins. Love the *Lord* with all your heart and soul. The *Lord* wants us to love deeper. He loves us with a perfect love. His love casts out all fear and doubt. This same love touches us so that we can touch others with love. As we keep loving, we see our lives changing. We see hope where there was none. We feel alive with joy that comes from *Jesus*!

With *Jesus*, our focus turns from past sins to present peace. His love and grace cover our sins. We are stirred by grace as we lean closer to His love. Our desires become one with *Jesus*. As we lean on *Jesus*, our hearts are abandoned of selfish desires and are turned to what *Jesus* desires for us.

New life is found in *Jesus Christ*. Let us walk confidently and joyfully in the Spirit and leave our past behind. As we do, we will be able to love one another. Our focus will shift from dwelling on ourselves and our problems, to loving and giving grace to those around us. Grace and love cover a multitude of sins. By grace, through His love, we have been saved! Rest in this truth and feel His eternal love and peace!

AUGUST 16

His Grace is Sufficient
2 Corinthians 12:9

My grace is sufficient for you, for my power is made perfect in weakness. The *Lord* has given you grace so that you can have life. His power and glory can be seen through His redeeming grace. The *Lord* shines through you and strengthens you when you make Him the *Lord* of your life. His grace covers you completely and has saved you. He is stronger when you are weaker.

Be of good courage and believe that He has good things planned for you. He has called you out and set you apart to meet Him wherever you are on your journey. His love has brought you to places you never thought possible. Your joy is complete when *Jesus* is the center of your life. When you are weak, He is strong.

Cling to *Jesus Christ* and look to Him for hope. He is the hope that you have been searching for over and over again. He is the peace that you need. He is the joy that you want. Finish the race that He has set before you by keeping the faith. Do not give up but keep pursuing *Jesus*. He is your friend and your best yes. His grace is sufficient for you!

AUGUST 17

Give Thanks for Loved Ones
Ephesians 1:16

I do not cease to give thanks for you; remembering you in my prayers. Praise the *Lord* for our family and friends who love us! We are thankful for those who walk in faith with us to lead us closer to *Christ*. We praise the *Lord* for those people in our lives who build us up and encourage us every step of the way. Every day spent in fellowship with our loved ones is a reminder of *God's* amazing love for us.

We pray for those who mean so much to us and give *God* the glory for giving us these people in our life to love. We are connected by the Spirit to our friends in *Christ*. We are all part of the family of *God*. Our hearts are linked to our *Lord* and our brothers and sisters in *Christ*. We are stronger together with *Christ* as our foundation and center of all our relationships.

When one in the body of *Christ* is hurting, we all hurt and grieve with them. Each part of the body needs the other to function effectively for the *Lord*. Let us put aside our desires and wants and look to the interests of others in the body who need us. Let us pray for our family and friends fervently and without ceasing. Let us love unconditionally like *Christ* has loved us. Let us find the joy of *Jesus* and feel His everlasting love by loving and praying for others. We give thanks and praise to our *Lord* and *Savior*.

HEARTS ON FIRE

AUGUST 18

Forgive as You have been Forgiven
Ephesians 4:32

Be kind to one another, tenderhearted, forgiving one another, as God in Christ forgave you. As you show your kindness and gentleness to others, you will be showing them *Jesus*. He wants you to forgive like He has forgiven you. Be willing to put aside your past offenses and put on the fullness of *Christ*. You will find freedom when you forgive. *Jesus Christ* is the one who has saved you and set you free. He is the one who has rescued you from the dark and put His light within you. Shine his radiant light and come out of the darkness!

Live with the Spirit of *Christ* active inside of you and make the *Holy Spirit* your friend. Find comfort in the grace of *Jesus* and lean on the love of *God*. Let go of control and feel the peace that comes with surrender. You do not have to be afraid anymore. With *Christ* in your heart, you can be free to love everyone again.

Trust Him and feel His amazing grace covering you completely. He loves you and has forgiven you. He is waiting for you to fully surrender and find freedom in His forgiveness. Do not wait another day as the time has come. It's time to find the peace that awaits you around the corner from your pain. The love of *Jesus* conquers all!

AUGUST 19

The Lord Knows Your Heart
Romans 13:14

Put on the Lord Jesus Christ, and make no provision for the flesh, to gratify its desires. Put on His truth found in His word and follow His commands to love one another and live in harmony. Make no room for anger, malice, or vengeance, but let the *Lord* avenge for you. He is the one who will judge as He wishes. There will be a day when we all will give account for our actions. Are you putting on His Spirit of love and grace?

He knows your heart and your intentions. He sees all and knows all. Put on the love of *Christ* by seeking to do good to all. Let others see the joy flowing out from you as you love *Jesus*. He is waiting for you to step away from the desires of the flesh, to step into a spirit-filled life. Love, peace, joy, patience, goodness, kindness, gentleness, faithfulness, and self-control will be the fruits of the Spirit that you will grow for *Jesus* as you draw closer to the Spirit. Step away from the flesh and step into the Spirit! *Jesus* is waiting for you to come to Him with a renewed desire to repent and give your heart to Him. Return to the *Lord* with your whole heart and let go of the flesh. Come back to the peace that flows from the power of *Holy Spirit*. Put on *Jesus Christ* and let His Spirit come alive in you!

AUGUST 20

Fear the Lord to Find the Way
Proverbs 9:10

The fear of the Lord is the beginning of wisdom, and the knowledge of the Holy One is insight. The *Lord* wants you to fear Him by loving and honoring Him. He has much to show you when you stay connected to Him. He will give you knowledge and insight as you draw deeper to Him. His will for you will become clear as you fear Him and not your circumstances. Keep looking for your wisdom from the *Lord*!

His Spirit will come alive in you as you continue drawing closer to Him and activate the *Holy Spirit* in you. He has given you this most special gift! Use this gift as He wills for you. Seek counsel from the *Most High* and you will know what to do. Quit turning to the world for answers but turn to the *Lord* who knows all and promises good to you.

Are you seeking the *Lord* and His counsel and comfort? Are you praying for healing? Are you drawing wisdom and insight from the one who has anointed you with power from on high? Seek His power and wisdom and you will be able to do what He has called you to do. There is no stopping a move of the *Holy Spirit* of the living *God*! He needs you to believe and faithfully follow His promptings. Listen and choose His way as the way!

AUGUST 21

Let Your Heart Rejoice
Proverbs 15:30

The light of the eyes rejoices the heart, and good news refreshes the bones. Let your eyes see His glory through His marvelous light. You will find Him when you seek Him with all your heart. Are you seeking Him with your whole heart or only following your ways? Do you want to live in the light? Have you rejoiced at the faithfulness of the Lord as you count His many blessings and answered prayers? Let your heart rejoice and seek the light that comes from the *Lord Jesus.*

Listen to the truth of the gospel and find hope in its message. His ways are higher and His plans for you are better. Your heart will rejoice, and your bones will be refreshed when you strive to make *Jesus* the *Lord* of your life. The good news of salvation to all who believe is worth telling and believing. All who believe in *Jesus* and want to make Him *Lord* of their life will be saved by His grace!

Are you looking for refreshment and rejuvenation for your soul? Have you tried finding all in *Jesus*? He is the living hope you have been searching for! He is the one who will make your heart and soul come alive with a new joy that you cannot find anywhere else. Find *Jesus* and watch Him change your life forever!

AUGUST 22

Fly Above it All
Isaiah 40:31

They who wait for the Lord shall renew their strength; they shall mount up with wings like eagles; they shall run and not be weary; they shall walk and not faint. Yes, we must wait on the *Lord*. He will give us renewed strength and restored hope when we look to Him and believe. We will fly like eagles, soaring high above it all. Even our painful circumstances and our struggles will be below us. Only the *Lord* can give us the wings we need to soar above it all. Wait upon Him, and you will fly freely.

When you are weary, run to the *Father's* arms and let Him carry you. He knows your desires and your needs before you ask Him. He is ready to catch you before you fall. All you need is a trusting and faithful heart turned towards the *Lord*.

Your joy will be revived. Your soul will be full of new life centered on *Christ*. You will be whole and satisfied in a new way. Your new self will come alive with more joy than you ever thought possible. Believe and find your way to the keeper of your soul. He is ready to bless you and show you the way. Be still, wait for the *Lord,* and know that He is *God*. He can do anything He desires for you in His will and His timing. Just ask and believe that He will surely do it!

AUGUST 23

Walk with Confidence
2 Corinthians 5:17

Therefore, if anyone is in Christ, he is a new creation; the old has passed away; behold the new has come! Yes, *Jesus Christ* lives in you when you let Him in your heart. You will be transformed and made new in His image. Your old self will disappear, and your new self will be made complete and whole again in *Christ*. Keep trusting and believing your *Lord* and *Savior*. He loves you and wants you to find joy in Him. His Spirit of life will set you free. Walk in His life-giving Spirit and not in the flesh that leads to death.

Hope in the things that are yours when you trust completely in the one who gave you life. You are conformed in the image of *Jesus* and called to your purpose in His kingdom. Be patient for the timing of the *Lord* in all things. You may not understand, but He is all knowing and is doing what is best for you. Let His peace guard your heart and your mind and let His hope flood your soul. You must keep persevering and trusting *God* in everything. He is with you in the valleys and on the mountaintops. He is always right by your side holding your hand. Lean on Him completely and He will strengthen you. Trust Him with all your heart and He will show you the way that leads to life!

AUGUST 24

Two are Better than One
Ecclesiastes 4:9-10

Two are better than one, because they have a good reward for their toil. For if they fall, one will lift up his fellow. This person will lift him up and encourage him to press on to accomplish the task that *God* has given them. When *Christ* is in the center, there is no stopping the work that can be done together. The completion of the task at hand is possible, so keep working together as the *Lord* has called you. You are trying to do it all by yourself and that is not how *God* intended. He wants you to partner with Him so that He can show you what He needs you to do. Then, He will show you who He desires for you to work with to fulfill the ministry that He purposes for you. Keep faithfully serving and the *Lord* will honor your obedience and hard work with many blessings and eternal rewards.

Are you struggling to find your *God*-given purpose? Do you need someone to help you with the great task you have been given? Call upon the *Lord* for counsel and help. He will show you who He needs you to work with and what He needs you to do. He will faithfully provide all the answers and open doors for you. He wants you to succeed and be secure in Him. Walk faithfully in His will and work for His glory and you will rise!

AUGUST 25

We are being Renewed Day by Day
2 Corinthians 4:16

So we do not lose heart. Though our outer self is wasting away, our inner self is being renewed day by day. Only *Jesus* can renew us and restore us with His abundant life. Believe Him and cling to His promises. Our bodies are a temple to the living *God*. We are made by the *Father* in His image so that we can serve and love Him. Our outer bodies will age, and our youth will fade away, but our inner souls will continue to be restored and renewed day by day if we cling to *Jesus*. Our inner nature will continue to thrive with life from the one who is life.

We were made to love Him and lean on Him. When we surrender all to Him, He will revive us and make us new. Day by day we will see the life-giving power of *Jesus Christ*. We will not lose heart because our hearts will be renewed, and our souls will be invigorated with His life! Only *Jesus Christ* can give us this power. Only His power can set us free. He has suffered much for our gain. His grace continues to save and restore us. Come to the place of revival with *Jesus*. He will fix our broken hearts and He will guard our hearts. Do not lose heart, faithful servants of the living *God*. Let us come and find our restoration and renewal in *Christ* alone, our hope, our joy, and our peace!

AUGUST 26

Boldly Proclaim the
Greatness of the Lord
2 Corinthians 3:12

Since we have such a hope, we are very bold.
We are ready to bring your word to those who do not
know you. We are eager to share your hope as we
spread your love far and wide. We are called
according to your purpose and we will faithfully serve
you. Thank you for making a way in the darkness for
us. We are drawn to your glorious light as we work
for you and your glory *Lord*. We hear you calling us
out and we will lean on you and stand on your
promises.

Thank you, *Lord,* for making us stronger.
When we are weak, you are strong for us. When we
feel pain, you comfort us. We will comfort others as
you call us to be your hands and feet. We will boldly
proclaim your greatness so that others may know this
hope we have in you. You are all powerful, all
knowing, and all loving! We will open our hearts to
hear you and open eyes to see you. We are stronger
and bolder each day because you have lifted us up to
that higher place with you. We know your joy and we
will not stop praising you, *Lord*. Even if things do not
go our way, we will continue walking and working in
faith and put our hope in you, *Lord*. Your will is best,
and we will surrender and trust you completely!

AUGUST 27

It is Possible with God
Luke 18:27

What is impossible with man is possible with God. Believe that this is true. The *Lord* can do more than you can ever dream or imagine. *God* is greater than your problem or circumstance. He will show you a better way if you choose to trust Him. You will see Him when you choose to obey Him and walk in His light. His power will lift you higher. His Spirit will come alive in you. Activate the *Holy Spirit* and feel His Spirit directing your steps. Each Spirit-led step you take with *Christ* will give you more joy! Choose joy, resist evil, and turn towards the light of *Christ*.

The path is clearer with *Christ*. When you think there is no way, *God* will show you that there is a way! Just believe and have faith. With *God*, all things are possible! Yes, all things are possible if you believe. Will you believe and walk in the way that leads to life? Will you stop doubting and start acting in faith? You are free to choose and free to believe.

Forget your past and come anew to *Christ*. You are one step away from a life of abundant joy here on earth. With *Jesus*, you have inherited all that is yours through Him. The promise of eternal life in heaven is your reward for your faithfulness. Seek all that *Christ* wants to give you in heaven and on earth by seeking Him first. His amazing grace is enough!

AUGUST 28

Run to Jesus
Mark 4:40

Why are you so afraid? Have you still no faith? Keep believing and trusting the *Lord*. He will guide you into truth if you let Him. He wants to be your friend and companion. He wants a deeper relationship with you. Are you going to let Him in your life? Will you trust Him completely?

Walk with Him in faith giving Him your whole heart and see what a difference He makes in your life! Your fears will disappear, and your faith will increase when you cling to *Christ*. You will see your chains of despair disappear and your hope increase.

Stay the course and be stronger and more confident. Let your love be grounded and rooted in your *Savior*. He wants to bless you if you will let Him.

All good and perfect gifts come from above. The *Lord* works out everything in His timing and in His will. He will show you the way. Run to Him and find your freedom! Let your chains of sin fall away forever. He has already forgiven you and healed you. Only *Christ* gives you the perfect healing you are searching for. You are made in His perfect image to be His friend. He desires more of you. Seek more of His presence in your life and watch your joy increase!

AUGUST 29

Make the Lord Your Dwelling Place
Psalm 91:9-10

Because you have made the Lord your dwelling place, the Most High who is my refuge, no evil shall be allowed to befall you, no plague come near your tent. Yes, the *Lord* is your refuge and strength. He covers you with protection and keeps you from harm. Believe that He is watching over you and will help you. Only the *Lord* can save you. Nothing can separate you from His abundant and eternal love! No evil can take over you as you are His child. You have been covered by the blood of *Jesus Christ*! As you have believed, your heart has been healed, your mind has been transformed, and your soul has been renewed. You are different than you have ever been before because you are His. You belong to the living *God* because you have chosen to surrender to Him. You have chosen life because *Jesus* lives inside of you.

Keep Him close to you and you will feel His strong arms of protection. You will not give in to temptations or evil when you are serving your mighty *God* with your whole armor of God. Keep your sword of the Spirit close to you so you will know how to face the enemy. *God* will be there for you always. Trust Him completely and confidently! Make the *Lord* your dwelling place!

AUGUST 30

His Throne is Established in the Heavens
Psalm 103:19

The Lord has established His throne in the heavens, and His kingdom rules over all. The *Lord* watches over you and from His mighty throne. His outstretched arms reach for you so that He can carry you. He lifts you up to a higher place with Him. Look up and see Him in the heavens. His glory shines in you when you come to Him.

The *Lord* will stand by you and strengthen you. He will be your refuge and strength and a very present help in trouble. Turn to Him and trust that He will bring good to you! His glory is constantly displayed all around you. He manifests Himself to those who love Him and walk in obedience. You will see Him if you are looking for Him and walking by faith. See the *Lord* in the beauty of all His creations. He wants you to enjoy life and live it to the fullest.

Life is found in the living spirit of *Jesus* given to you by the grace of the *Father*. Keep walking with *Jesus* by faith and see your life change instantly. You were once lost but will be found as you give your heart completely to *Jesus Christ*, your *Savior*.

In Him is the promise of abundant life on earth and eternal life in heaven so take up your cross and follow *Jesus*. His glory awaits you!

AUGUST 31

The Only Way to Peace
John 14:6

Jesus said to him, "I am the way, and the truth, and the life. No one comes to the Father except through me." Jesus is the only way to peace. Take it and let it cover your entire body, heart, and soul. Soak up His love and feel His presence comforting you like nothing or no one else can. Your fears will vanish when you cling to *Jesus*.

With *Jesus*, you will be released from your pain and your struggle. He loves you so much that He gives you complete peace if you choose to take it. Let His arms hold you up right now, weary one. Take hope in Him and find your rest with your *Savior*.

The peace that the world tries to give you will not last, but the peace from *Jesus* is eternal. Cling to His peace.

Come to His light and be filled with joy once again. Come out of the darkness and see His hope calling you to a brighter future. Delight in the *Lord* and He will give you the desires of your heart. Only *Jesus* can give you everything you really need. Believe that He will bless you with life and come to His fountain of living water set aside for you. Take a drink and let it nourish you from the inside out. Come to His peace and come to life with *Jesus*!

PRAYER TO JESUS

Dear *Lord,*

Thank you for carrying my burdens and filling my life with joy as I cast all my burdens upon you. You will sustain me as you have promised. My righteousness comes from making you the *Lord* of my life and obeying your commands. You will not permit me to be moved away from your love because I am securely anchored in you. You sacrificed all for me on the cross and have given me grace so that I can experience salvation. My inheritance is secure in you and I will not be shaken! Thank you for saving me by grace! You have bestowed many blessings on my life and I am thankful for each one of them. My trials have made me grow closer to you and have increased my faith. You meant it all for good and I can see it now. I praise your mighty name that is above all names!

I will keep you close to my heart forever as it burns with a fire for more of you. I will run with endurance as I know you will be with me every step of the way. Thank you, *Lord,* for showing me the victory that is mine in *Jesus Christ.* I am yours forever!

In *Jesus* name,

Amen.

Have I not
commanded you?
Be strong
AND COURAGEOUS.
Do not be frightened,
and do not be dismayed,
FOR THE LORD
YOUR GOD
is with you
WHEREVER YOU
GO.
JOSHUA 1:9

SEPTEMBER 1

Make a Difference
1 Corinthians 15:58

Therefore, beloved brothers, be steadfast, immovable, always abounding in the work of the Lord, knowing that in the Lord your labor is not in vain. The *Lord* knows how you are working and He sees you serving Him faithfully. Stand firm and do not be moved from the position where He has placed you. He needs you and will reward your efforts. Your work is never in vain when you are working for *Christ*. You are securing eternal treasures in heaven.

Have you given up because you do not see the results of the seeds you are planting? Have you stopped making a difference in the Kingdom and moved on to just pursuing worldly desires? Have you grown weak, disillusioned, and frustrated? This world cannot provide what you need. Only *Jesus* can give you the life you are seeking.

Come back to *Jesus*. Make a difference for Him by serving Him diligently even when you do not always see the results of what you have planted in faith. In due time, the harvest will grow if you do not give up and grow weary in doing good. The seeds you have planted in faith will grow if they are rooted in the love of *Jesus Christ!* Keep sowing and reaping for the fields are ripe today and *God* needs you!

SEPTEMBER 2

All Things Made New in Jesus
Isaiah 42:9

Behold the former things have come to pass; and the new things I now declare; before they spring forth, I tell you of them. Yes, the old things and ways will come to pass as the *Lord* makes all things new. He is ready to bring forth justice and reveal truth in His time. Never fear for your righteousness and good works will shine forth as you keep drawing to the Spirit. Your life will be full of joy and you will experience personal revival in your heart and soul when you keep faithfully aiming to please the audience of one, the *Lord Jesus Christ*. He is the way to a new covenant relationship with the *Father*.

The world and its ways will not prevail over the *Lord* and His ways! His ways are higher and always better. Are you struggling to find a way out of the mess you find yourself in? Do you want to find joy but seem to be living only in your current circumstances? These are real issues commonly dealt with by God's people today.

Look to *Jesus Christ* who gives you steadfast love and abundant grace no matter what you have done. He is the only way to the *Father*. Accept His gift of the *Holy Spirit* that is yours when you believe, so that your life will be made new in Him. All things are made new in *Jesus Christ* and that includes you!

SEPTEMBER 3

Walk By the Spirit
Galatians 5:16

But I say, walk by the Spirit, and you will not gratify the desires of the flesh. Your new life will be infused with a fresh wind and a fresh fire of the Spirit that will change your desires. Your old desires will fade away as new desires will be embedded in you. Walk in the power of the Spirit that leads to a super abundant life. Your new life in the Spirit will produce good fruit as you start seeking the will of your *Father* in everything you do.

You will wake up with a new desire to serve and work in your purpose. You will see your world differently through the eyes of *Jesus*. His compassion will grow deeper in you as you see ways you can make a difference for the glory of *God*! As you serve faithfully where you are led, your faith will grow deep roots. As you sow seeds of love and hope in others, you shall reap a harvest of joy! Do not grow weary of doing good, for at the proper time you will reap a bountiful harvest. Do not give up, for there is a new life ahead of you. Keep seeking the *Lord* and praise the *Lord* for His grace, mercy, and blessings that He pours over you. Your joy will be renewed every morning when you wake up each day with the joy of the *Lord* in your heart and your soul! Walk by the Spirit and you will have new life!

SEPTEMBER 4

Seek the Approval of God
Galatians 1:10

For am I now seeking the approval of man or of God? Or am I trying to please man? If I were still trying to please man, I would not be a servant of Christ. Serving *Christ* means letting go of your need to please man, but instead asking the *Lord* how you can please Him. What is His will for you and are you following it?

A follower of *Christ* means you might need to make sacrifices and decisions that are not popular. You will be called to stand up in ways that might not always please man. But *God* will not have you do anything that quenches the Spirit. The fruit of the Spirit will be in you as you serve Him. Good things will come to those who wait on Him. Your eternal reward awaits you, faithful servant. Ask for His power to come alive inside you so you can work faithfully for Him.

Your faith will be alive and grow in you the more you aim to please your *Lord*. He will show you the way to go so you don't have to go alone. You will not need to worry with *Christ* on your side. The world may tell you no, but *Christ* will always be your encourager. Don't lose heart, you have the light of the world with you. The *Lord* will stand by you and strengthen you!

SEPTEMBER 5

Put on the Joy of Jesus
James 5:9

Do not grumble against one another, brothers, so that you may not be judged; behold, the Judge is standing at the door. You will be judged as you judge and fight others. Your joy will be gone when you keep trying to control your life without God. You will be unhappy when you turn away from *God.*

Be still and let *God* fight for you. He will fight your battles and He always wins! Your bitterness and anger are quenching the power of the *Holy Spirit.* The more you argue and throw out insults, the farther away from the *Holy Spirit* you will be. The more you forgive and love, and act with gentleness and kindness, the closer you will be to His love. Try putting on the joy of *Jesus* by clinging to His word and His power. Seek revival of your spirit and seek the *Holy Spirit.* He will guide you into truth so that you can see the truth. There will be others who will be fooled by evil and untruths, but those who follow *Jesus* and activate the power of the *Holy Spirit* will see! Be patient for your blessing is just around the corner. Love, joy, and peace are waiting for you, faithful one. Your obedience to *God* will grant you blessings and favor in the eyes of the *Lord* and your faith will be your sight!

SEPTEMBER 6

Live with the Promise of Salvation in Your Soul
Colossians 1:17

And He is before all things, and in Him all things hold together. He is the one who goes before us. He is the one who puts all things together for our good. God's will and purpose will be lived through us as we listen and let His desires live in us. He will show us great miracles when we keep believing.

He will capture our heart and keep loving us through it all. Our prayers will bring us closer to Him. The truth we read in His word will become food for our soul. The light of *Christ* will shine in us through His unconditional and everlasting love. We are given that love so that we may live our lives to the fullest by giving more love away. Keep loving because *God* has loved you first. Love conquers all! The victory has already been won for us. We are conquerors for *Christ*!

Live with promise of salvation in your soul. Live with the hope that more will come to know this love if only they knew the truth. We can bring the light of *Christ* and the truth of the gospel by sharing it. This world is waiting to hear and see the good news that life on earth can be filled with joy when we have *Jesus* in our heart to stay. Nothing or no one can take that away!

SEPTEMBER 7

Sow to the Spirit
Galatians 6:8

For the one who sows to his own flesh will from the flesh reap corruption, but the one who sows to the Spirit will from the Spirit reap eternal life. Draw to the Spirit and find life that is everlasting. You are sowing seeds of eternal value when you live by the Spirit of the living *God*. All other ways of living that center only on the flesh and the ways of the world will lead to heartache and pain.

You are a child of light who the *Lord* created to live in the light with Him. Get out of the darkness and come back to the light of *Christ*. You have been struggling in the darkness of your sins too long and now you have become a prisoner to your own actions and addictions. The *Lord* sees you struggling and He is calling you to come back to Him. Remember He has never left you, but you are the one who has left Him! He loves you and has forgiven you for everything! Your sins have vanished in His eyes because of the grace that He has given you. You are made clean and whole through the blood of *Jesus*. Live by the Spirit and you will not be drawn to the desires of the world. These fleshly desires will disappear, as you choose to reap eternal treasures that bring life. Sow to the Spirit and you will reap the rewards of eternal life!

SEPTEMBER 8

Lose Your Life for the Sake of Jesus
Matthew 16:25

For whoever would save his life would lose it, but whoever loses his life for my sake and will find it. When you try to save your life by doing only your will and acting selfishly, you will lose your life. You will not know the pure joy that comes from letting the *Lord* guide you. You will be lost without your *Savior*. Let go of control and give your life to *Jesus*. You will be saved when you let go and let Him take over.

Now is the time to trust the *Lord* to bring you through that fire. He is ready to carry you to His place of refuge and hope. Do not be afraid to trust Him completely. There is joy in submission because you have a powerful and mighty *God* on your side. With *God* on your side, who can be against you? He will fight for you. He will conquer all your fears. He will bring you to the other side with Him. He will be your strength when you are weak. He will be your comforter when you are hurting. He will give you wisdom when you seek His counsel and live by His truth in the Gospel. Lose your life in *Jesus*. You will find life when you come to Him fully surrendered to live out the calling and purpose He has for you. Abide in *Jesus Christ* now and He will abide in you for eternity!

SEPTEMBER 9

Share in His Comfort
2 Corinthians 1:7

Our hope for you is unshaken, for we know that as you share in our sufferings, you will also share in our comfort. The *Lord* will comfort you and help you when you suffer. Rely on Him and stand firm knowing that He has you wrapped inside His arms. Whatever you are facing is not too hard for *Christ*. He has already suffered much for you and His grace has been poured over you. He has delivered you from sin and He will deliver you again. Keep praying and keep your focus on the *Lord*. The *Father* of all mercies will comfort you in your affliction. Wait patiently on Him and He will surely deliver you. You will experience total peace through your salvation.

Let Him be the one to strengthen your spiritual legs so that you can stand firmly on His promises. He has anointed you to go out and strive for success by trusting in Him alone. He is your best yes! The Spirit of the living *God* lives in you, faithful one. His Spirit will set you apart and guide you into truth. Be still and know that He is *God*. He loves you with an everlasting love. He will lift you higher than you have ever been before without Him. The veil has been removed and the light is shining through you. Your heart and your soul are glowing with His glorious light! You are beautiful!

SEPTEMBER 10

Speak Boldly with Confidence
Ephesians 6:19

Words may be given to me in opening my mouth boldly to proclaim the mystery of the gospel. When we seek Him, the *Holy Spirit* will give us words to speak as we proclaim the greatness of the *Lord*. May we speak boldly and with confidence to share the good news of salvation through *Jesus*. May we share the security that comes with *Jesus* as the foundation. The love of *Christ* needs to be shared far and wide. Let us open our mouth and speak of our hope that is found in *Jesus Christ* We can show our love as we share the hope that is found in following and serving *Jesus*. Our prayers and our words of encouragement will strengthen others. Our faith will give us boldness when we speak about *Jesus* and pray with others. As we draw nearer to *Jesus* and activate the *Holy Spirit* in our lives, He will intercede to give us the words to say as we speak and as we pray.

Do not be afraid to speak. Your words will plant seeds of faith that will eventually produce good fruit. Be patient and wait on the *Lord* to sow these seeds. They must be planted in love by us as we are the hands and feet of *Jesus*. Work for His glory and do not wait another day to tell your story of love for Jesus!

SEPTEMBER 11

Peace is Possible with Jesus
Hebrews 12:14

Strive for peace with everyone, and for the holiness without which no one will see the Lord. Yes, *Jesus* is the answer to the peace we have been looking for. Through His flesh, He has broken down the wall of separation and division. He is the Prince of Peace who has come to give us perfect peace. He wants us to come together and be united in our efforts. There is still hope when we include *Jesus* in our lives and let Him lead us instead of trying to control everything ourselves.

Are we laying aside our selfish ways to let *Jesus* lead us? Are we letting go of anger and bitterness in our hearts to find new life again? Are we striving for peace with others or are we living with an offended and unforgiving heart? Peace is only possible with *Jesus*, the author and perfecter of our faith.

He is the way, the truth, and the life. Come to Him and you will find all these things. All things are possible when you are living with *Jesus* in your heart and the power of the *Holy Spirit* guiding and directing you 24/7! Are you looking to recharge and revive your life? If so, come to *Jesus Christ* who will energize and awaken you to perfect peace, pure joy, and living hope!

SEPTEMBER 12

Sealed with the Holy Spirit
Ephesians 1:13

In Him you also, when you heard the word of truth, the gospel of your salvation, and believed in Him, were sealed with the promised Holy Spirit. You have the *Holy Spirit* living inside of you, so are you letting the *Holy Spirit* do His work in you? Are you living with His power that He has made available to you? Do you know that you have been given this gift to unwrap and enjoy to enrich and empower your life?

The *Holy Spirit* will change your life in such a way that you will feel many blessings of great joy. You have been sealed with the power of the *Holy Spirit* and He is waiting to bless your life as you let Him work in you. Activate His power and let Him fall fresh on you today. You are missing so much in your life when you do not surrender and let His Spirit work in you.

Unwrap His gift and soften your heart to *Jesus*. There is a life of hope, love, and joy waiting for you as you give your whole heart to *Jesus*! Make Him your first love and He will shower you with blessings of His love and grace. Allow the *Holy Spirit* to work in your life as you have believed and receive all that is yours in *Christ*!

SEPTEMBER 13

Feed Your Heart with Jesus
Ephesians 5:8

For at one time you were darkness, but now you are light in the Lord. Walk as children of light. Let the *Lord* show you the way. He has made a perfect way for you when you follow His light. Do not be afraid but keep following Him. When you make the *Lord* your deliverer in the storms, your disappointment will disappear, and a beacon of new hope will appear for you on the horizon.

Are you struggling today because the darkness of the world is strangling and surrounding you? Do you feel you are in deep waters being tossed about without direction or hope of rescue? Maybe you have come to the light before, but the fire that once burned brightly in your heart for *Jesus* needs igniting again. It only takes a single spark to relight that fire. That spark is *Jesus Christ*. He will ignite you!

Everybody has a hungry heart. What are you feeding yours with? If you had a heart to heart talk with *Jesus*, could you tell Him that you are hungry for Him? Is His daily bread and living water sustaining you? Maybe you have not really talked to *Jesus* lately. He has so much to tell you as you are His child of light. Listen and lean in closely so you do not miss a single blessing. He wants to light up your life!

SEPTEMBER 14

Jesus Brings Us Higher
Psalm 71:20

You who have made me see many troubles and calamities will revive me again; from the depths of the earth you will bring me up again. We are made new with you, *Lord.* You are the one who carries us over to the other side of joy. Your love lifts us higher, your hope strengthens us, and your peace comforts us. We need you to rebuild us into the person you need us to be to minister to the flock you have given us. We are ready to serve and be your hands and feet.

We have seen things that tear us apart. Our hearts have been broken and our souls have been hurting. But you *Lord* can bring us up higher with you. We see the good through all the bad and we have found the joy you have promised us! Your light shines through the dark skies reminding us that with you everything will be good again. We are revived and made new through you!

We need not worry or fear with you here. All the pieces of our heart have been put together even stronger than before the trial. We are made whole again only through you. Nothing will be able to separate us from your love! Yes, nothing can come between us as we rest in your presence now and forevermore!

SEPTEMBER 15

Be Strong in the Lord
Ephesians 6:10

Finally, be strong in the Lord and in the strength of His might. Put your full faith in His powerful presence. He gives you the energy you need each day when you seek His help. Find your refuge in the *Lord* and let Him rescue and redeem you. His power will help you overcome your weakness, so trust Him to be your strong tower and surrender all to *Jesus*.

As you let *Jesus* in your life, your life will shine and sparkle with a joy that will revive your heart and awaken your soul. He will open your eyes to His beauty and grace. Tears of joy will flow as you feel His Spirit coming alive in you. Hope will enter your heart once again. Peace will settle in the depths of your soul and you will be free.

Jesus Christ is the one who will set you free! Discover the real freedom in the saving grace of *Jesus* and come closer to His love. Only His love can set your heart on fire and only His grace can break the chains of sin. Come alive with *Jesus* by saying yes to Him and experience true freedom in the power of His love and grace!

SEPTEMBER 16

Seek the Lord with Your Whole Heart
Psalm 119:10

With my whole heart I seek you; let me not wander from your commandments! We need you, *Lord,* and we will give our whole hearts to you. We want to obey your commandments and be guided by the truth in your word. There is hope in you, *Lord.* You have given us the gift of hope that comes only from you. We want this hope in the depth of our souls, so we will seek you with everything that is in us.

You are the one who loves us unconditionally. You have forgiven us and given us life everlasting. You have put your *Spirit* inside us so that we may know joy here on earth. We seek to know you better and we will start by reading your gospel and praying with you. We need a stronger and deeper relationship with you. All you want from us is our heart. Your love flows in us and through us to encourage and build us up. We want you to mold us and make us better servants so that we can spread your love to build others up and encourage them. Your love has lifted us higher and we are soaring with new life and spirit. We praise you, *Lord,* for giving us the freedom that we so desire. It is the desire of our hearts to please you. Let us keep your word inside of us. We see the light as we draw closer to you.

SEPTEMBER 17

Perfect Submission
Luke 6:21

Blessed are you who are hungry now, for you shall be satisfied. Blessed are you who weep now, for you shall laugh. Your hunger will be satisfied by *Jesus*. Let His word feed you and His Spirit fill you. You will not be hungry when you cling to *Jesus* to nourish you and sustain you.

When you weep, He will weep with you. With *Jesus*, your weeping will turn into shouts of joy! You do not need to be sad anymore because your *Lord Jesus* will give you a new song of victory. His love will be enough. His joy will be your strength and your sorrow will disappear. You are complete in *Jesus Christ*!

Have faith in the one who remains faithful. Delight in the *Lord* and He will give you the desires of your heart. You will sing a new song of hope when you come to *Jesus*. His grace is enough to sustain you. His love will conquer all your fears. He promises good to all those who trust in Him. Give Him your whole heart and feel alive in a new way. Abandon your old ways and be made new in *Jesus*. Perfect submission will be yours when you give it all to *Jesus Christ*. Praise your *Savior* and sing a new song of joy with Him!

SEPTEMBER 18

Sweet Freedom in Jesus
Psalm 62:2

He only is my rock and my salvation, my fortress; I shall not be greatly shaken. We are stronger because of our trials and hardships. Our faith grows deeper each day when our hearts are connected to *Christ*. When we are weak, He is strong for us. Our soul waits patiently for the *Lord* because we know that He will come through for us. We stand on our rock, our *Lord Jesus Christ*. We put our faith in the only one who will save us. Our soul clings to the cross of our salvation. We look upon our *Lord* in His sanctuary and behold His power and glory. We sing praises to His holy name and give thanks for His great power and love.

Let us magnify the *Lord* and constantly exalt His name together. His steadfast love extends to the heavens and His faithfulness to the clouds. We will take refuge in the *Lord* who is our firm foundation. All other ground is unstable and changing. Our *Lord* and *Savior* never changes. Let us commit our way to the *Lord* and trust in Him and He will act. Our steps are established by Him when we delight in Him and seek Him first in all our ways. Hope in the *Lord* and cast all your anxieties on Him because He cares for you deeply! Praise Him in the heavy storms and in the sprinkling light rain and let Him reign in You!

SEPTEMBER 19

Your Destiny is in Jesus
Philippians 1:6

And I am sure of this, He who began a good work in you will bring it to completion at the day of Jesus Christ. You have been destined for work for His kingdom purposes. The *Lord* has called you to a purpose so that His glory can shine in you. Keep believing in the power of the *Holy Spirit* to guide you as you continue trusting Him and leaning on *Jesus.* He will be by your side as you continue working. He knows what you need to complete each task and will provide everything you need. Depend on the *Lord* in all you do as you make the most of your time each day. Give Him your whole heart so that He can use you to make a difference in the lives of others. Wake up every morning asking the *Lord* how you can serve Him today. Your joy will be full, and your hope will be real as you use your gifts and talents for *God's* greater glory!

Do you believe that there is good work for you to do for the *Lord*? Have you found your *God-*given purpose and trusted Him to help you fulfill this calling? We all have good work to do, but not all have looked to *God* to find it. Lean on the *Lord* and call upon Him and He will surely show you the way to your destiny.

SEPTEMBER 20

His Covenant Promises are for You
2 Chronicles 6:14

O Lord, God of Israel, there is no God like you, in heaven or on earth, keeping covenant and showing steadfast love to your servants who walk before you with all their heart. You are so faithful to us and we strive to be faithful to you. We thank you for watching over us like you do. Your hand is upon us as we work and serve you diligently and passionately. Your covenant with us is real and your love for us is everlasting.

Only you can show us the way to freedom through your amazing grace and sacrifice. You are our living hope and we stand firm on your promises. Thank you for delivering us from the storms and making a way for us when there seems to be no way. We love you with all our heart and soul. We come to you in our brokenness and heartache ready to be healed! Only your love can save and restore us as you lift us up out of the pit of despair and disappointment. We are made new and whole in your presence. We have come alive with your mighty presence and power. In our weakness, you are our strength and our stability. Your saving grace is enough! We are forever changed and made whole in you and we pray that we will step out of the way and let the *Holy Spirit* guide our way every day!

SEPTEMBER 21

Come Alive with a New Passion
Psalm 145:3

Great is the Lord, and greatly to be praised, and His greatness is unsearchable. Always praise the *Lord* and give thanks for His mighty power in your life. His love for you is unfathomable. His awesome deeds are indescribable. His faith is undeniable.

Know His voice by spending time with Him. Make the *Lord* your highest priority, pursuit, and passion. Put Him first by making time for Him with a deep yearning in your soul to know Him better. Run to the *Lord* and make Him the love of your life. You are the love of His life. Abide in His love and He will abide in you. The *Lord* is near to all who call on Him in truth. Call on the *Lord* and bless His name forever and ever. Open your heart and come alive with a new passion deep inside of you. The *Lord* is abundantly good and righteous in all His ways.

Cling to his promise to never leave or forsake you. He loves you with an everlasting love that remains strong no matter what. Even if you do not understand, keep believing and walking by faith. Faith without works is dead. Trust and obey and find peace. This peace that only the *Lord* can bring will guard your heart and your mind and keep you stronger and wiser. Bless the *Lord* every day and praise His greatness in your life forever and ever!

SEPTEMBER 22

We Can Dwell Forever in His Tent
Psalm 61:4

Let me dwell in your tent forever! Let me take refuge under the shelter of your wings! Lord, we need you to comfort us like only you can do. Your shelter is a sanctuary for us. Your wings cover us and protect us like a mother who protects her children. You wrap us in your loving arms and hold us tightly. We are safe and happy when we are in your tent. You welcome us in your loving arms to stay. *Lord*, you never leave us, but you give us continual grace and mercy.

We praise you for being present with us. We need you in every part of our life. When we struggle, you lift us up! When we doubt, you give us hope again! When we cry, you wipe away our tears. We are never alone because you are never far away from us. You hold us tightly and won't let go and we feel your presence inside of us. Your spirit is strong and real. We feel you and see you everywhere we look for you. The same spirit lives in all who believe.

Surrender your heart and activate the *Holy Spirit* inside of you. Turn to the *Lord* and the peace of *Christ* will rule your heart once again. He wants to help you and be your refuge and strength so let His love cover you completely!

SEPTEMBER 23

Cast Your Fears into His Arms
1 Peter 5:6-7

Humble yourselves, therefore; under the mighty hand of God, so that at the proper time He may exalt you, casting all your anxieties on Him because He cares for you. Let *Jesus* take all your burdens and your worries. Give Him your anxieties and your fears. He will take them all away.

Be still and know that He is waiting to release you. He is wanting to save you from that struggle. *Jesus* is ready to bless your life with joy through His love. The joy He gives is everlasting and real. Give up the struggle and surrender all to *Jesus*. Let go of all control and hold on to Him. He promises good to those who love the *Lord* and walk in righteousness with Him. Follow Him to a place of peace. Cast your fears into His arms so that He can take them from you. Don't be afraid but trust the *Lord* to carry you. He will bring you through the flood or the fire.

Jesus Christ has forgiven you and His blood has cleansed you. All you must do is believe! Say yes to *Jesus* and release everything to Him. All your worries will disappear as His peace covers all of you. Let *Jesus* wrap you up. Let His love overwhelm you. Your home is in His arms right where you belong!

SEPTEMBER 24

The Lord is Patient with You
Matthew 6:10

Your kingdom come, your will be done, on earth as it is in heaven. The *Lord* will act in His will and His timing. Keep trusting that He is doing everything for His glory and purpose. You may not understand why things are happening to you, but you will see the joy in it all if you just let go and let *God* work all things out. Keep believing and asking for more of His love and you will receive. Keep honoring Him by putting Him first in your life. He will bless your life with countless blessings if you wait upon Him. Be patient and let go of your worries and your fears. Take His hand and walk into the light where there is no more pain or suffering. Do not be afraid. Keep trusting and just let go and let Him fill you. Open the eyes of your heart. Fill it with hope once again.

The *Lord* is ready and able to give you more than you could ever ask or imagine. A life filled with abundant blessings of great joy is waiting for the one who endures to the end. Keep fighting the good fight of faith and finish the race He has given you. He will bless you along the journey to the victory that He has already won for you. You are saved by His grace, so walk confidently and bravely with your *Lord Jesus Christ.*

SEPTEMBER 25

His Light Shines Brighter
in the Darkness
1 John 1:5

God is light and in Him is no darkness at all. Come to the light and see *Jesus*. He is ready to bless you with His overwhelming love. Turn to the light and surrender all control. He is ready to hold you in His arms. He can give you all that you need. Your every need is fulfilled in *Jesus*. Your eternal hope can be found in *Jesus Christ*!

Praise *God* for giving you the light and praise Him for the glory He shows you every day. His light shines through the dark skies and showers you with joy. Look around and see Him working out all things for you. You are complete in Him when you choose Him and walk the path that leads to life. Your faith will continue to hold you up.

Your joy will be found in the *Lord*. You will lack nothing but will gain everything when you choose the light. He lights up the sky for you to show you His glory. He showers you with joy when you believe.

Look up and see His face of grace and mercy. He covers you completely and forgives you repeatedly so find your victory in *Jesus*. Run to Him and be forgiven and free!

SEPTEMBER 26

Jesus Christ is All You Need
1 Peter 1:8

Though you have not seen Him, you love Him. Though you do not see Him now, you believe in Him and rejoice with joy that is inexpressible and filled with glory! Your love for *Jesus* is real and your faith has lifted you up higher to His light. You are not going to be down because you have *Jesus* inside of you. You are stronger than you have ever been before. When life seems to be pulling you down, you will be lifted higher with *Jesus Christ,* your redeemer.

He has forgiven you for everything and He has washed away your every sin. He has saved you, so draw deeper into Him. He will wrap you up in His arms of comfort and protection. Never again will you be alone or afraid when you have *Jesus Christ.* He is the one who will be with you always through it all.

Trust Him and look to Him for hope. Let Him rescue you. Let Him love you. Let Him hold you. Let Him fill you with His joy. Let Him save you once and for all! Look through the clouds and see His light shining brightly. He is there in the light even though you cannot see Him. Love Him and open your heart to the overflowing and abundant joy that comes from trusting Him completely. Your faith will make you stronger even in the toughest times. *Jesus* is all you need. Believe in Him and His promises!

SEPTEMBER 27

Sing a New Song of Praise Every Day
Psalm 40:3

He put a new song in my mouth, a song of praise to our God. Many will see and fear and put their trust in the Lord. Yes, a new song of hope and praise has been given to you for our *God* is a good, good *Father*. He will answer you and give you the hope you have been searching for. He is your hope all the time. Sing praises for what you believe you will see and what you know *God* can do!

Keep seeking Him in all that you do. Get your boldness and your strength from *God*. Open your heart to His mercies and grace that He will give to you. Never fear with the *Lord* by your side, faithful one. The light has come to show you the way. Keep believing and hold fast to what is true. Many are watching you to see what you will do in your storm. Will you remain faithful no matter what? Will you be able to stand firm and proclaim His greatness? Will you sing a new song for the world to see? Yes, you will because you are a living example of the power of the living *God* inside of you. You will sing praises through your circumstances because you are looking up to *God* for everything! He is everything that you live for and He is your breath of joy in a world of heartache. Breathe Him in and be filled with new life to breathe out on those around you who need *Jesus*!

SEPTEMBER 28

Find Your Refuge in God
Psalm 46:10

Be still and know that I am God. He is the one who will never leave you. He is your refuge when things seem impossible and you are struggling. He is your strength when you are weak. He brings you joy through the pain.

Turn to *Jesus* and feel His love covering you. Open your heart to His love. Come fall in His arms and find rest. Draw to the *Lord* and you will find peace again even through your pain. He takes away every tear and every ounce of pain and heartache.

His arms are wide open for you. Come fall in His loving arms and find your rest weary one. He wants to help you through it all. He is the way, the truth, and the life. Only *Jesus* can give you the life you long to find. Turn towards *Jesus* and you will see the way to His light. His light shines brightly, so follow it out of the darkness. He is the only truth that will set you free.

Good things are waiting for you as you trust your *Lord* and *Savior*. Come now and receive life abundantly! The crown of life is waiting for you, faithful one. You have fought the good fight and you have finished the race! Oh, what joy to see *Jesus* face to face! You are home with Him!

SEPTEMBER 29

Your Healing is in the Hands of the Lord
Psalm 54:4

Behold God is my helper; the Lord is the upholder of my life. God will defend you and help you, so will you let Him? Look to Him and not your circumstances. Reach out and touch Him and you will be healed. He has a physical and spiritual healing waiting for you to receive. Ask and you shall receive. Through *Jesus* you will be revived and made new. You who are weary will find your rest and your strength in Him. Believe He has a life of joy waiting for you around the corner from your pain and heartache. He promises good to all those who put their faith and trust in Him alone.

Seek first the kingdom of *God* and all good things will come to you. Do not let your fears take over but remain in His love. His amazing grace is running through your veins. In Him, your soul is saved.

Be strong and let *God* work all these things out in His will and His way. His timing is perfect. Just keep trusting and keep believing and you will see His perfect plan made just for you. He is the way, the truth, and the life!

SEPTEMBER 30

Remain Steadfast in the Lord
James 1:12

Blessed is the man who remains steadfast under trial, for when he has stood the test, he will receive the crown of life, which God has promised to those who love Him. Remain steadfast and unmovable with the *Lord* by your side. All your hope comes from *Jesus*. He has already given you victory through the cross. His blood was shed for you so that you can walk in freedom. The crown of life is waiting for you! All authority comes from the *Lord* who loves you with an everlasting love. He gives you authority when you give Him your heart. He will not leave or abandon you. He promises good to all those who trust Him.

Keep walking by faith and trusting the *Lord*. Draw to Him for your strength and courage. He will fill you with so much joy and peace that you will be able to overcome any trial you face on this earth. Walk hand in hand with *Jesus*. He is ready to fill you with hope and bless your life to the fullest. Trust in the *Lord* with all our heart and lean not on your own understanding. Even when things are not clear, *Jesus* is there. Acknowledge *Jesus* in all your ways and He will direct your path. Walk with Him and He will show you the way. Never fear, your *Savior* is here for you!

PRAYER TO JESUS

Dear *Lord*,

Today I am praising you for your glory and grace in my life. I have seen your miracles. I know that you answer prayers. I have seen reminders of your great love for me as you show your glory in the heavens. For your steadfast love is great to the heavens, your faithfulness to the clouds!

I feel your saving grace covering me all over even when I make mistakes. You have fully forgiven me as you laid my sins out on your cross and took them from me. My salvation is secure in you forever and I am eternally grateful and filled with praise and thanksgiving!

I will worship you in Spirit and truth and give you honor and praise as I rejoice for your many blessings in my life! My heart is overflowing with joy and my soul is at peace today. I know that you love me abundantly and unconditionally and all is well with my soul!

In *Jesus* name,

Amen.

THEREFORE,
IF ANYONE IS
in Christ,
HE IS
a new creation.
The old has
passed away;
Behold,
THE NEW HAS
COME.
2 CORINTHIANS 5:17

OCTOBER 1

Press on Towards the Prize
Philippians 3:14

I press on toward the goal for the prize of the upward call of God in Christ Jesus. Together we press on closer to *Jesus*. He is the one who gives us strength as we keep on the path of righteousness with Him. He cheers us on as we see manifestations of His glory all around us!

Our *Lord* is with us each step of our race when we include Him in our journey of life. He gives us His *Holy Spirit,* so we can have His power working inside us every moment. He gives us divine appointments so that we see Him working all around us. He renews us spiritually day by day. Are we including our *Lord* in our daily thoughts and actions so that He can strengthen us, or are we pushing Him out of our lives so we can run our race alone?

When our goal is the prize of the upward call of *God* in *Christ Jesus*, we will find that unexplainable joy and satisfaction that only comes from spiritual blessings. Our life on earth will have a new infusion of hope and joy through the mighty power of *God* through *Christ Jesus.* The flesh is weak without the spiritual strength of *Jesus*. He yearns to rejuvenate us for the race set before us and desires that we delight in Him, so He can give us the desires of our heart! Run with *Jesus* and finish strong!

OCTOBER 2

Infusion of Power
Philippians 4:13

I can do all things through Him who strengthens me. You are infused with power from the *Holy Spirit* when you are a child of the living *God*. The same power that lives in *Jesus* lives in you and your fellow brother and sister in *Christ*. Why are you not drawing to this power to strengthen and fill each day? Why are you trying to live without all the spiritual blessings that *God* has for you?

Forge ahead with new stamina and energy from the *Lord*. He gives you everlasting power and protection that you cannot find anywhere else. He helps you when you are weak and gives you courage for the journey. Only *Jesus* can bring you everlasting joy and perfect peace. Put your hope in *Jesus* and be filled with His great love and mighty power.

It is *Christ* who gives you the freedom that you desire. He is the answer to every question, so let Him into your life and ask so that you can receive. Call to Him and seek more of His presence and power in your life so that your joy may be complete in Him! Knock and He will open the door for you to have an abundant life of eternal blessings!

OCTOBER 3

Walk in the Love of Jesus
Colossians 2:6

Therefore, as you have received Christ Jesus the Lord, so walk in Him. Keep your feet secure in the *Lord* and your heart connected to His and you will find everlasting joy. All His love has been poured over you, faithful one, as you have believed and walked in His grace. By His grace you have been saved and His grace has allowed you to walk in freedom and security.

Are you struggling because you are being pulled away from what you know is right and putting your hope in temporal things? Are you losing hope because you do not see any way out of your circumstances? Are you clinging to self and not letting *Christ* save you?

Wake up to the promise of new hope and put your trust in *Jesus*. He wants to walk with you, but you are not letting Him in. He wants to surround you with His presence and He yearns to comfort you with His promises. He lives in you so that you can live! As you walk with Him, you will discover His love is enough. He gives you just what you need for each moment. Make your moments come alive with the joy that only comes from *Jesus Christ*.

OCTOBER 4

Abide in the Love of Jesus
John 15:7

If you abide in Him and His words abide in you, ask whatever you wish and it will be done for you. Keep abiding and drawing closer to *Jesus* each day. He wants you to depend on Him and seek Him. As you abide in Him daily, He will show you great and mighty things that you may not have known. His power will overwhelm you as you totally rely on Him and see Him at work in your life.

Pray without ceasing as you abide in the love of the *Lord*. He loves to see you abiding in Him and asking Him for all that you need. Pray for what you hope for believing that *God* will bring it to pass if it is His will for you. He loves to see you praying faithfully. Keep abiding in His love so that you can know His will for you.

The more you abide, the more good fruit He can produce in you. Live connected to *Christ* and make the most out of the days He has given you on this earth. Your days will be full of joy when you choose to lean on the *Lord* and love Him with all your heart, soul, body, and mind! Keep the faith and live fully in the precious love of *Jesus*!

OCTOBER 5

Complete Peace in Jesus
Luke 24:36

Peace to you! Jesus gives His peace to you. The peace that Jesus gives is a deep peace that never ends. This peace in your soul covers you completely and sustains and comforts you. You can have the peace that gives strength when you do not think you can make it anymore. Only the peace from the *Lord* will help you when you feel helpless. Whatever you face in this world, keep His peace. The storm will pass so be still and know that *God* is your peacemaker.

Give Him your heart and soul so that you will know this peace that is beyond all understanding. This peace will help you in times of great need. The calm waters are coming if you just wait on Him.

Come to Him with your eyes wide open and your heart ready to be filled with His everlasting love. Feel His mighty hand of protection over you, child of faith. His Spirit will fill you completely if you surrender to Him. Do not be afraid but be encouraged, for you are about to be filled with the fullness of the Spirit when you say yes to *Jesus*. Seek more of Him and you will find His peace! This peace is a complete peace that never ends!

OCTOBER 6

The Lord is Your Hiding Place
Psalm 32:7

You are a hiding place for me; you preserve me from trouble; you surround us with shouts of deliverance. We come to you and seek you with all our hearts. You provide a safe place for us to rest in your presence. When we are weak, you are strong. We need you to deliver us from this pain and heartache. We are desperate without your hand of protection over us. We need your comfort right now and we will seek you, *Lord Jesus*. We need you to cover us with blankets of protection and comfort. Help us to be faithful and to be wise to listen to you *Lord*. We need you, *Jesus,* to come rescue us!

We release control and ask for you to make us whole again. We have suffered alone because we have not asked for your protection. We have heard you calling us and we have not answered. Forgive us for turning our backs on you and seeking our own will and our own ways.

Lord, make us whole and strong in you. With your strength, we can overcome all. With your love, we are redeemed and delivered. We come to you for healing and wholeness. We will shout with joy as we are born again in you, *Jesus*! Thank you for saving sinners like us! Thank you for coming to our rescue! In you, we are forgiven and free!

OCTOBER 7

Set Your Mind on the Spirit
Romans 8:6

To set the mind on the flesh is death, but to set the mind on the Spirit is life and peace. The Spirit is waiting for you to find Him and find life. You must host the presence of the Spirit for Him to come alive inside of you. Turn away from the flesh and turn towards the Spirit. Your life will be full when you seek more of *Jesus*. He wants to empower you with more life as He is waiting for you to come to Him fully surrendered.

The *Lord* smiles through rainbows when He sees His children walking faithfully and obediently. Do not let fear stop you from finding your *God*-given purpose and walking in it. When you choose to step out in faith, your life will burst open with joy and peace that lasts. You will be overcome with more love and peace than you ever thought possible.

Tears of joy will fall down your face as you feel the Spirit of the living *God* moving inside you. He will direct you and guide you. He will show you the way. He will be your strength when you are weak. He will be your friend. He will be your comforter. Set your mind and your heart on the Spirit and you will find everything you have been searching for!

OCTOBER 8

Your Trial is His Triumph
Romans 12:12

Rejoice in hope, be patient in tribulation, be constant in prayer. Rejoice in hope knowing that the *Lord* loves you more than you can ever imagine and that He hears your prayers. Be hopeful knowing that He is in control of all things and wants the best for His children. Cling to the *God* of hope right now and let Him work out all things for good. Be patient when the storms come, for He builds your faith and endurance during these times of tribulation. There is joy waiting for you in this trial. God works all things out for the good of those who love Him and are called according to His purpose.

Always be constant in prayer, for *God* will answer your prayers in His will and in His timing. Praise Him and do not ever stop believing and praying. Seek *God* first in all that you do, and He will show you the way. He will lead you to the place of rest where you can be still in His presence and feel His love covering you. Yes, even in the hard times you will find joy with the *Lord* when He is your beacon of hope. Focus on Him and not the problem or circumstances you are facing. Ask Him to deliver you and take over. His Spirit will give you life, so keep drawing into Him and He will give you the power to endure and to overcome!

OCTOBER 9

Make the Lord Your Stronghold
Psalm 27:1

The Lord is my light and my salvation; whom shall I fear? The Lord is the stronghold of my life; of whom shall I be afraid? Yes, the *Lord* will protect us completely and He loves us deeply. He is the stronghold of our life and He will fill us full of hope when we allow His light to shine upon us. He comes to us in the storm and lifts us up higher to a place of calmness and peace. Only the *Lord* can do that! He has redeemed us and taken us out of the pit of despair. Once we truly surrender, our heart will be filled with complete peace and joy. Our fears vanish, and our hope increases with the *Lord* by our side.

With the *Lord*, we are forgiven and free and released from our sins that once kept us from living life to the fullest. We are transformed by the renewal of our minds and our hearts when our joy is found in the *Lord*! We no longer struggle and focus on the problem because our eyes are fixed upward on *Jesus Christ.* He is our prize and our peacemaker. The *Prince of Peace* is holding us every step of the way. When we let His love cover every part of us, we will be filled with a peace beyond understanding. Come to His fountain of life and be forgiven and free. A new life fully immersed in *Jesus* is available to all who believe!

OCTOBER 10

You are Radiant
Psalm 34:5

Those who look to Him are radiant; and their faces shall never be ashamed. His light shines through you when you are looking to His light. Keep looking up and be drawn to Him and His radiance. He is perfectly positioned for you to draw to Him for your every need. Right in the center of your life is the best place to put the Lord Jesus Christ. He is your cornerstone and the foundation of your faith. Put Him there and be filled with His blessings!

Have faith and be of good courage. Your *Lord* will raise you up and position you for the blessings He wants to give you. All you must do is trust the *Lord* and open your heart to receive these blessings.

Turn towards the *Lord* when you are weak, and He will strengthen you. Turn towards the *Lord* when you are discouraged, and He will encourage you. He will give you full joy and love as you let Him lead you out of the dark place you are in right now. Come to the light and come to *Jesus* just as you are. He fixes your broken heart and infuses your empty soul with life! Look to Him and be filled with the radiance of the *Lord* and shine for *Jesus Christ*!

OCTOBER 11

Experience Awe and Wonder Today
Acts 2:43

And awe came upon every soul, and many wonders and signs were being done through the apostles. At Pentecost after the *Holy Spirit* came, all the believers came together and had all things in common. They devoted themselves to fellowship, prayer, teaching, and the breaking of bread. They believed with their souls and praised *God* all day long for His favor and blessings. These believers were made new. They found joy and peace together as one in *Christ* with the power of the *Holy Spirit* inside them. They were saved by the blood of *Jesus* and freed by the power of the *Holy Spirit*!

Today we can experience these same wonders and signs from *God* through the power of the *Holy Spirit* working in us. Miracles are not only for the past but can be experienced in the present. We can see the power of the *Holy Spirit* if we just believe and activate it in our lives. The *Holy Spirit* was alive in the people at Pentecost and is alive in us today. Once we choose to receive the *Holy Spirit*, we will be given the manifestation of the Spirit for the common good.

Let us be ready to see wonders and signs with awe in our souls. Glory to *God* in the highest as our souls are in awe again today!

OCTOBER 12

Many Spiritual Gifts are Waiting for You
Colossians 4:2

Continue steadfastly in prayer, being watchful in it with thanksgiving. Keep praying and look to the *Lord* for answers. He is listening and ready to bless your life with much joy! Come to Him with your requests believing that He will surely answer you. Ask and you shall receive. Knock and the *Lord* will open the door for you. He is always available for you and ready to listen. Pray in faith that you will see answers to your prayers. Praise the *Lord* for His mighty power and enduring love poured out upon you! With a grateful heart, come to the *Lord* and humbly ask. If you do not ask, you will not receive! He gives generously and loves abundantly. Let the Spirit of the *Lord* come upon you and praise His heavenly name for His grace and mercy upon you.

He has clothed you with the garments of salvation. He has put His seal of the Spirit inside you as you have believed. Now, ask for *Jesus* to give you everything He has for you. There are many spiritual gifts waiting for you. All you must do is activate the *Holy Spirit* within you by surrendering to *Jesus* and asking for Him to baptize you in the *Holy Spirit*. Your life will be complete in Him!

OCTOBER 13

Call Upon the Lord
Romans 10:13

For everyone who calls on the name of the Lord will be saved. You need a *Savior* and He is ready and waiting for you to call upon Him. His arms are open for you, so come and give Him your heart. Do not let fear keep you from completely surrendering all. Cast all your cares, anxieties, and burdens upon *Jesus*. He will take all the pain, guilt, and shame from your past sins. He will trade your sorrows for joy! Believe that you can be free in *Jesus Christ*. You are free to experience all that He is ready to give you as His love for you is everlasting and His grace covers you completely. His mercies are new every morning. Hope in the *Lord* who gives His grace to you generously and abundantly and believe that He always loves you. Be still and know that He is *God* and rest in His presence once again.

Let go and let *God* take you away with Him. He is right there as He has never left your side. He is not angry, bitter, or disappointed in you. He will make beauty out of ashes. Everyone who calls upon His name will be saved. And that means you! Call upon *Jesus* right now. Pray to Him and give Him all your heart, mind, and soul. You will find the freedom you have been searching for in total surrender to *Christ*!

OCTOBER 14

Work Together for God in Harmony
Philemon 4-5

I thank my God always when I remember you in my prayers, because I hear of your love and of the faith that you have toward the Lord Jesus and for all the saints. Yes, we give thanks and praise to our *Lord* for giving us fellow believers who encourage us and build us up. We are thankful for our friends who work alongside us to build up the kingdom of *God.* The *Lord* puts these fellow servants in our life at times of greatest need. We know that only *God* could orchestrate everything in perfect accord to meet our needs. We desire to work together in perfect harmony with other believers for *Christ.* We receive much comfort and joy from those who meet us where and when we need them. The *Lord* puts these friends in our life who He knows will share the same burden that He places within our heart. The *Lord* gives us friends who will share our faith and desire to be an effective servant for the sake of *Christ.*

We share our struggles and we celebrate our joys together. With the *Lord God*, we are one. We can live in unity and peace if we decide to work together towards that common goal. The *Lord* desires that His people come together and live and work in unity with love and peace in their hearts.

OCTOBER 15

His Presence Manifests All Around You
Joel 2:30

And I will show wonders in the heavens and on the earth, blood, and fire and columns of smoke. Yes, the *Lord* shows His glory and His presence manifests all around you. As the day approaches for His return, you will see even more signs. The heavens and the earth are full of His glory now and forever. Open your eyes to see His glory. The goodness of *God* is all around you. Feel His presence and open your heart to His blessings and favor.

The *Holy Spirit* comes like a fresh wind and fire that you can experience completely when you allow His presence to be alive in you. Your soul will rejoice as you experience abundant joy and love through His power within you. Your heart will sing of His grace and mercy when you let Him bring you out of the darkness and into His great light!

Rejoice for this is the day that the *Lord* has made for you! He has given you His Spirit of joy so that you can go and spread the hope that is within you. He has given you peace so that you may rest in Him. He has given you His love so that you can give His love to those around you. Go and make much of *Jesus* today!

OCTOBER 16

Trust in the Lord with All Your Heart
Proverbs 3:5-6

Trust in the Lord with all your heart, and do not lean on your own understanding. In all your ways acknowledge Him, and He will make straight your paths. Give Him all your heart and surrender control to Him. He wants to know you better so that He can give you the desires of your heart. Lean on Him and His ways. His ways and His thoughts are higher than yours.

He knows your past, present, and future and He loves every part of you. He will make beauty out of ashes and will wipe away every tear. Come to Him and release the chains that keep you from fully trusting Him. He does not remember your sins but rejoices in your victories! Acknowledge the *Lord* in all your ways by continuing to grow in your relationship with Him. You can draw closer to Him through your prayers. The *Lord* will speak to you as you read His word and listen to His voice directing and guiding you. Only the *Lord* can make your paths straight. If you try to go alone, you will not receive all the spiritual blessings that He has for you. Lay your burdens down and come rest in His arms. Believe and be made new in Christ. Trust Him to do what seems impossible and give glory to *God* for the great things He has done for you!

OCTOBER 17

New Life in Jesus Christ
Proverbs 9:11

For by me your days will be multiplied and years will be added to your life. Yes, the *Lord* promises new life to those who come to Him. Abundant life will be yours when you give your heart to Him. Years in this new life will be added to you. You are born again in *Christ* and made new when you give your heart to Him. Your heart will be full and overflowing with His great joy. Your days will be filled with gladness and hope.

You will see the presence of *God* everywhere you go as He lives in you. His Spirit becomes your power and your strength. The *Holy Spirit* becomes your helper and your friend who remains with you when you choose to welcome Him in your life.

Through *Jesus Christ*, you are redeemed, and His grace has saved you. Keep living for Him and with Him and your life will be fulfilled. Your dreams and desires will become reality when you start seeking *God's* will and purpose for you. Today is the day to start living for *Jesus*. He is ready and waiting for you to come see what He has for you. It will be glorious and more magnificent than you could ever dream or imagine! Today is the day that the *Lord* has made for you, so rejoice and be glad in it!

OCTOBER 18

Throw off Your Chains
Romans 3:23-24

For all have sinned and fall short of the glory of God, and are justified by His grace as a gift. God gives us His grace as a gift so that our sins are fully forgiven. The blood of *Jesus* has cleansed us from our iniquities and wiped us clean. The chains of sin are gone now that *Jesus* has come to set us free. He bore our sins on the cross with each stripe of pain He suffered. He died for us so that we could have a relationship with the *Father*. All authority from heaven and earth has been given to us through *Jesus*.

He yearns for us to come to Him and throw off the chains that bind us. *Jesus* is the way, the truth, and the life. Come to the *Father* through *Jesus Christ*. He forgives you for everything! Throw off any sin from your past and take on your new inheritance in *Christ*. You are new in *Christ* when you invite Him into your heart and let Him transform you. You will be clothed with the power of the *Holy Spirit* as you believe and receive your gift. This power will come alive inside of you as you surrender and seek to live by the power of the *Holy Spirit*. *Jesus* gives you the choice to have it all. You must decide to take up your cross, surrender to His will, and follow Him into the light. What are you waiting for? Today is the day for you to find everlasting life when you come to Jesus!

OCTOBER 19

Spirit of the Living God
Ephesians 3:16

According to the riches of his glory he may grant you to be strengthened with power through his Spirit in your inner being. An abundant spirit-filled life is waiting for you as you trust the *Lord Jesus* and come to Him for life. Ask for the *Holy Spirit* to come alive inside of you. Hunger for more of His presence in your life. Surrender all control. Let go of your fears and doubts. Go with the *Lord* and experience freedom!

He will direct your path when you let Him. It is your choice to come. You must choose to live a spirit-filled life to experience all that the *Lord* has for you. He has more than just your eternal salvation. Your life on this earth can be more joyful and peaceful if you let the Spirit of the living *God* actively live inside of you. A new hunger will be ignited in you as you let the Spirit move inside you starting a fire in your soul. This holy fire will burn increasingly brighter and stronger as you spend more time in the word and in prayer.

Host the presence of the spirit of the *Lord* and let the spirit rest upon you. Surrender to Him today and you will walk with purity and power with the *Holy Spirit* alive and active within you!

OCTOBER 20

The Lord Smiles at You
1 Thessalonians 1:4

For we know brothers loved by God, that He has chosen you. The *Lord* has handpicked you for the work that He has for you. He knows your gifts as He has created you and given you a God-given purpose. Have you been searching for your purpose? Are you hoping to find your why? Have you discovered that you have many opportunities to work for the *Lord* to bring Him glory? The *Lord* is eager for you to find it all today.

He is looking far and wide for someone with a heart like yours. He knows that you can make a difference to bring many to know *Jesus* through your active faith. He sees your compassion for others and it makes the *Lord* smile. He knows that you love Him with all your heart and soul. He rejoices because you are living out your faith!

There will come a day when your faith will be your eyes and you will see what He has promised you. There will also be glimpses of His glory as well as manifestations of His power for you to experience on earth, faithful one. Remember you have been chosen by *God* to receive these spiritual blessings! Take all that is yours in *Christ* today and be strengthened and encouraged to press on to the rewards that await you in heaven!

OCTOBER 21

The Lord Will Revive Us
Hosea 6:2

After two days he will revive us; on the third day he will raise us up, that we may live before him. The *Lord* wants us to surrender our heart to Him. His desire is that we will return to Him with all our heart and not just some of our heart. He yearns for us to return to Him so that He can fill us with His love. He hopes that we will share this love with others so that they may experience the powerful love that flows from Him. This love is pure and brings real joy. He will open our hearts in a new way as we seek more of Him. He will revive us when our hearts are connected to His. The *Lord* knows how much we need Him and is always there for us. Let us be open to His love so that we can experience true joy that never ends.

Come home to your *Lord* by opening your heart completely to Him. He will show you great and mighty things that you have not known before! He will bring you more joy than you ever thought possible! He has given you *Jesus* so that you can live by grace. He has given you the *Holy Spirit* so that you can live in His power. Return home and live with the *Father* above you, *Jesus* beside you, and the *Holy Spirit* inside you!

OCTOBER 22

Wait for Your Abundant Blessings
Lamentations 3:25

The Lord is good to those who wait for Him, to the soul who seeks Him. Wait upon the *Lord* so that He can bless you abundantly. You will miss blessings if you try to forge ahead without the *Lord*. He will be with you if you let Him lead you. Make the *Lord* your portion and feel His countless blessings flow to you.

He will overflow your cup with abundant blessings. You will be amazed at how much He really does love you as your soul is enriched with the presence of *Jesus* and the power of the *Holy Spirit* Why are you not waiting for the *Lord*? Have you grown impatient while the *Lord* is working on your behalf? Do not let your impatience stop you from counting the blessings that await you!

He wants you to seek Him with your whole heart and give thanks with a grateful heart. Be persistent and not impatient with the *Lord*. He knows what your heart desires and He wants to give it all to you. All good things will come to you when you wait upon the *Lord*. You will rise with wings like eagles and fly with hope like never before. Your faith will come alive and you will feel the favor of the *Lord* upon you! Put faith first and rise above it all with the *Lord* guiding you to victory!

OCTOBER 23

Find Brighter Days with Jesus
Isaiah 60:1

Arise, shine, for your light has come, and the glory of the Lord has risen upon you. Yes, the light has come to the darkness. This light is everlasting and brightly shining upon you. See the light and let it brighten your way out of the darkness. There is only one true light. When you come to the light of the world, *Jesus Christ*, you will be filled with brighter days and the glory of the *Lord* will rise upon you!

Your *Savior* has delivered you to a better place where you can experience the fullest joy and the greatest peace than you can ever imagine. Come to this place of deliverance and freedom with your *Lord* and *Savior*. You will never walk alone with *Jesus*. He will carry you through it all as you trust more in the one who will never leave your side.

Jesus Christ is the way, the truth, and the life. No one comes to the *Father* except through Him. Come claim your victory in *Jesus*. He has won the victory for you, so repent and believe you can be free. With *Jesus*, you will experience a total transformation of your soul and renewal of your heart and mind. He is ready to give it all to you, so come just as you are, and *Jesus* will put all the broken pieces of your life back together. Come let His glory shine upon you!

OCTOBER 24

Blessed are the Meek and Faithful
Matthew 5:5

Blessed are the meek, for they shall inherit the earth. Be gentle and kind and put others before yourself knowing that it is right and a good thing not to always be first. The true blessings come from being the giver. Give humbly and serve quietly giving all the glory to *God* and not yourself. Let your pride fall away and keep your eyes fixed on *Jesus Christ* because He is the one who will satisfy your every desire when you choose to follow Him.

Be filled with the Spirit and walk humbly serving Him with joy and gladness. Your life will be filled with blessings beyond measure as you continue trusting and obeying the promptings of the *Holy Spirit*. In order to do this, you must live connected to the Spirit by your surrender of self. Give the *Lord* all control and ask for Him to give you all the spiritual blessings that are yours. *Jesus* will baptize you in the *Holy Spirit* as you surrender all to Him and ask. Your faith and surrender will change your life forever.

All things are new again when you are saved and when you are baptized with the *Holy Spirit*. You will become a disciple for *Christ*. He is ready and waiting for you, His faithful and meek servant. Do not delay another day, come and find your new life in the Spirit!

OCTOBER 25

Remain Steadfast
James 1:2-3

Count it all joy, my brothers, when you meet trials of various kinds, for you know that the testing of your faith produces steadfastness. Remain steadfast in your trial and *God* will reward you. You must keep standing to see His glory.

He is the one who will redeem you and make you whole by delivering you. When your faith is tested, you will grow perseverance and character if you stay the course. Keep the faith and keep fighting the good fight with *God* by your side.

The *Lord* will give you everything you need when you give your whole heart to Him. His love will be poured over you and His peace will be made perfect in you. You will be comforted when you let Him comfort you. You will find hope when you put your trust in Him. There is no need to worry and be afraid when *God* is by your side. He will show you great and marvelous things as you continue walking by faith in obedience.

Your test is surely coming as the storms of life are certain. But take heart because with *Jesus* in your whole heart and the *Holy Spirit* active deep within your soul, you will be able to survive! Your *Lord* is your deliverer!

OCTOBER 26

Sow the Peace of Christ
James 3:18

A harvest of righteousness is sown in peace by those who make peace. The peace of *Christ* which surpasses all understanding will guard your heart and your mind when you choose *Jesus*. His righteousness will be harvested in you as you seek to live peacefully with others. You have a choice how you will live and treat others. Choose *Jesus* and choose a life of complete joy!

Jesus looks at you with eyes that see your heart. May your heart be full of the joy of *Jesus* to do the work He has called you to do. He searches for those who will live faithfully and peacefully to accomplish much for His kingdom. He needs you to see others with His eyes of compassion and kindness. He needs you to be a peacemaker. He needs you to be a light in this dark world.

Keep your destiny and identity in *Christ Jesus* and show others that your confidence comes from Him. Bring the good news of salvation as you display peace to those around you. This seed of peace will spread far and wide. A harvest of righteousness is sown in this peace. This peace has been given to you by *Jesus*. Now take His gift and be a peacemaker for *Jesus*!

OCTOBER 27

He Hems You In
Psalm 139:5

You hem me in, behind and before, and lay your hand upon me. Yes, the *Lord* is the one who protects and keeps you safe. He goes before you and behind you. Follow the *Lord* to places of hope and peace. He wants to take you with Him on a journey where He will be your guide and protector.

When you are afraid, put your trust in *God*. When the road seems rocky and the journey seems impossible, keep your eyes fixed upon *Jesus* who will show you the straight and narrow path. He will never leave or forsake you.

Believe that He loves you and wants the best for you. Keep seeking more of *Jesus* and find the well of life that will quench your thirst forever. His joy will overflow in you as you keep trusting Him more. He will show you the way because He is the way and the truth. You cannot get where you need to go alone. You must draw the living water of *Jesus* to be saved. Your salvation rests in *Jesus*, your mighty *Savior*. Believe in Him and have everything you have been looking for. Follow Him to places of joy where you can be free because He gives you life in abundance. Drink of His living water and be filled with life!

OCTOBER 28

The Lord is Your Refuge
Psalm 142:5

I cry to you, O Lord. I say, "You are my refuge; my portion in the land of the living." Cry out to Him and He will certainly hear us. He will comfort us and give us rest. He will bring us peace and protection when we seek Him and ask. He hears us calling Him in the night. He is holding our hand through it all. Believe that He will be our refuge and our hope. He is a very present hope in trouble.

Come to the fountain of everlasting life. Draw the living water from *Jesus* and trust that His life will spring forth in us when we call upon Him. Only the *Lord Jesus* can give us a new life filled with His complete peace that never fades. This inner peace from his spirit stays inside us at all times. When we are struggling, His peace comforts us. When we are coming out of the fire, unharmed, His peace calms us. When we are weary, His peace covers us.

Let us draw closer to Him than we have ever been and seek to be filled completely. A double portion of blessing is waiting for each of us. We will be blessed beyond measure the more we seek Him. Let us find Him and be filled with His bountiful blessings!

OCTOBER 29

Lead the Next Generation
Psalm 145:4

One generation shall commend your works to another, and shall declare your mighty acts. Our generation of believers are to lead the next generation. We are to show them the truth that is found in *Christ Jesus*. The *Lord* will surely reveal His glory through His mighty acts. The *Lord* is ready for us to bring hope by sharing the truth!

The *Lord* is so great and powerful. There is nothing that He cannot do. The *Lord* does as He chooses in His will. We have our hope in Him no matter what our circumstances may be. We are called to share that hope with the next generation. We are to be doers of the word by leading, teaching, sharing, giving, and loving the next generation.

The *Lord* is looking for those people who have the faith to accomplish His mighty plan without seeing all the details. He wants us to serve Him with our whole heart one day at a time, one person at a time. We are planting seeds in the hearts of future leaders for *Christ*. Do not grow weary of doing good, for at the proper time you shall see the harvest. Stay the course and finish the great task you have given for His glory and not for yours. There is a great difference when you work for His glory! To *God* be the glory forever and ever!

OCTOBER 30

Be Faithful
Psalm 25:10

All the paths of the Lord are steadfast love and faithfulness, for those who keep his covenant and his testimonies. You were called to be a faithful servant of the *Lord*, so go where He has called you. Keep walking in your purpose. Not all will understand your purpose, but when *God* places it in your heart, He will show you the way. Your path will be clear when your heart is connected to *Christ*. Remain faithful as the *Lord* is always faithful to you. He will protect you in all your ways and help you. Serve Him obediently and see His abundant blessings poured over your life. He rewards those who serve even when they don't see all the details. Faith is believing in the thing hoped for without seeing. Believe and live out your *God*-sized dream!

Keep serving the *Lord* steadfastly with your heart directed to Him. He will give you the strength to start and the will to finish. Take that first step of faith today. He is waiting to give you His complete joy that will surely come to you, faithful servant. Surrender your will to His will and be filled with the power of the *Holy Spirit*. Open your eyes and give Him all the glory for what He will do for you. Not all have faith, but the *Lord* is faithful!

OCTOBER 31

Give to Receive
Acts 20:35

It is more blessed to give than to receive. Yes, this truth from *Jesus* will bring much joy and blessing to your life. Try giving instead of always wanting. Seek to be the giver instead of the receiver. When you give, your life will overflow with abundant blessings. When you pour your heart into others, you will experience the double-portion blessing that comes from your gift. The better gift flows out from the giver.

Sit at the feet of *Jesus* and hear Him calling you to serve. Spend time with *Jesus.* He is so real and wants to have a real relationship with you. As you strive to keep giving and serving, the *Lord* will open more doors of opportunity and blessing for you. Each new door is filled with a greater blessing. Victory is found with each step as you walk by the Spirit with *Jesus.* You are His workmanship, created in *Christ Jesus* for good works, which *God* has prepared especially for you so that you would walk in them. He can do far more abundantly in you than all you could ask or think. His power is at work within you when you choose to walk in it. Be filled with the fullness of *God* and press on to your new life of abundant blessings and favor with the power of *Jesus Christ* actively working inside of you!

PRAYER TO JESUS

Dear *Lord*,

I come to you, *Lord,* and speak all that is in my heart and on my mind. As I fall on my knees in your presence, I feel thankfulness flood my soul. I know that you will listen and attend to the voice of my prayer. I am so grateful that you are there whenever I call your name!

I do not ever need to make an appointment with you because you are never too busy for me. I am the one who gets too busy for you as I worry about my responsibilities and plans for my day without including you. Thank you for always being available and ready to listen to me whenever I need you!

I need you in every detail of my life, *Lord,* and I will strive to pray often so that our relationship can grow deeper and stronger. I want to know you more, so I will seek you by spending more time with you in prayer starting today. Not just prayers for what I need, but prayers for what you want for me. Your will to be done in my life is what I will pray. *Lord*, your will be done in my life as your servant is listening!

In *Jesus* name,

Amen.

Give thanks
IN ALL
CIRCUMSTANCES;
FOR THIS IS
the will of God
in Christ Jesus
for you.
1 THESSALONIANS 5:18

NOVEMBER 1

Give Thanks
2 Thessalonians 1:3

We ought always to give thanks to God for you, brothers, as is right, because your faith is growing abundantly, and the love of every one of you for another is increasing. God sees you trying to make a difference by your love. He sees you loving your fellow brother and sister like He desires. He sees you growing in faith and He is well pleased. He knows that you are living by faith first and that is why you are able to love those who have hurt and betrayed you. *God* has forgiven you and expects you to forgive and love others.

Make peace with your neighbor and love those who have not always been lovable, as everyone needs love. You will find peace on earth as you make peace. *God* will reward your faithfulness by giving you the crown of life as your eternal reward. Abundant spiritual blessings await you, faithful one. You can have it all when you make *Jesus* the *Lord* of your life! Start living for *Jesus* and not for just yourself. Seek the treasures above and many blessings will be added to your life. *God* is ready to shine His favor upon you. This world would be a better place if all would strive together to live in harmony and unity in the love of *Jesus* and in the power of the *Holy Spirit*!

NOVEMBER 2

He is Our Hope of Glory
Colossians 1:27

Christ in you, the hope of glory! When you choose to give your heart to the *Lord*, you receive His hope and His glory! He works within you giving you the power and the energy to proclaim the truth of the gospel. He breathes life into your body and peace into your soul. He gives you everlasting love and enduring grace that covers a multitude of sins. He fills you with knowledge and wisdom to understand these spiritual truths when you seek Him through prayer and reading His word.

He strengthens you so that you will have patience, endurance, and determination to finish your race. He gives you peace so that you can rest in His presence and feel His love. He wants a relationship with you, His beloved child. Come to Him and cast all your cares and anxieties on Him because He cares deeply for you. Set your mind on the *Lord* and the things above, not the things of this earth. He will comfort you and give your weary body rest. Lay it all down and let go. It's time to trust Him completely as the *Lord* will save you. Sit with Him and listen and trust Him and obey as you hear Him calling you. Save us, *Savior* of the world, our hope of glory!

NOVEMBER 3

How Majestic is Your Name
in All the Earth
Psalm 8:1

O Lord, our Lord, how majestic is your name in all the earth! You have set your glory above the heavens! We look up to you to see your majesty and glory! You have given us hope again. We have restored peace that only comes from you in this storm we are facing. Your awesome and overpowering love has taken us straight into your arms. There is no other place we would rather be!

Our faith is renewed in you. Your love has taken us higher and we are full of faith as we see evidence of your love all around us. You light up the skies to show us that you can do the impossible. Our faith has healed us and made us whole! We pray for healing for those around us. Many need physical, emotional, and spiritual healing. We lift our voices to you and cry out for miracles that only you can give us. Our faith has strengthened us! You continue to light up the sky to show us that we can depend on you. Because of you, *Jesus*, we have a new hunger for you and we are redeemed and are not who we used to be. Our chains are gone as we cling to you and your promise to always be with us. Your love takes us higher! Thank you, *Jesus Christ* our *Lord,* for setting us free!

NOVEMBER 4

Find Your Way Home to the Lord
Proverbs 1:7

The fear of the Lord is the beginning of knowledge, fools despise wisdom and instruction. Fear the *Lord* your *God* and look to Him for His power, wisdom, and knowledge. His power will be your strength and His wisdom will fill you with knowledge. Trust in the *Lord* with all your heart. Get to know the *Lord* better each day by spending time with Him by prayer and reading His word. You cannot trust Him if you do not know Him. You will know Him when you seek Him. Spend your days wisely by seeking the *Lord* at every turn. He will show you the way to live and will direct your path.

He wants to give you a life full of hope. You must elect to spend time with Him to know Him. It is your choice whether to make the *Lord* your sanctuary. He is a living sanctuary for you. He has prepared a way for you.

Take the path with the *Lord* and find your way home. You will not be lost anymore when you come to Him. Live with His grace and you will find life. Live with His hope and you will find joy. Live in His word and His Spirit and you will be fulfilled all the days of your life!

NOVEMBER 5

Feed His Sheep
John 21:17

"Do you love me?" *Jesus* asked this important question to His disciple and said that if he loved Him, he would feed His sheep. He asks us this same question today. We show our love for *Jesus* by constantly tending and feeding His sheep. Are we seeking those He has put in our flock? Are we ministering and loving them. Our family and our friends become a ministry of love for us. We also go out where we are called and seek those who are lost and need us to show them the love of *Jesus*.

Jesus wants us to follow Him and make disciples as all authority in heaven and earth has been given to Him. We are to observe and follow all that *Jesus* has commanded and show others the unconditional love that comes from Him as He is with us until the end of the age. The time is now to go out and find the sheep and love these sheep so that they can become disciples for *Christ*.

Jesus is longing for us to be His disciples and eager for us to spread His light all around our community. Our love for Him will be seen as we follow *Jesus* and feed His sheep. Do you love *Jesus*? Then follow Him and feed His sheep!

NOVEMBER 6

He Works Powerfully Within Us
Colossians 1:29

For this I toil, struggling with all His energy that He powerfully works within me. Yes, we get our strength from *Jesus*. We have our hope in *Jesus* when we place our trust in Him. He is the one who will never leave or forsake us. He keeps giving us His power to energize us for the work He has called us to do. We will not struggle alone when we have the living power from the *Lord*. Let us activate this power from the *Holy Spirit* that works within us. The *Holy Spirit* will transform our hearts and our minds when we decide to surrender all to Him. Our surrender equals His power. This power is the same power that rose *Jesus* from the dead and it lives in us.

God desires the best for us, His children, and He is pleased when we obey. Our acts of obedience become acts of love for our *Father* as we follow His commands. Keep trusting and obeying and experience more life!

Let us get our energy from the *Lord Jesus*. He has given us His living Spirit as a gift for us to experience life from a spiritual perspective. Let us continually look to Him and place our trust in the one who will surely deliver!

NOVEMBER 7

Find Life in Jesus
John 10:10

I came that they may have life and have it abundantly. Through Him, you will find your life and you will find your identity. He brings abundant joy and perfect peace that cannot be found in the world but only through Him. His joy will be complete in you when you abide in Him and His love. He loves you so much and wants you to live a life full of blessings.

Your Savior, *Jesus Christ,* died so that you would have this abundant life. Your *Father*, out of His love for you, gave up His son so that you could have eternal life and salvation through Him. All you must do is believe that you have received salvation through His death and resurrection and take this gift of life through *Jesus Christ.*

You will be blessed beyond measure by your *Lord* and you will see your world differently through His eyes. The eyes of *Jesus* love and do not hate. These eyes have compassion and kindness and not bitterness and anger. These eyes see beauty instead of ashes. These eyes see hope instead of hopelessness. Cling to *Jesus* and see your world through the eyes of your *Lord*.

NOVEMBER 8

Born Again
John 3:5

"Truly, truly, I say to you, unless one is born of the water and the Spirit, he cannot enter the kingdom of God." To be born again and have eternal life, we must be born of the water and the Spirit. We are born into this world physically through water. But as we believe in *Jesus* and give our hearts to Him, we are filled with the living power of the *Holy Spirit* from the *Lord* who gives His Spirit to live inside of us. We must allow the Spirit who resides in us, as we are born again, to be alive and active within us. We do so by recognizing this power and surrendering our self to the *Holy Spirit* We activate this power through our surrender and service. We have the same power living within us that raised *Jesus* from the dead!

We are given this gift of the Spirit because we were first loved by *God* and we love Him and want to draw closer to Him. As we abide more in our *Lord*, our desires will become His desires. We will show our love through our obedience to Him. He will bless our lives more and more as we obey more. The *Holy Spirit* becomes our guide as we put aside our selfish desires and allow Him to direct our lives. Let us be born again and seek the eternal kingdom of *God* by serving Him faithfully!

NOVEMBER 9

He Chose You and Set You Apart
John 15:16

You did not choose me, but I chose you and appointed you that you should go and bear fruit and that your fruit should abide, so that whatever you ask of the Father in my name, He may give it to you. Yes, the *Lord* has chosen you, set you apart, and has called you friend. Go and serve where you are planted and spread your good seeds that will bear good fruit. Abide in the love of *Jesus* so that His love will remain in you and your joy may be full.

Spread the good news of hope that is found by trusting your *Father*. He gives generously to those who seek His will and follow Him obediently. Ask anything of your *Father* by prayer believing that you will receive. Your *Father* knows what you need even before you ask Him. Ask anything in the name of *Jesus* and you shall receive. Whoever keeps the commandments of the *Lord* and follows Him shows His love for Him. He who loves *Jesus* will be loved by the *Father* and will see His love manifested in their life. He longs for your love and wants you to follow Him. He loved you first so that you would know His love and would be free to love one another. Remain in Him and He will remain in you. His love will grow good fruit in you. You will be firmly planted in this love and bloom!

NOVEMBER 10

God Will Deliver You
From Any Temptation
1 Corinthians 10:13

God is faithful, and He will not let you be tempted beyond your ability, but with the temptation He will also provide the way of escape, that you may be able to endure it. Yes, we will certainly face temptations in this world, but God can deliver us from any temptation we might face. He is the one who will provide another way for you. Look to Him and not yourself for the way you should go. Seek the path of righteousness with the *Lord* by your side.

When faced with a choice, choose *Jesus*. Seek His will above your own and find peace. Ask the *Lord Jesus* to help you and He most definitely will be there for you. Call upon the Him to rescue you and comfort you. He promises to never leave or forsake you and will keep His promises. People might abandon, betray, or hurt you, but the *Lord* your *Savior* will stand strong with you always. Stand firm for Him and His word. Ask *Jesus* to give you His power from the *Holy Spirit* so that you can know Him better. Surrender your thoughts and will to Him. Let Him guide you into truth today and always. Give your heart to the one who will change your life completely. Have faith for *God* is faithful to you. Never fear because your *God* is always near!

NOVEMBER 11

The Glory of the Lord Fills the Earth
Isaiah 6:3

Holy, holy, holy is the Lord of hosts; the whole earth is full of His glory! His glory is magnified, and His blessings are all around us. The *Lord* is so mighty and powerful and there is nothing that He cannot do so let us praise *God* in His sanctuary! Let us praise Him in His mighty heavens! Praise Him for His mighty deeds. His blessings await us in abundance!

Trust Him to bring you through that storm you are facing. Lean on Him and know that this trial will strengthen your faith. Believe that you will find joy through it all. *God* will use this trial for your good even though you may not understand. God promises good to you when you believe, and your faith will grow deeper if you just believe. He wants to bless you in abundance but needs you to trust and lean on Him completely. He will take you where you need to go if you allow Him to guide you. His Spirit will come alive in you as you allow Him to come in.

Jesus is waiting for you to believe to receive your gift of the *Holy Spirit*. The *Lord* will send you where He wants you to go as you activate the Spirit in your life. Open your heart and be ready to answer the call. Live out your purpose in *Jesus Christ* with the *Holy Spirit* and you will find life everlasting!

NOVEMBER 12

Shine on as a Child of the Light
1 Thessalonians 5:5

For you are all children of light, children of the day. We are not of the night or of the darkness. As believers, we are full of His great light and we shine brightly for all the world to see! We become beacons of light shining brightly through darkness. We are beautifully and wonderfully made in His image to be His children. As we grow in spiritual maturity and wisdom, we grow closer to *Jesus Christ*. He lives within us to revive and restore us to greater heights with Him. We fly on new wings of hope for the glory of *God*. Our hope is the foundation of our faith as we know that we are set apart and made whole through *Jesus Christ*. We have an inheritance in *Christ* as believers and we trust our *Lord* to get us through the flood or the fire. Our hope runs deep and wide into the depths of our soul with *Jesus* as our anchor. We no longer cling to worldly things, but we reach for the stars of hope that can only be found in *Jesus*.

Shine His light, little children, through your love. Love one another and forgive one another as *Christ* has surely forgiven you. Spread the seeds of love and grace and watch the good fruit grow abundantly in your garden of hope filled with rays of light from *Jesus Christ*. Shine on and be filled with the Spirit!

NOVEMBER 13

Just Believe
Acts 16:31

Believe in the Lord Jesus, and you will be saved, you and your household. He will rejoice when you put your trust and faith in Him by believing. You will rejoice in your new life with *Christ* your *Savior*. When you believe, your life will be enriched by the power of the *Holy Spirit* living inside of you. Your heart will be full of the joy of the *Lord*. Your soul will be nourished by spiritual blessings of hope. You will rejoice for the *Lord* will transform you from the inside out!

Every moment spent with *Jesus* will be fulfilling for you. He gives the good portion and your cup will overflow in abundance with blessings. These blessings and favor will be yours in *Christ Jesus.*

Search no more for life found in the things of the world but seek the treasures in heaven that come as you put your trust in the one true king of your heart. As you do this, you will see *God* work in your life in ways you could never dream or imagine. Our *God* is bigger and can do anything He pleases for you. Ask and you shall receive. With man it is impossible, but not with *God*. For all things are possible with *God*! Just believe!

NOVEMBER 14

Stand Firm in Jesus Christ
2 Thessalonians 2:15

Stand firm and hold to the traditions that you were taught by us, either by our spoken word or by our letter. Brothers and sisters loved by *God*, stand firm and stand apart for the truth. Keep working and do not give up. Do not worry or be anxious for you know that your steadfastness in the *Lord* will be rewarded. He will surely do it, faithful servant!

Do not grow weary of doing good, for in *God's* time you will reap the rewards of your sacrifices. Your work for *God* becomes your joy and your strength is found through renewed hope. What once was lost, will be found through the *Lord*. He will give you eternal comfort and peace as you continue working by faith. Therefore, continue encouraging one another and build one another up just as you are already doing. Rejoice in your sufferings knowing that your suffering will produce endurance. That endurance will produce character which will in turn produce hope for you. The *Holy Spirit* has been given to you so that you would continue walking in the hope of your calling. Be guided by the Spirit of truth and stand firm in the only hope, *Jesus Christ*. He stood up for you at Calvary and sacrificed all so that you would be forgiven and free! Stand up for the truth and come to life in *Jesus*!

NOVEMBER 15

Commit Your Work to the Lord
Proverbs 16:3

Commit your work to the Lord, and your plans will be established. The *Lord* will show you the direction to go when you let Him establish your steps. He will lead you on the path that leads to peace and joy everlasting. The *Lord* knows all your thoughts, desires, and dreams. When you give your whole heart to Him, your thoughts, desires, and dreams become aligned with *God* and His plan for you. He has a divine direction for you, but you must choose to follow Him. The *Lord* has a purpose for you and He wants to see that purpose lived out in you. Keep striving and do not give up. He hears your prayers and will answer your pleas for mercy.

Come to the fountain of life with your *Lord*, the maker of heaven and earth. Be still and know that He is the *God* who will lead you into all truth. Trust and obey the one who can do more than you could ever dream or imagine. Do not limit *God* in your prayers as He can do more. Dream big and pray bigger. Be patient and see your *God*-sized dream become reality. Know that He hears you and will answer if it is His will. Seek His will above all else and His desires will become the desires of your heart. *God* will respond to you when you call His name.

NOVEMBER 16

Seek the Favor of the Lord
Proverbs 22:1

A good name is to be chosen rather than riches, and favor is better than silver or gold. Seek the favor of the *Lord* by loving Him and obeying Him. If you love Him, you will keep His commandments and honor Him. Your home will be with the *Lord* as you believe and follow Him with all your heart.

Rejoice when you see His favor and bask in the glory of His love for you. Abide in the *Lord* and His love and He will abide in you! He has chosen you, brothers and sisters loved by *God.* Now you must choose Him. Once you have believed, seek the things that are above where *Christ* is seated at the right hand of *God.* Find your treasure in His riches which are everlasting. Make your home with *Christ* and put on humility, gentleness, kindness, patience, and compassion.

Stand firm in one spirit standing strong with *Christ* in you. With His strength, you can do more than you ever thought possible. *God* is working in you for His will and His good pleasure. Seek the unity of the spirit in the bond of His peace and find your hope in *Jesus Christ*, your *Lord* and your *Savior*!

NOVEMBER 17

Fight the Good Fight of Faith
2 Timothy 4:7

I have fought the good fight, I have finished the race, I have kept the faith. God has been right beside you cheering you on as you go. Don't give up. Stay the course and keep on working where He has called you. Your race will take you to places with the *Lord* that you never thought possible. Your faith will bring you through the toughest roads and biggest valleys. You will be able to climb any mountain because you have the power of the *Lord* giving you extra strength and energy each step of the way. There is nothing that your *Lord* cannot do for you. Choose His way and not yours.

Give up fighting your own battles and try asking the *Lord* to fight the good fight of faith with you. You will be able to finish strong with His lead.

Your race has just begun when you fully surrender to the *Lord* and His *Holy Spirit*. He will infuse you with so much joy that you will be overflowing with hope in your calling.

His favor and blessings will be poured upon you, beloved child of *God*. Believe and keep running the race set before you with a new song of joy in your heart and His praise on your lips! You are His new creation, made perfect in His image!

NOVEMBER 18

Believe that He Reveals Mysteries
Daniel 2:28

But there is a God in heaven who reveals mysteries. He will reveal so much to you if you choose to see. Open the eyes of your heart and look around to see all the beauty around you. He has made beauty out of your ashes and has given you hope out of your hopelessness. Through your disappointments, you will find pure joy. Through your heartache, you will feel a greater love that has no end.

The *Lord* will show you the better way through trusting Him. His plan is the best plan and you will finally see now that His mysteries are being revealed to you one step at a time. Each step you take in faith becomes a big step toward *God*. You must take that first step of faith without knowing all the details. When He calls you, go! Draw your strength from the *Lord* who gives in abundance to all who seek Him. Reach for *Jesus* and find a new door of opportunity to serve opened to you. Through your faith, you see His plan for you revealed. His plan and purpose for you is better than anything you can ever imagine. Look up and see the heavens and the earth that the *Lord* made in His power. Nothing is too hard for the *Lord* and He will accomplish everything He has planned through you. Trust Him and obey and see your world with the eyes of your heart!

NOVEMBER 19

There is Joy in the God
of Your Salvation
Habakkuk 3:18

I will rejoice in the Lord, I will take joy in the God of my salvation. Come to the heart of worship and praise. The *Lord* is your portion and your song for He gives you more than you can ever dream or imagine. The *Lord* is doing more in you than you ever thought possible. Trust Him to carry you in the storm and lean on Him and His ways. He will bring you through the flood and the fire. He is the one holding your right hand.

Believe that the *Lord* will deliver you. Trust Him to be there for you. Allow His loving arms to wrap joy around you. Let Him be the one to comfort you and give you peace.

Be still and know that He is *God*, your redeemer and your rock of salvation. The victory has been secured through *Jesus Christ* your *Lord*. Claim your victory through *Jesus* and let His living spirit cover you with love and power. This power is the same power that rose *Jesus* from the dead and it lives in you. Come to the joy of the *Lord* and be free to live and love again covered by His grace and infused with His power. Let Him reign in you and be revived and restored! Rejoice in the *Lord*, rejoice in His mighty name!

NOVEMBER 20

Covenant of Peace for You
Isaiah 54:10

My steadfast love shall not depart from you, and my covenant of peace shall not be removed, says the Lord, who has compassion on you. His love, compassion, gentleness, and kindness will be with you always. His amazing grace covers you and sustains you. His peace will be great with you when you trust in Him with all your heart. He gives you all that you need when you believe and give Him your soul. His joy will be complete in you and your joy will be full when you fully abide in Him and He abides in you. *Jesus Christ* saved you by His blood that He poured out on the cross. The *Father* forgave your sins by the great sacrifice of His son. He suffered and gave you grace. His grace is sufficient for you for His power is made perfect in weakness!

Believe in the power of the *Holy Spirit* given to you so that you may have this same power that rose *Jesus* from the dead. This power lived in you when you first believed. Activate and energize the Spirit inside of you by surrendering all and letting the Spirit who lives within you guide you into all truth.

He will lead you and give you peace. Receive the *Holy Spirit* that has come upon you and live an abundant life! Find your identity and your destiny in *Christ*, the *Savior* of the world!

NOVEMBER 21

Give Thanks to the Lord
Psalm 100:4

Enter His gates with thanksgiving and His courts with praise! Give thanks to Him; bless His name! Come to the *Lord* and see all the blessings He has for you. He has made the heavens and the earth and all that is within it. He has made you in His image when He formed you in your mother's womb. He knows your every thought and your heart.

Praise Him for making you just how you are, beautiful one. You are His child and He loves you so much. Give thanks for all the wonderful blessings that He has bestowed on you!

The *Lord* knows you from the inside out. Give Him all of you; your heart, mind, body, and soul. He will mold you and give you all that you need when you surrender all to Him. Because He lives, you can face tomorrow. All fears are gone when your heart is connected to *Jesus*.

He takes away all your pain and replaces it with joy. He is your anchor of hope. Rest in His presence and let Him give you peace. His love will cover you from head to toe and He won't let go!

NOVEMBER 22

Guarantee is with the Lord
Matthew 24:13

But the one who endures to the end will be saved. Yes, keep believing and keep working as your faith will increase as your love for the *Lord* increases. You are saved by your faith in the *Lord Jesus*. Some will grow cold and fall away, but you who are pure in heart will remain strong in the *Lord* to the end of times. *God* rewards those who keep the faith and keep going as they are called to witness and give their testimony. Be ready to tell your story as you meet your next divine appointment. Be eager to share the good news of salvation. Be loving as *Christ* has loved you. You have been set apart to stand out for *Christ*. People need to know the *Lord* in the lowest valleys and on the highest mountain. They need to meet *Jesus* everywhere. Show *Jesus* to everyone you meet by your kindness and compassion. Share your hope in *Christ* before it's too late. We are not guaranteed tomorrow on this earth, but our guarantee is with our *Lord* in heaven when we are saved. Blessed is the servant who is serving the *Lord* when He returns.

Let Him find you working for His good purpose. Let Him see you actively seeking the Spirit as you are led by Him. Let Him find you faithful because the one who endures to the end will be saved!

NOVEMBER 23

Surrender All and Be Saved
Joel 2:28

And it shall come to pass afterward, that I will pour my Spirit on all flesh; your sons and your daughters shall prophesy, your old men shall dream dreams; and your young men shall see visions. In these days of the *Lord*, He will pour His Spirit upon all so that we will know His great power. Dreams, visions, and prophesy will occur and all who call upon the name of the *Lord* shall be saved!

We have salvation through *Jesus Christ* as we have believed. We have a relationship with the *Father* through *Jesus Christ*. We have the gift of the *Holy Spirit* through *Jesus Christ*. Our salvation, relationship, and Spirit are all possible only through *Jesus*! He is the way to salvation, as He is the truth and the life! We can have a relationship with His *Father* only through believing in Him by confessing with our mouth and believing with our heart that *Jesus Christ* is *Lord* of all! Once we believe and repent of our former ways, we are given freedom from all our sins! The perfect gift of salvation by grace is wrapped up with a gift from *Jesus* of the *Holy Spirit* for us to unwrap and use in our lives. The power of the Spirit is real and available to all who make *Jesus* their *Savior*. Surrender all and be saved by His grace today!

NOVEMBER 24

Overcome Evil with Good
Romans 12:21

Do not be overcome by evil, but overcome evil with good. God will rejoice when you are at peace with your brothers and sisters. Hold fast to what is good and continue walking in your righteousness. You were made to be peacemakers and not avengers. The *Lord* will repay the unrighteous as He desires. Do what is good and love one another. By your love, others will know your *Lord* because they see *Jesus* in you.

Jesus loved His enemies and forgave those who hurt Him. He was mocked, persecuted, beaten, and put to death, but yet He showed mercy and grace to His enemies. He loved the very ones who hated Him. He forgave the ones who betrayed Him. He prayed to the *Father* to forgive them for they did not know what they were doing.

In the same way, you were called by *God* to live peacefully by forgiving those who hurt you. You will be set free from your anger, bitterness, and hatred as you forgive. As you forgive, you will see more peace and hope in your life. The *Holy Spirit* will rest upon you and not be quenched by the desires of the flesh. His Spirit of peace and life will control you and your heart and soul will rejoice once again!

NOVEMBER 25

Praise the Lord in His Sanctuary
Psalm 150:1

Praise the Lord! Praise God in His sanctuary; praise Him in His mighty heavens! Our hope is in our God almighty! He is the real and sure thing in a changing and unsure world. Trust in Him because He loves you. Seek Him because He wants to be your help and your hope. He completely heals your brokenness and sadness with the touch of His hand.

He gave His only Son, *Jesus,* to die on a cross out of His great love for you. He wants you to know Him more and have a relationship with Him. Confess, repent, and believe! He has already forgiven you for everything you have ever done. Believe this and ask Him into your whole heart today. Give the *Lord* all of you and you will experience a new life of joy and peace that will overwhelm you. He will never forsake you or leave you. He will carry you through whatever storm you are facing and lead you to still waters of comfort and joy. Blessed are those who seek and walk with the protection of the *Lord.* He restores and revives you when you dwell in the shelter of the *Most High* and abide in the shadow of the *Almighty*! He will hold fast to you and deliver you! Abide in Him and His powerful love and you will be filled with the hope of the promise of eternal salvation in heaven and a life of peace on earth.

NOVEMBER 26

Draw Near to God
James 4:8

Draw near to God and He will draw near to you. He hears you calling in the night and He will answer you. Keep praying and asking because if you do not ask, you will not receive. He delights in your prayers and your praises and answers your pleas for healing.

Purify your heart and submit yourself to the *Lord.* Confess your sins to one another and pray for one another that you may be healed. The prayers of a righteous person have great power and are working. Lean on the power of *Christ* in you and stand on His promises! He will never leave or forsake you. When you submit to the *Lord,* believe more deeply and lean on Him, you will see the mighty hand of *God* exalting you at the proper time. Humble yourself before the *Lord* and He will exalt you. He can do far more than you can ask or think according to the power at work within you. *Christ* dwells in your heart through faith and that faith grows love. When you love others and serve the *Lord* with eagerness and gladness, you will experience full joy. The joy of the *Lord* will be your strength forevermore. Keep believing and fight the good fight of faith!

NOVEMBER 27

Worship with Praise and Thanksgiving
Psalm 95:2

Let us come into His presence with thanksgiving; let us make a joyful noise to Him with songs of praise! We are here to worship His Holy name with praise and thanksgiving! He is mighty to save and will save us. Praise the *Lord* for making us whole again. Nothing is too hard for our *God*!

He brings wisdom and courage into our hearts as we put Him first in our lives. He brings hope to us as He calls us out of our hiding place into His place of refuge. He lifts us up and strengthens us when we are weak. He is the bread of life that will satisfy our hungry souls. His living water will quench our thirst. Living waters will flow out of our heart as we believe in the *Lord* and His abundant power in our lives.

The *Lord* can do great and mighty things through us by His great power that He puts in us. We must claim this same power that rose *Jesus* from the dead and activate it in our lives. His power will direct us and strengthen us as He calls us to His greater purpose. Our fears will vanish as we see *God* at work in our life. Let us take heart and keep the faith and we will be healed. Let us set our minds on the Spirit and find life and peace. Let us hope for what we do not see and wait for it with patient longing. It will be done for us, His faithful servants! Just believe!

NOVEMBER 28

Be Sold to Your Savior
2 Timothy 2:22

So flee youthful passions and pursue righteousness, faith, love, and peace along with those who call on the Lord with a pure heart. Seek the power of the *Lord* who gives more than you can ever dream or imagine when you decide to follow Him and His ways. He is ready to bless your life and give you more when you decide to step out and pursue Him more with all your heart. Make Him the *Lord* of your life and be sold to Him as He has already paid the price for your sins through His blood shed on the cross.

Greater love, faith, righteousness, and peace will be yours as you trust and obey the *Lord*. You will be a witness for *Christ* as you put His desires first! He knows and notices everything you do. He sees you reaching out with compassion and love and He is well pleased. He loves a cheerful giver who never expects anything in return. He rewards those who put faith first above all circumstances. He blesses the humble and gives grace to the meek. He is patient with you, so patiently wait upon Him. He hears you praying and sees you serving, faithful one! Keep in step with the Spirit and in tune with His power as you are about to rise with wings and soar higher than ever before!

NOVEMBER 29

Count Your Blessings
Nahum 1:15

Behold upon the mountains the feet of him who brings good news, who publishes peace! God brings peace to all who will receive it and want to be revived by His truth. Take His peace and bring peace to others. Be a peacemaker by being the hands and feet of *Jesus*. Spread His love to those who need to feel love.

Spend time thinking of your blessings and not worrying about your problems. Give thanks to the *Lord* who gives generously to you. He is waiting to bless your life abundantly and bountifully. There are many blessings waiting for you so be ready to receive them one by one. Count your blessings, not your troubles and you will feel His peace flood your heart and soul once again. Are you struggling to find peace? Are you stressed and worried about problems and not focusing on *Jesus*? Take your mind off your problems and put your mind on the things above. Think of the things that are pure, lovely, joyful, peaceful, and praiseworthy and keep your focus on these things of *Jesus*. What are "these things" for you? Maybe you just need to shift your attention away from the things that take your time away from *Jesus* and refocus on *Jesus Christ* who is the true answer to all you want and need!

NOVEMBER 30

The Lord Will Shower You
with His Power
John 14:14

If you ask me anything in my name, I will do it. The *Lord* is just waiting for you to ask. He is ready to give you every good and perfect gift from above when you seek Him. When you seek Him with all your heart, you will find Him. He will open the door to you when you knock. Keep asking, seeking, and knocking.

Believe that you will receive and keep asking in prayer with thanksgiving. The *Lord* is ready to give you more than you could ever ask or imagine. He will shower you with His power because He is a mighty and powerful *God.* He wants to give you more than your heart's desire. He needs you to trust and obey Him first by walking and acting in faith fully surrendered to Him. He will direct your heart and your mind to His perfect will for you. Your purpose will be fulfilled in Him as you show your love through your obedience to what He has called you to do. He will know that you love Him by your actions so trust the *Lord* with all your heart and lean not on your own understanding. Acknowledge Him in all your ways and He will make your paths straight. He is waiting for you, so come just as you are and let *Jesus* open the door for you!

PRAYER TO JESUS

Dear *Lord*,

For you, O *Lord*, are my hope and my trust. O *Lord*, from my youth. I know the way I should go, and I will follow you. You bring me such joy and fill me with renewed hope once again. I am stronger because your power has energized me. I can reach new heights as I fly securely with wings like eagles and soar with you!

You have set your Spirit within me and I am living freely away from all that is hindering me. I am focusing on the joy that you have given me. Thank you for carrying my burdens and giving me life!

I am praising you more and worrying less. I will choose to live with you guiding me in all areas of my life as I am connected to you, my living hope. I am trusting you to lead me on the right path. Your path leads to truth and justice and your glory shines brightly for all to see! I see, and I believe!

In *Jesus* name,

Amen.

GLORY TO GOD
IN THE HIGHEST,
and on earth
PEACE
among those with whom
he is pleased.
LUKE 2:14

DECEMBER 1

Perfect Gifts Come from
the Father Above
James 1:17

Every good gift and every perfect gift is from above, coming down from the Father of lights, with whom there is no variation or shadow due to change. The Father of heavenly lights gives to us generously. He does not change like shifting shadows but remains constant and reliable as His light illuminates the world. He shows us His glory in the nighttime sky filled with bright stars on a dark night. We see His majesty in the beautiful sunrises and sunsets.

We see hope as we gaze into the eyes of a newborn child. The hope of the world was born in the small town of Bethlehem years ago. That child, *Jesus*, your Savior and King, came as the answer to all your needs and desires. His love is everlasting and will comfort you in the darkest of nights. His Spirit will sustain you and His joy will enlighten you. He came into this world to bring joy to the world.

Keep reaching with joy for *Jesus*. Receive this gift of His love and give the love of *Jesus* to others this Christmas season. *Jesus* is the best gift you can ever give! Every good and perfect gift is from heaven above!

DECEMBER 2

Lift Your Eyes to the Lord
Psalm 121:1-2

I lift my eyes to the hills. From where does my help come? My help comes from the Lord who made heaven and earth. In this world, you will be faced with choices and decisions that will challenge you. As you search for answers, know that your help comes from the *Lord*. Lift your eyes to the *Lord*, the maker of heaven and earth. He has made you in His image as a child with needs and desires that He can fulfill. Come out of the darkness and into His arms of love and grace. The *Lord* loves you and wants to give you everything He has made for you.

Look up to the hills and seek His face. Your fears will disappear the closer you get to the true light of the world. Step out of yourself and run into His arms of safety and security where you can be comforted like a child. Your heart will be filled with joy and your soul will be comforted with the perfect peace of *Christ*.

The answers will be clearer as you trust the *Lord* to guide you. He has the perfect plan for you. His plans are to give you hope and a purpose that He can fulfill in you. The closer you get to your Father, the greater your joy will be! Run into his arms and know that He is your Father and you are His child. Feel His unconditional love for you like never before!

DECEMBER 3

Let Every Tongue Confess
that Jesus Christ is Lord
Philippians 2:10-11

At the name of Jesus every knee shall bow, in heaven and on earth and under the earth, and every tongue confess that Jesus Christ is Lord, to the glory of God the Father. Jesus Christ is over all and He is exalted high at the right hand of the Father in heaven above! It is our joy to worship Him with honor and praise. We give thanks to our *Lord* and pray without ceasing in the name of *Jesus*. At His great name, every knee shall bow and every tongue shall confess that He is *Lord*.

He gave us life so that we could be made whole again from the sin that entered our lives. We are no longer slaves to our sins but are free with the living spirit of the *Lord* in our hearts. As we believe and we live for *Christ*, our minds are transformed to be like His. We are one in our spirit and in our mind with our savior, *Jesus Christ,* when we say yes to His power in our lives. He who began a good work in us will bring it to completion at the day of *Jesus Christ*.

Keep on believing as you pray, watching as you serve, and waiting as you worship Him in spirit and in truth. You will see *Jesus* by obediently following Him in faith. You will know *Jesus* more as you trust Him more completely.

DECEMBER 4

Trust in the Lord Always
Psalm 62:8

Trust in Him at all times, O people; pour out your heart before Him, God is a refuge for us. God is your refuge and strength and He is a very present help in trouble. He is right beside you ready to catch you when you fall and hold you up when you are weak. He will be your rock in the times of difficulty and times of peace.

Trust in Him to lead you with the power of the *Holy Spirit* that He gives to you. He makes all things possible to those that believe and trust Him with all their hearts. Ask and you shall receive if you ask in the name of *Jesus* in the will of your *Father*. He loves to give to His children who ask in the name of *Jesus*. If you do not ask, you will not receive. Be bold in your prayers to the *Father,* in the name of *Jesus,* and pray big without ceasing. He is the one who turns all your dreams into reality as you seek His will for your life. The peace you are missing and the joy that you are seeking will come like a flood into your heart and soul the more you put your trust first in *Him*. His everlasting love is the answer to all your needs. Take and receive this love and give it freely to those around you. Be a faithful witness by sharing the love of *Jesus* as you keep believing and trusting in the *Lord* above all else!

DECEMBER 5

Let Your Mouth Declare the Mighty Works of the Lord
Jeremiah 1:9

Behold, I have put my words in your mouth. Do not be afraid when the *Lord* commands you to speak. He will put His words in your mouth as you trust Him and speak with power and authority from the *Lord*. The words He gives you to speak will declare His witness in a mighty way. The blessings from the *Lord* will be poured over you as you proclaim His glory. He appointed you as His witness to share the good news of salvation through your words and your actions. Serve Him with gladness. He will renew your mind, restore your soul, and revive your heart so that your new identity will be in *Christ*.

As you grow in *Christ*, you will be made new as your old self will pass away and your new self will be born again. New life will emerge in your Spirit. You will grow good fruit where you are planted as your roots will be firmly planted in *Christ*. This sweet fruit will satisfy your every desire and will be enough for you to share with others. As you share, you will be planting new seeds that will produce good fruit for *Christ*. This fruit of the Spirit is never out of season. Keep planting and believing and you will see miracles like never before!

DECEMBER 6

Spread His Message of Hope
1 John 4:4

He who is in you is greater than he who is in the world. He is the one who will sustain you and lift you up as He is mighty to save. The *Lord* promises to never leave or forsake you and He always keeps His promises. He is the great fulfiller of joy, peace, love, and hope in a world filled with heartache. As you trust in the *Lord*, your heart will be revived, and your soul will be refreshed. As you seek His will for your life, He will show you great and mighty things He wants to do through you. Believe that He needs you!

He is looking to and fro to find those that who have hearts for *Christ* and will keep their eyes fixed on the prize of the upward calling of *Jesus Christ.* Be the one He needs you to be to further His kingdom. He is searching for you. Stand firm and believe that you can help by spreading His message of hope through the gospel of peace. Share His love by loving others as *Jesus* loves you. Reach out and touch those that need this hope and love. Just as you have believed, the *Lord* has given you the power of the *Holy Spirit* inside of you to direct you and guide you into all truth. Use this power from the *Lord* and know that you can do all things through Him who is greater than the world.

DECEMBER 7

Immeasurable Love
Acts 17:28

In Him we live and move and have our being. Everything that we are is possible because of who He is. His love for us is immeasurable. He loves us so much that He gave us victory through His son, *Jesus,* who paid the price for our sin through His death on the cross. We live because He died! We can live in this freedom and peace as we are indeed His. To live with the peace of *Christ*, we must let go of the chains that bind us and walk freely with His Spirit guiding us every step of our way. We must repent of our sins and seek to exist in the will of the *Father* by living in the truth of the word. Let us hunger for more of His Spirit by pouring out our hearts to Him in prayer and thanksgiving. He will speak to us if we will open our hearts, listen, and obey. As we prayerfully act with obedience and live in His Spirit and Truth, we will come alive with the hope that only comes from the *Lord*. We will sing a new song of joy as we bask in the glory of His beauty and majesty. Praise the *Lord* and bless His Holy name!

DECEMBER 8

The Lord Knows You
Psalm 139:5

You hem me in, behind and before, and you lay your hand upon me. The *Lord* knows you from the inside out. He knows your thoughts and your desires. He is with you when you lay down and when you rise. He is your safe place, so remain in Him and be still and know that He is *God*. His hand will lead you through the darkest times as He holds you firmly.

You are precious to the one who formed you in your mother's womb. You are fearfully and wonderfully made in the image of *God* who loved you even before you were born. Give your heart to the *Lord* who loves you with an everlasting love. He is your strength when you are weak. He is the fresh breath of hope when you are hopeless. Breathe in His Spirit and feel His peace covering you like a warm, soft blanket. His touch will open your heart and your soul to a new hunger for Him.

Only the *Lord* can completely fill the empty places in your life. Let Him be the one who brings you life and fills your cup. Your cup will be overflowing with the greatest joy you have ever felt when you put your trust in the *Lord Jesus Christ.* Drink of His living water and you will never be thirsty again!

DECEMBER 9

Food that is Needful for Me
Proverbs 30:8

Feed me with the food that is needful for me.
The *Lord* will feed you the Spirit and the truth, when
you trust Him to nourish your body and your soul.
His food is needful for you and will fill you up so that
you will never be hungry or thirsty again. Seek Him
above all else and see the *Lord* transform you
entirely. His truth will give you security and His spirit
will give you peace. His word will speak everlasting
truth into your life. The grass withers and the flower
fades, but the word of our God will stand forever. His
word will not return void but will surely accomplish
what the *Lord* desires to prosper and grow. When you
spread His word, good fruit will grow from its
plantings. Hold onto these truths and desire the sweet
fruit of the Spirit of the *Lord*.

Your body is a temple of the *Holy Spirit* living
inside of you and given to you by *God*. Honor Him by
offering your body as a living sacrifice, holy and
pleasing to *God* who sacrificed His only Son for you.
Be transformed by the renewing of your mind and
your soul as you worship Him in Spirit and Truth.
Live by faith with the power of the living Spirit of
God inside you. Open your mouth and your heart so
that He can fill you completely.

DECEMBER 10

Find Your Joy in Jesus Christ
John 15:11

These things I have spoken to you, that my joy may be in you, and that your joy may be full. Jesus is your joy! He chose you and gives you joy in abundance. You will be full of His joy when you trust and love him with all your heart. This joy becomes part of you as *Jesus* makes His home inside your heart. Love Him and you can love one another.

His righteousness will cover you as you trust and obey His words of truth. Take your requests to the *Lord* and seek Him by drawing nearer to Him in prayer. He will certainly answer you when you pray according to His will for you. Ask and you shall receive all that is yours in *Christ*. Knock and the door of joy will be opened to you. Believe that He has everlasting joy waiting for you.

All you need to do is to openly receive this gift of His joy by surrendering to your *Lord Jesus Christ*. Take hold of *Jesus* and yield to the *Holy Spirit*. Your life will be filled with beauty and grace and your heart will be full of the joy of *Jesus*! His love does conquer all. Believe this and become one with your *Savior*. He has redeemed you and has given you everything you need. Fill any void or emptiness with the joy that will make you complete in *Jesus Christ*!

DECEMBER 11

Let Your Soul Magnify the Lord
Luke 1:46

"My soul magnifies the Lord, and my spirit rejoices in God my Savior!" Mary, the mother of *Jesus*, the Son of the Most High, spoke about her love for the *Lord* by saying," my soul magnifies the *Lord*." Her soul and her spirit rejoiced as the *Lord* looked upon her, His humble servant, with favor to be the mother of the Savior of the world. She gave Him all the glory and praise for this amazing, magnificent, and glorious gift. His promise was fulfilled in her and she gave birth to *Jesus*. Her soul was filled with great joy through the power of the *Holy Spirit*.

Rejoice in *God* with your Spirit as He has looked upon you with mercy and sacrificed His only Son because He loves you. He has given you His amazing grace by forgiving all your sins. Spread the love and joy given to you freely by your Savior.

Your joy will be full when you abide in the love of your Savior and love one another. You will be known as a follower of *Christ* as you love one another. Your soul will rejoice as you see the *Holy Spirit* working through you to give the love of *Jesus*. You will live with the light of *Christ* inside you as you believe in His promises. Your mouth will sing of His glory and your heart will be full of His joy. Seek the joy of *Jesus* and let your soul magnify the *Lord*!

DECEMBER 12

Desire the Higher Gifts
1 Corinthians 12:31

But, earnestly desire the higher gifts. And I will show you a still more excellent way. Let the *Lord* mold you into something beautiful as you allow Him to be the master potter of your life. His hands have made you one of His beautiful masterpieces created in His image. You are uniquely made and called by *God* to do great things for Him.

His ways are higher than your ways and His thoughts are more excellent. He knows what is best for you so trust Him to direct your path. Lean on Him and be a willing vessel ready to be filled with all the good things from the *Lord*. He can be your best friend and the one who you can put your trust in completely. He has great plans for you if you will let go and let Him show you the excellent way with Him.

You are a member of the body of *Christ* adorned with spiritual gifts and treasures of the heart. Use these gifts to serve the *Lord* with joy and gladness. Walk hand in hand with the *Lord* as you show others His great love. Be patient and kind and love one another with the love of *Christ*. This love will take you higher and make you stronger. Give Him your best and you will see things that you never thought were possible. With *God* all things are possible!

DECEMBER 13

Rejoice in the Lord Always
Philippians 4:4

Rejoice in the Lord always, again I will say rejoice! He wants you to come to Him with all your requests and praise Him for His blessings. Trust Him to work all things for your good. Do not be anxious about anything, but in everything, by prayer and supplication with thanksgiving, let your requests be known to *God.* He will supply every need of yours according to His will for you in *Christ Jesus*

Give Him glory and praise for His answers to your faithful prayers. In times of need, keep praying, rejoicing, and trusting. Trust that His plan for you is good and that He knows what is best for you. Be joyful in hope, patient in affliction, and persistent in prayer giving thanks to *God* in all circumstances. As you rise with Him you will rise above your circumstances, His light will shine in you for all the world to see. Be a light for *Christ* and rejoice for the *Lord* is good all the time. You can do all things through *Christ* who strengthens you time after time. When you are weak, He is strong. Let His grace and peace cover you and keep His flame of hope burning inside of you. Think about the things that are worthy of His praise. Pray with certainty expecting answers to your prayers. Come to the *Lord* and rejoice!

DECEMBER 14

All for the Glory of the Lord
1 Corinthians 10:31

Whatever you do, do all to the glory of God! Whatever you say, say it all for the glory of the *Lord*. He deserves all your honor and praise for the things He has done for you and through you, faithful servant. He rewards those who put their full faith and trust in Him. Favor rests on those that love the *Lord* with all their heart and soul and show this love and faith through their obedience.

Without faith, it is impossible to please *God* as He looks for those who will remain faithful even when they do not see or understand. Do not shrink back when you are tested but persevere and keep walking by faith through your *Lord Jesus Christ*.

Run your race with endurance and hope of things yet to come by giving *God* all the glory each step of the way. He will never leave your side. He is your rock and your refuge, and His very presence brings peace and joy to any situation as His peace and joy is everlasting and will remain in your heart, child of *God*. Once your heart is fully opened to His love, you will be ready to share His love with others and spread your wings. Keep seeking Him above all else and you will rise with eagles' wings and fly fearlessly with a heart that beats strongly for *Christ*!

DECEMBER 15

Rise to a Higher Place of Mercy, Peace, and Love
Jude 1:2

May mercy, peace and love be multiplied to you. The *Lord* will multiply these gifts in you as you seek Him daily with your heart, soul, and mind. Your mind will be renewed, and your soul will be restored through His peace and mercy. Your heart will be revived through His everlasting love that never fails.

Give the *Lord* your best each day as you follow Him. Come to the *Lord* with a grateful heart and sing His praises for His mercy and grace for you. Cast your anxieties and worries on Him because He cares for you and always wants to be your help. He loves you with a love that can overcome anything.

Keep the faith and walk in His love so that you can rise to a higher place of peace and joy with your *Lord*. You are His beloved so let Him be the master of your heart. Pray in the *Holy Spirit* as this will build your faith. Keep seeking truth in the word of the *Lord* which leads to life. Worship Him with thanksgiving and with a grateful heart. Make a difference for *Christ* today and serve Him so that others may see *Christ* in you!

DECEMBER 16

Let Your Faith Rest
in the Power of God
2 Chronicles 16:9

For the eyes of the Lord run to and fro throughout the whole earth, to give strong support to those whose heart is blameless toward him. He will give you power from the *Holy Spirit* that will sustain you and carry you throughout your life. Trust Him to be with you in all times. When you are weak, He is your strength. When you are afraid, He will fight for you. Take His hand and go with Him to places of joy and peace.

No eye has seen, no ear has heard, and no heart has imagined what *God* has prepared for those that love Him. Love the *Lord* your *God* with all your heart, soul, and mind. He has searched you and knows every part of you. He sees your brokenness and knows your fears. Take these things captive to the *Lord* and be free. He wants to save you and bring you hope. The *Lord* is near to you, so rest in His presence. You are His child whom He loves deeply. Boast in the *Lord* and see His love flow through you to others around you as you proclaim His glory. He is the source of your faith and you have victory through *Christ Jesus*. Proclaim His excellence and see the power of *God* work in and through you as you give glory to *God* in the Highest!

DECEMBER 17

Present Peace in His Presence
Acts 3:20

That times of refreshing may come from the presence of the Lord, and that he may send the Christ appointed for you, Jesus. Look to the *Lord* for your peace. His peace is everlasting and fulfilling. His peace is beyond all human understanding. Always trust the Lord and lean not on your own understanding. He will give you peace if you ask Him. When you seek Him with all your heart, you will find Him waiting for you. Knock and He will open the door for you to rest in His presence of peace. His peace will cover you completely and you will rise with the *Lord* to greater heights.

Believe in His promise that He will be your peace. Don't hesitate to trust the *Lord* with all your heart. He will take you out of darkness into His great light. Every second spent with the *Lord* by your side will enrich your life magnificently. You are chosen and called by *God* as His blessed child. All you must do is come to your *Lord, Jesus Christ,* with hearts open to be filled with more love, joy, hope, and peace than you can ever imagine! He is ready and waiting just for you. Come to the Most High where you will find peace as you live with the *Lord* by your side every moment of your life.

DECEMBER 18

Go in Grace and Peace
Psalm 136:26

Give thanks to the God of heaven, for his steadfast love endures forever. He will lead you on the straight and narrow path if you choose to follow His direction from the *Holy Spirit*. His ways are pure and holy and will lead you to the path of righteousness. Look to the *Lord* and lean not on yourself or your own understanding. Lean on Him and He will guide you into all truth and wisdom in every situation. His powerful love will overwhelm you with joy and His *Holy Spirit* will cover you with peace.

Not all will understand or have faith, but the *Lord* is faithful, and He wants you to remain faithful and fruitful for His kingdom. Keep walking in your purpose and steadfastly persevere with your heart directed to the love of *God*. You can do all things with joy and strength that comes from *Jesus Christ*. The grace and peace of the *Lord Jesus Christ* is with you.

Therefore, encourage one another and build one another up in *Christ* just as you are doing. Share His love and keep your faith. He needs you to help spread the good news of salvation to a lost and broken world. Go in peace and grace as you help feed hungry souls with *Jesus Christ*, the bread of life!

DECEMBER 19

Engraved in the Palms of His Hands
Isaiah 49:16

Behold, I have engraved you on the palms of my hands. He is powerful and mighty and works all things for good. His plans are best for you and He has plans to give you hope as you walk in your purpose. Keep your faith and continue seeking Him with your whole heart and He will bring joy and peace to you!

The *Lord* searches for those who will continue to love Him faithfully with all their heart and who obey His will. Let the *Lord* find you serving Him with joy and gladness as He equips you each step of the way. The *Lord* reveals deep and hidden things to you when you draw close to Him. He makes everything beautiful in its time so trust the *Lord* to bring you out of the darkness into His marvelous light where you will shine. His light will dwell inside you as you walk by the light of His holy fire and come nearer to the *Lord*.

He has engraved you on the palms of His hands and is waiting for you to keep Him close to you. Come near to the *Lord* and rest with Him. He knows you from the inside out and will uphold you with His righteous right hand. Hold His hand, be strong and courageous, and walk with confidence and wisdom with the *Lord*!

DECEMBER 20

Be an Overcomer
1 John 5:4

For everyone who has been born of God overcomes the world. And this is the victory that has overcome the world... our faith. You are an overcomer as a child of *God*. When you are born again of *God*, you have the victory through your faith in *Jesus Christ*. Everyone who believes in Him has been saved. He loves you and yearns for you to just believe in Him with all your heart. Give the *Lord* your heart and come alive with the *Holy Spirit* inside of you.

Keep your faith alive by trusting the *Lord* more each day. Sit in His presence and rest in His love for you. You are seated with Him in the heavens as the *Lord* has blessed you with every spiritual blessing in the heavenly places in *Christ*. We are not saved by works, but by grace through faith. God made us to sit with Him as we keep our faith alive in *Christ*. We must put our utter dependence upon the *Lord Jesus*. Surrender to Him and find your place of rest in union with Him in the spiritual places. Your life will be perfected and blessed by His gift of the Spirit inside of you. The kingdom of *God* is near so go out and proclaim the good news of salvation to the world. The victory has been secured for all in the sweet name of *Jesus Christ*!

DECEMBER 21

Be Courageous for Christ
Psalm 112:1

Praise the Lord! Blessed is the man who fears the Lord, who greatly delights in His commandments! He loves to bless those who follow His path of righteousness. He shows himself to those who trust and obey His laws. He is good to those who desire to please Him. Keep the *Lord* close to your heart and look to Him for comfort and strength.

He pours out His love generously to all. Love the *Lord* your *God* with all your heart and seek Him first above all else. He will set you free and give you courage to achieve great things in His name. He forgives you for all your sins when you ask for forgiveness. Repent for the time has come for you to be courageous for *Christ*. Those who fear Him will not be afraid anymore because the *Lord* is on their side. Do not be afraid or discouraged for the *Lord* will be with you always.

Trust in Him and find favor and blessings forevermore. His light dawns in the darkness for the faithful servant. Give freely and serve the *Lord* where He calls you. The righteous follower will never be moved. Glory to *God* in the Highest!

DECEMBER 22

The Word of God Dwells Richly in You
Colossians 3:16

Let the word of Christ dwell in you richly. Worship Him with a thankful heart. Teach and encourage one another in wisdom and truth as you share the love of *Christ*. Sing psalms and hymns with joy as you seek the *Lord* with all your heart. Pray in the Spirit giving thanks to *God* the *Father* through *Jesus Christ* He is worthy of your thankfulness and praise!

Live peacefully with others as you seek the *Lord* in all that you do. Let the peace of *Christ* rule in your heart and put on His love which binds everything together in perfect harmony. Forgive one another as *Christ* has forgiven you and be a witness of His love and peace. Salvation is given to those who believe!

Glorify Him in all that you do and let the power of the *Holy Spirit* work in your life by guiding you into all truth. Seek His kingdom and all His righteousness, and all good things will be added to you in the name of the *Lord Jesus Christ* He reigns in you when you let Him reign in you as your *Lord* and *Savior*. Let His Spirit dwell in you and find your home in Him.

DECEMBER 23

Anchor of Our Soul
Hebrews 6:19

We have this as a sure and steadfast anchor of the soul. When we place our faith in *Jesus Christ* we can finally experience the intimacy with *God* that He intended for us. Our hearts were made to be one with our *Lord Jesus.* He is the anchor of our soul that keeps us steady and strong throughout our life. He will give us security and safety as we place our hope in Him. The *Lord* is our peace and only His gospel of peace can stabilize our hearts in this world of constant ups and downs.

Let us anchor our hearts firmly to Him and be thankful for the peace of *God* that is ours to cultivate. The anchoring and guiding peace of *God* is already in us as a divine gift given at the moment of salvation. We are given all the fruits of His Spirit to empower us on earth. Our task is to make sure we are constantly developing and exhibiting this fruit basket of gifts He gave us to serve others.

By serving, we are blessed by the peace and joy of *Christ* which grows inside of us. Let us experience all that *Christ* intended for us! The only one who can truly satisfy the soul is the one who made it. He is the *Lord* of our heart and anchor of our soul.

DECEMBER 24

Believe in Jesus Christ
to Have Eternal Life
John 3:15

Whoever believes in Him may have eternal life. Believe that the baby *Jesus* was born in the tiny town of Bethlehem in a manger for you to have eternal life. He was born and died for your salvation and inheritance in Him. He lives inside you when you invite Him into your heart. As you surrender all to *Jesus*, He will give you another Helper, the *Holy Spirit*. This Spirit dwells in you and gives you the power of hope, love, joy, and peace.

Grab ahold of your destiny and live in *Christ*. He will deliver you and set you apart as you soar high with His mighty power inside of you. Your heavenly reward will be great as will the blessings you will see on earth as you serve Him with all your heart. The joy of *Jesus Christ* will reign true for you when you believe and bear fruit for His kingdom. If you love Him, you will keep His commandments and find freedom in obedience. When you believe in Him and love Him, you will find the hope and the joy you have lost. His peace will settle inside you where you will find comfort and rest. You will live because *Christ* lives in you. Let your hearts not be troubled. Believe in *God* the *Father*, His son *Jesus Christ,* and the *Holy Spirit* and find life everlasting!

DECEMBER 25

Glory to God in the Highest
Luke 2:14

"Glory to God in the highest, and on earth peace among those with whom he is pleased!" Rejoice for unto you is born a Savior who is Christ the Lord! Rejoice for He brings peace on earth and good will to all with whom He is pleased.

He has come to give you peace, hope, joy, and love. He was born to be your Savior and King. *Jesus* has come to give you life. He will be with you always as you let Him guide you. His light will give you hope as He lights your path in the darkness. He will fill your heart with His saving grace because He loves you. He gives you His peace freely and graciously.

Seek Him and find your joy in *Jesus Christ*. These good gifts He gives to all who will take them. Take your gifts from *Jesus* and be renewed and revived by His powerful, redeeming, overwhelming, and compassionate love for you. As you celebrate His birth, let the power of *Jesus Christ* come alive inside of you to make you all that you were meant to be in *Christ*. Give your gift of the love of *Jesus* given freely to you. Be all that *Christ* wants you to be and rejoice for your Savior reigns in your heart forever! Hallelujah! *Christ* is born in you! Merry *Christ*mas!

DECEMBER 26

Rejoice in the Salvation of Jesus
Isaiah 25:9

Behold, this is our God; we have waited for Him, that He might save us. Let us praise His name for He has done mighty and wonderful things and His plans are faithful and true. Let us rejoice and be glad for the salvation He brings to us! He brings us great joy forever because we trust in Him alone. He is our rock and our fortress of strength and hope.

We are humbled by His great and powerful love that He pours over sinners like us. He forgives us and washes us clean when we repent and come to His throne of mercy and grace. His love covers a multitude of sins. He will keep us in perfect peace as our mind stays on Him and trusts Him above all else. Let us put our faith and trust in *Jesus Christ* our Prince of Peace. When we come to the place of rest with the *Lord*, we will find strength in His love.

Those who believe in Him will not perish but will have everlasting life. Come to the *Lord* and find hope at the cross. The light of the world is shining ever so brightly at the cross. If you repent and seek Him, you will find Him waiting just for you. Taste and see that the *Lord* is so good all the time!

DECEMBER 27

You are a Dwelling Place for God
Ephesians 2:22

In Him you also are being built together into a dwelling place for God by the Spirit. Let His Spirit guide you into all truth as you put your faith and trust in Him. The *Lord* is able to do far more than you can ever ask or think according to the power of *Christ* within you. His love surpasses all knowledge and covers you with a fullness of peace that is beyond understanding.

Come to His dwelling place and rest in His love for you. Put your hope in the *Lord* your *God* who can do all things. The *Holy Spirit* will fill you with a never ending peace and joy that will sustain you and raise you up to a place where you will be alive with *Christ*. Yield all to the *Holy Spirit* and let Him work through you to do the good works you were created to do in *Christ*.

You have a rich inheritance in *Christ* having been predestined according to His purpose. Praise the *Lord* for giving you a new hope so that you can overcome all that is in the world by your faith in Him. Praise the *Lord* and rejoice for *Christ* defeated death and won the victory on our behalf. Walk as a child of *God* and awaken from your sleep because the light of *Christ* is shining on you to spread to the world. You are a child of the light, so walk in it with confidence.

DECEMBER 28

He Will Increase the
Strength of Your Soul
Isaiah 43:2

When you pass through the waters, I will be with you; and through the rivers, they shall not overwhelm you; when you walk through fire you shall not be burned, and the flame shall not consume you. The *Lord* will answer you. Call to Him and He will increase the strength of your soul and give you boldness to accomplish what He has called you to do. The *Lord* will fulfill His purpose for you. He will preserve you and hold your hand as you walk through the fire or the flood. Give Him your whole heart and give thanks to the *Lord* for His steadfast love and faithfulness. Remain obedient and persevere with your heart directed to the love of the master of your heart. Believe that He loves you steadfastly and that He will be with you. You can do all things through *Christ* who strengthens you. He has heard you call Him and He will lead you into all truth. He knows your every thought and desire. You cannot hide from your *Father* who loves you so much. Trust in Him to lead you to a place of peace and joy. Stand firm and rise above your circumstances to victory with *Christ*. He has overcome all so that you can live in freedom and truth. Choose to live your life in His strength and purpose and find your joy in *Jesus Christ*!

DECEMBER 29

Work in His Will
and for His Good Pleasure
Philippians 2:13

For it is God who works in you both to will and to work for His good pleasure. As you obey and trust in the *Lord*, your actions will please the *Lord* your *God*. Your faith in action through *Christ* inside you will bring His light to the dark places of this world.

Be glad and rejoice when one who is lost comes to *Christ*. Only *Christ* can set the sinner free. Share this good news and you will not labor in vain. As you work, stand firm with other believers in one spirit, striving side by side for the faith of the gospel. The *Lord* is raising up an army of warriors to fight His good fight of faith to the end. The *Lord* is always by your side, so you will have the armor you need for victory. Do not fear but be strong and courageous knowing that the *Lord* is the one who will fight your battles. He is the one who began a good work in you and He is the one who will help you bring it to completion at the day of *Jesus Christ*. Work heartily for *Christ* and not for men as He loves to see you working for His good pleasure. Seek Him and His righteousness and all good things that come from the *Lord* will be added to you. Believe and receive all that is yours in *Christ*!

DECEMBER 30

Citizenship is in Heaven
Philippians 3:20

Our citizenship is in heaven and from it we await a Savior, the Lord Jesus Christ You will inherit the kingdom He has prepared for you from the foundation of the world. Work out your salvation with honor and respect for the *Lord* who has saved you as you have believed in Him. The *Lord* has looked upon you, His child, with love.

Believe *God* and walk in the footsteps of faith. Your righteousness will be born through your unwavering faith. Grow your faith as you believe that *God* can do what He has promised. He has promised to show himself magnificently to those that believe.

The *Lord* will come again, so keep pressing forward to the goal of the prize of the upward call of *God* in *Christ Jesus*. Honor and serve the *Lord* with your obedience. He will come again when you least expect it so let Him find you serving Him. Be wise, prepared, watchful, and ready as you work to please your *Lord*. Keep working with joy as you wait for His return in all glory. Celebrate your new life in *Christ* with shouts of joy and praise for the *Lord* is so good to you. He loves you and wants the best for you, beloved child of the most holy *God*!

DECEMBER 31

A New Thing Springs Forth in You in the New Year
Isaiah 43:19

Behold, I am doing a new thing; now it springs forth; do you not perceive it? The *Lord* is working all around you for peace and joy to enter the hearts of His people just as He intended. He will make all things beautiful in His time through His constant and steadfast love that never ends.

There is good news of great joy all around you if you just believe. Joy is yours forever if you choose to follow the *Lord Jesus Christ* with all your heart. As you give your heart to Him, you become a new creation in *Christ*. You were made in His image to love Him as He loves you. He needs you to join your heart with His as you begin your journey as a new creation in *Christ*. He will make a way for you in all that you do when you trust Him and love Him. His love is the key that opens hearts. Love one another with the love of *Christ* as you make *Christ* your priority by trusting Him more each day. End this year by making a commitment to connect deeper to *Christ* and see this new thing spring forth in you in the new year! *Jesus* will ignite a fire in your heart as you spend time devoted to Him!

Looking for more?

Check out Jill's previous book:

ABOUT THE AUTHOR

Jill Lowry is an ardent follower of Jesus who has a desire and passion to communicate His truth. Her writings combine the accuracy of a scholar with the practicality of a wife and mother. Jill grew up in San Antonio, Texas. She graduated from the University of Texas with a Bachelor of Business Administration in Marketing and holds a law degree from St. Mary's University in San Antonio. She resides in northeast Texas with her husband and two children.

Her ministries include helping mentor and feed at-risk students, co-leading a women's bible study, co-hosting a weekly radio show that answers questions of faith, and praying with fellow believers in a weekly community prayer group.

Jill is the founder and president of a student mentoring and food program, Mt Vernon Cares, created for at-risk students at the local Junior High and High School. She is also one of the hosts of a faith-based weekly radio talk show, Real Life Real People Radio and Coffee Talk.

Jill takes every opportunity to pray with friends and neighbors in need and considers intercessory prayer a vital part of her ministry. She is part of a weekly community prayer group which meets on the Downtown Square to pray for revival in her community and beyond.

This is her second book. Her desire is that you will be encouraged to find your joy in Jesus through the application of scripture and truth from the Holy Spirit found in this book.

Made in the USA
San Bernardino, CA
05 December 2018